"Tricia Booker's *The Place o*
and the bonds that form th
she's a red-headed, salty sto,
international family came to be with verve and unflinching honesty."
~ Neely Tucker, the Washington Post, author of the memoir *Love in
the Driest Season*

"In her gorgeous memoir, Booker takes you on a candid, funny,
heart-wrenching, and poignant journey to and through parenthood.
With three adopted children, two dogs, a husband, and a household
to manage, Booker hilariously describes the chaos of her life. But
it is the tender motherhood moments that cling to your skin like a
soothing balm – the exhausting and beautiful search for peace for a
son whose own skin feels foreign and false to him. It's the decision to
downsize, to find happiness and contentment with less … on the way
to discovering so much more. These are the moments that stick, that
catch in your throat, that ease their way into your heart. Booker is a
brilliantly talented new voice with a story that is as much ours as it is
hers: the story of searching, of finding, of accepting. It is the story
of imperfectly perfect, unconditional love." ~ Katrina Anne Willis,
author of *Parting Gifts* and *Table for Six*

"Tricia Booker is a good, honest and absorbing writer whose
storytelling bluntly conveys the raw emotions, vulnerabilities and
complexities of individuals living in a family. This book, inhabited by
a loving couple, their hopes and adopted children as well as doctors,
therapists and dogs, is also a personal journey through sometimes
hellish terrain. As the author persists through a series of perplexing
battlefields with courage, intelligence and sacrifice, she discovers how
personal fulfillment often comes from the hard-fought struggle to
meet the needs of others." ~ Kerry Temple, author of *Back to Earth:
A Backpacker's Journey into Self and Soul*

"Tricia Booker's *The Place of Peace and Crickets* is a richly moving
mediation on the unexpected heartbreaks and joys that accompany
the creation of a family—and how those painful closed doors can

sometimes open breathtakingly beautiful windows in a life. *The Place of Peace and Crickets* is a blisteringly honest, very funny, and totally unforgettable memoir." ~ Laura van den Berg, author of *Find Me*

"Tricia Booker has written a gripping story of the fiercest kind of love: that of a mother moving heaven and earth to save her child. With wit, humility and self-deprecation she writes honestly of the ups and downs so familiar to any parent who has a child who doesn't quite fit the mold. She goes through a litany of experts, treatments and diagnoses, searching for the key that will unlock the mysteries of her son's struggles. Every mother of a child with special needs will recognize this battle, but few of us wage it with such humor and honesty." ~ Valle Dwight, Director of Communications at Whole Children, a New England center for children with disabilities

The Place of Peace and Crickets

How adoption, heartache and love built a family

Tricia Booker

Twisted Road Publications LLC

This is a work of creative nonfiction. While all the stories in this book are true, some names and identifying details have been changed to protect the privacy of the people involved.

www.twistedroadpublications.com

For my three little bugs.
Thanks for letting me be your mom.

PROLOGUE

"Create a womb," my husband says.

I'm transplanting hydrangea bushes from pots into my garden. The analogy startles me. But he's right, that's what I need to do. I dig big holes and add a little fertilizer, then fill the holes with water and swish the dirt around to create a hearty primordial soup; I plop in my horticultural embryos. I place each plant carefully into its bed, then tuck in the dark earth around it.

I never really gardened before. Houseplants wither at my touch, and the scant impatiens I've always shoved into the ground each spring usually wilt by July.

But I'm sick of looking at spiky grass stretching across my backyard like a green suburban desert. If life won't spring from me, I want it to spring from my soil. I want blooms to smile at me like satisfied children, and I want birds to eat sunflower seeds from my feeder while I watch. I want to tend to a garden like a hen tends her eggs. I want photosynthesis to occur before my eyes.

"I'll believe it when I see it," says my neighbor. He thinks I'm a slacker because I nap every day.

One Sunday afternoon I pick up a shovel and start digging up the grass around the perimeter of my yard. Periodically I hit big old roots, or bricks left from long-ago construction, and I get down on my knees and claw into the ground until I uproot the culprits. The earthworms squirm between my fingers as I carefully lift them out of the reach of my shovel.

The dirt blackens my knees and stains my overalls. It settles beneath my fingernails and mutes the gold on my wedding ring. I dig for hours, till blisters pop up on my hands and my back feels stiff as a pine tree.

The next day I begin searching for flora in need of a home. At first I think big. Roses, maybe? But I want to be practical.

Jason works at the nursery near my house. He has long blond dreadlocks held back by a bandana. "Bluebird hydrangeas," he tells me. "Man, they're awesome."

"I don't have a lot of sun," I say. But hydrangeas like shade, it turns out. I buy some.

I consult a landscape designer, and she offers her ideas about what will thrive where. "What do you like?" she asks. "I like things that live," I tell her.

She points me toward some althea hibiscus. Bush daisies, native azaleas, holly ferns, lantana, African irises, and a gardenia bush. Also some dianthus. And a tiny King Sago palm.

I love the lantana, but my dog likes it more. He uses his teeth to pluck the yellow blooms right off the stem, like a party guest nibbling a miniature hot dog off a toothpick. Jason says lantana is poisonous, but it doesn't seem to bother my dog.

When I'm away from the house, I think about my plants. When the afternoon sun glares down, I feel myself dry out. I imagine my little azaleas, their leaves drooping like arid tongues.

The dianthus doesn't want to bloom. I didn't create a womb for them, and I bet that's the problem. Also, I bought them from The Home Depot, which I now know is like buying a dog from a pet store. Classic *Failure to Thrive* syndrome.

My neighbor tells me my gardenia will probably get a disease and die, and I want to hit her. After she leaves, I search it for signs of stress. Sweet lemony blooms shine white against the dark green leaves. "I won't let you die," I whisper.

I decide to grow vegetables. A friend has some extra cherry tomato plants and she brings them to me. They're tiny, not much more than a few leaves on a stalk, barely four inches high. I'm nervous taking them into my custody. We dig furrowed aisles, which we fill with Black Cow manure. That night I dream there's liquid napalm roiling beneath my little tomatoes, and I wake up in a cold sweat.

My dad wants me to plant carrots. He thinks it'll be cool if I raise a carrot to the sky after pulling it out of the ground and shout, "As God is my witness, I will never go hungry again!" like Scarlett O'Hara. Take a picture, he says, and send it. But I think I'll just stage the photo with a carrot from the grocery store. Somehow, using one of my homegrown vegetables like a movie prop seems exploitative.

My friend Walter comes over to bring me a datil pepper plant and tells me everything I'm doing wrong. I listen to his advice on the fungus that's bothering my tomatoes and my hydrangeas' need for water. "Did you dig up all the roots before you planted?" he asks.

"Pretty much," I say.

On my deck sits a ficus tree growing in a clay pot, and Walter turns on the hose to water it. "Don't water that," I shout. "I hate that plant. I'm trying to kill it."

"That's terrible," he says. "If you don't want it, chop it up. Don't just let it suffer."

A month ago I would have laughed at him. But now I feel ashamed. Later I stand on the deck and observe my poor ficus tree. I know that I'll try to save it, for now I see that the tear-shaped leaves seem droopy with grief.

Hell, there are no rules here - we're trying to accomplish something.

-Thomas A. Edison

In the flush of love's light, we dare be brave. And suddenly we see that love costs all we are, and will ever be. Yet it is only love which sets us free.

-Maya Angelou

PART I

ONE

Sitting at my kitchen table, I pressed on my breast. Gently at first, like going to first base with myself, then a bit more insistently. I felt for pain - a tenderness, a swelling, any smidgen of discomfort might have meant I was pregnant. Sometimes, after prolonged pressing, I did have pain, although I knew from the bruises that I had caused it myself.

I focused on the rest of me, too. A slight wave of nausea made my heart sing, assuming it wasn't a hangover. A cramp was downright exciting, unless blood started gushing out of my vagina soon afterwards. Of course, no symptoms might mean pregnancy, too - I had read that somewhere.

Any real or imagined symptom sent me to the pharmacy for a pregnancy test. I never told my husband. If I told him, I definitely wouldn't be pregnant. We had been married for two years, together for six.

I counted off the days on the calendar a dozen times each day. When my period came due, or even if it wasn't quite due, I went into the bathroom and peed on the thin white wand, and waited three minutes to see how many blue lines showed up. I usually didn't have to wait three minutes. Usually I was so *not* pregnant that the one blue line appeared almost instantly, a colorful SO SORRY, MAYBE NEXT TIME billboard for only me to see. That night, I would usually get wasted.

I took more pregnancy tests than I could count, and always with the same outcome. But in the beginning—you know, back before I was supposed to be having sex—I was giddily grateful for only one line. For years, sexual encounters or near-sexual encounters led to days or weeks of agonizing about whether I was pregnant. Sometimes I took tests when I had not even had sex—I imagined I had been raped when I was drunk and did not remember it, or that a sneaky sperm, released in the heat of fully-clothed passion, had escaped and swum through two pairs of jeans.

When it first became an issue, in the late 1970s, early pregnancy tests weren't even early—they weren't accurate until after the first missed period. So, often, my fear resulted in expensive blood tests.

With the amount of money I spent on the tests, I could have paid for some of the expert fertility treatment I later underwent, which is ironic in an *Are you fucking kidding me?* sort of way.

But young Catholic girls have always harbored a particular fear of getting pregnant because we repeatedly were told it would lead to imminent ruination. We pondered it endlessly among ourselves. *What would you do? Oh, God, I'd kill myself. I'd run away.*

Before the fear of pregnancy, naturally, came the fear of sex, which also tormented us. Sex invaded our thoughts early due to the determination of the adults to keep it out of our minds. Sex was the major no-no. Pregnancy was simply the unspeakable shame that resulted from it, along with a dirty reputation and several trips to the confessional.

At the all-girls Catholic school I attended, I was one of the last in my class to learn the facts of life. I knew the word sex; I just didn't know what it meant. One day in 6th grade religion class, I asked Sr. Camden this awkward question: *Is oral sex against the Catholic Church?* Since I didn't know what oral sex was, it seemed like a reasonable question. The other girls were aghast. Sr. Camden blushed and flapped her hands as she spoke. "I don't know! But personally, I think it's disgusting!"

I learned more details in seventh grade religion class, the first one I'd had not taught by a nun. But if the nuns told us too little, Mrs. Klayman told us way too much—and not the stuff we wanted to know. She was about 50 years old, and the mother of ten. She had long, dull black hair pulled back in a ponytail, and her tinted glasses made her eyes look yellow.

She was assigned the task of teaching us sex education. All sex education, in fact, was taught through the religion classes, perhaps so we'd learn right away to connect it with sin.

Mrs. Klayman believed the way to educate us about *our* bodies was to tell us about *her* body. She went into graphic detail about childbirth. One day she told us childbearing had caused her to grow two additional breasts, one under each arm. I told my parents about Mrs. Klayman's four breasts over dinner that night. I imagine most of my friends did, too. Mrs. Klayman soon was quietly replaced.

One day before she left, as she tried to explain how the Virgin Mary had gotten pregnant without having sex, one of the cool girls began passing around a note. Everyone who read the note dissolved into giggles before passing it on.

When the note came to me, I read the pencil scrawl: *Did Joseph fuck Mary or did God fuck Mary?* I had no idea what *fuck* meant. But my pride was at stake, so I laughed before passing the note. Eventually, Mrs. Klayman confiscated it. "Do you think this is funny?" she screamed. We all laughed. "Who thinks this is funny?"

I had laughed, but I was crushed. Clearly all my friends knew what *fuck* meant. That afternoon, I rushed off the school bus and ran home. I found Mom in the laundry room folding clothes. "Mom," I said, through tears. "Mom, I'm 11 years old now, and I think I'm old enough to know what fuck means."

Later, Mom explained to me how men have penises, and they put them inside of their wives and make babies. I was grossed out, but now I knew what fuck meant. It sounded hideous. But I was intrigued. And I really liked boys, so I was excited to grow up enough to have sex. But first I had to see if I'd be "called."

The Calling, we were taught, is the Lord's way of telling young Catholics they have been chosen to serve the church. The nuns said The Calling revealed itself as a voice from above.

I tried to be a good Catholic—I went to church, confessed my sins once a week and prayed. I had never been on a date, never kissed a boy, and didn't lie (too often). I was a perfect candidate to be Called to be a nun, which I thought I could tolerate, but being a virgin nun seemed unreasonable. I began to pray for God to wait to "call" me until after I had lost my virginity. But as a good Catholic, I couldn't have sex before I was married, and if I got married, I would be ignoring The Calling. I felt vexed. The answer came to me during confession one afternoon: What if I had sex, then went to confession and got absolved? I would still be in the clear for The Calling.

At night, lying in bed, I imagined I heard voices, and I shut my eyes and ears in defiance. If I heard a noise, I'd start humming aloud, without taking time to determine whether the noise was God or the dishwasher. If I was humming, I thought, I wouldn't hear The Call.

Adolescence passed, the teen years engulfed me, and I eventually found my way to sex. Michael was a cast-off from one of the cool girls who smoked, had done drugs, and talked openly about how much she loved sex. I could not even dream of attaining her level of urbane maturity.

Michael was a lot like his ex-girlfriend—he smoked, did drugs, and talked a lot about sex. His brown hair was sun-streaked, and he talked in a long-winded drawl. His brown eyes peeked out from heavy stoner lids and he always wore a lopsided half-grin on his lips.

He thrilled me. I simply couldn't believe my luck. By this time, I had kissed my share of boys, and had even participated in some extended make-out sessions. But I had always stopped short because I was scared.

Michael validated me in a way that good grades, the basketball team, and my family never could. He was proof of my ability to keep up with the cool bad girls. Naturally, my parents weren't fond of Michael. He honked his horn instead of coming to the front door, telephoned me after 9:00 p.m., and occasionally stood me up. Still, I spent hours writing our names together in various styles of script.

One Saturday night, Michael picked me up to go to a party at a friend's house. The friend's parents were out of town, and he had invited about 150 of his closest, most troubled friends to drink beer and "Jungle Juice" - Hawaiian Fruit Punch mixed with grain alcohol. This was a common weekend activity for New Orleans youth. There was always someone hosting an "open" party, which meant no supervision, lots of liquor, and no limit on the guest list. The Jungle Juice concoction was served from a plastic garbage bin, and ladled into pint-sized plastic cups.

I downed one Jungle Juice, then another. Michael put his arm around me and suddenly he seemed positively gallant. It occurred to me that his drug habit actually added character. By the end of the night, I felt sure that I loved him. We left the party early and went to Audubon Park, where we trod over rotting oak leaves and kissed. And kissed more. I don't remember thinking, "Okay, this is it!" But I remember saying to myself, "Well, maybe I won't try too, too hard to stop him this time."

I might as well have flashed a green light at him, or held up a sign that read, "Open for business."

I closed my eyes. But at the crucial moment, I flashed them open. It hurt. My heart was breaking, and so was something else down there. It felt dreadfully, terribly wrong. I pushed him away. "No," I whispered.

After a minute or two of trying to coax me, Michael sat up. Shortly afterwards, we walked to the car and he drove me home. "I'll call you," he said as I walked up my drive. And then he was gone.

My bedroom was filled with remnants of my short life. Pictures of horses lined the walls, and my dolls and teddy bears stared at me balefully when I turned on the light. The glow-in-the-dark rosary my father had given to me was shining from around the bedpost where it hung.

I suddenly was horribly sober, and grieving for my evaporated impression of what losing my virginity would be like. My world had changed. I knew that God would forgive me, for never had I been sorrier for something I had done. But I also realized that it had all been for naught; I now knew for sure that I wouldn't get The Calling, and I didn't feel the least bit relieved about it. Even more pressing, though, was the sudden fear that I could be pregnant.

I spent most of that night on the phone with 24-hour crisis lines. Most of the conversations went like this:

"This is Diane. How may I help you?"

"I'M PREGNANT!"

"Okay. How old are you?"

"Seventeen."

"Tell me what happened."

"Well. My boyfriend and I … we … but it hurt … it wasn't all the way. It was, but I quit."

"I don't think you're pregnant." Cue detailed explanation about ejaculation.

"But are you sure?"

No one could be sure, which wasn't good enough for me. It was a long night.

When the sun finally rose, I showered and dressed before my family woke up. I drove to my grandmother's house so I wouldn't have to face my parents.

I spent that Sunday trying to feel things moving in my stomach and wondering if my increasing nausea was morning sickness or a hangover.

After another sleepless night, I left the house early Monday morning. It was some holiday - no school. I drove to the nearest Planned Parenthood and tried to look grown up as I walked through the doors. The receptionist pulled aside the plastic window separating the office from the waiting room. "Can I help you?"

"Do you have the morning-after pill?" I asked. I had vaguely heard of such a thing. She looked at me for a long moment. "No," she said. "We don't."

I suppose, looking back, I had heard of some promising research, or perhaps a story about a plan to develop a "morning-after pill." Maybe in my desperation, I had created its existence in my mind. I spent the next six hours going to women's health clinics all over the city of New Orleans. Everywhere I went, I asked for the morning-after pill. No one seemed able to help me, or even understand what I was talking about. As the day dragged on, my hope sagged, and my faith that the Lord would provide disappeared.

Finally, I arrived at the very last place listed in the yellow pages. The woman at the front desk smiled at me, giving me a final shard of hope, and so I asked for the morning-after pill.

Her smile faded, and she looked at me sympathetically. "There's no such thing," she said.

All hope was gone. My plans for college melted before me like an ice cube on hot concrete. I was pregnant, I would have to leave home, get a job at Denny's, and change my name so as not to mortify my family. Goodbye, privileged life.

I took a deep breath and tried to say thank you. Instead, I fainted.

The receptionist and her manager helped me up and walked me to a cot in the back of the clinic.

"I'm sorry," I said. I convulsed into tears. "I just don't know what to do. I'm afraid I'm pregnant and I don't know what to do."

"Have you taken a pregnancy test?" the doctor asked.

"No," I said.

Again I went through the whole story. By this time it had become so routine that I was adding in details like how long we'd been dating and how many glasses of jungle juice I had consumed.

For a few minutes they talked to each other quietly, asked about my last period, then told me not to worry. "You're not pregnant," the doctor said.

"Positively?" I asked. "For sure?"

"Well, nothing is for sure, but …"

I started hyperventilating. Even one more hour of considering the possibility would be too much for me to handle. I thought of just throwing in the towel, telling my parents and getting on with the imminent ruination.

The nurse, probably worried I'd faint again, sat down next to me and put her arm on my shoulders.

The doctor left the room. He returned with a pack of birth control pills. He told me to take one every eight hours for the next two days, until my period started. Then I would know for sure I wasn't pregnant.

And so my tummy didn't swell. The only part of me that grew was the certainty that I had done something irreversible.

Michael didn't call the day after he broke my heart, nor did he call the next day. I should have known then this guy was trouble, but I felt more connected to him than ever. I ached to hear his voice, to hear him tell me what had happened was okay, and that it meant something aside from panic and pain and birth control pills.

He finally called. He took me to my senior prom—he stopped to get stoned before picking me up, left the dance to make out with my friend, and was gone so long I had to take a cab home. I never heard from him again.

Later—much later—as my husband and I embarked on a long, painful journey filled with needles and drugs and artificial insemination, I would wonder if the ultimate penance for those early wild days was the one thing—a *real* pregnancy—I wouldn't have been willing to give.

TWO

Before I settled down with a good man, I dated a series of losers. My true love, I thought, was a divorced father of two who smoked Marlboros and had only been arrested once. But he was older than me, and lived 1,000 miles away—by then I worked at a newspaper on Cape Cod.

Bob was one of my co-workers. We were great friends; we had lunch together often, and we enjoyed going on long runs and bike rides. One night, our company softball game was cancelled, and we got drunk instead. Drinking led to skinny-dipping, and when the police arrived, Bob pressed up against me as we hid behind a rock in the lake; inappropriate inter-office relations ensued. Work was awkward for several weeks, but eventually, we moved in together, and four years after that, we married. I was 30 years old. I had stopped taking birth control pills several months prior, and because my rebellion against conservative Catholic values had begun, I dreamed of being pregnant at my wedding because it would be badass and scandalous. My parents were already a tiny bit disappointed because our union would be formalized by a judge instead of a priest. Getting knocked up beforehand would be just short of a shotgun wedding. But then I wouldn't be able to drink at the reception, which would be a bummer. I loved to drink.

After the wedding, my husband and I settled back into our lives with pretty plates, a new Cuisinart, and a lot of sex. We assumed we were on our way to a traditional family with red-haired (me), short (him) children. We waited. When I stopped using birth control, it was like letting go of a rope swing. I was hoping, of course, to land in cool spring waters, the magic place meant to awaken in me a hidden woman endowed with milk-filled breasts and patience. But for months I felt nothing more than a passing pang when my period started. I thought about other things. I thought about getting a dog.

We had moved around a bit for work, but were pretty settled in Florida. One hot summer afternoon, we went to look at a litter of yellow Labrador Retrievers, which is like looking at plate of brownies. One little guy followed my husband, nipping at his heels, and when the other puppies lost interest in me, chasing instead the sound of a plane overhead, he plopped in my lap.

We named him Boston, the city closest to where my husband and I had met, and a place special to both of us. I worked as a freelance writer at the time, so I was mostly unemployed. I became a stay-at-home puppy mom, focused on raising my canine baby. I called my vet at least twice a week. *He's blinking his eyes really hard. Should I bring him in? He ate cat crap! What's wrong with him? I fussed at him and now he seems depressed. What should I do?*

Boston grew out of puppyhood, and bragging about him started to seem weird. Why wasn't I pregnant? Finally, I called the doctor.

Dr. Gee had no concerns about my fertility. "Don't worry, we'll get you pregnant," he said. "I think you'll look so cute with a big old belly." He rattled off a few tests he thought we should do. The first one was designed to see whether my husband and I were "compatible." Apparently, just because a man and a woman live together happily doesn't mean their sperm and eggs get along. Sometimes, the doctor explained, the woman's antibodies don't let the man's sperm live long enough to hook up with any eggs. I found this shocking.

In order to conduct the test, I had to figure out when I was ovulating by peeing on an ovulation predictor stick. When an extra blue line appeared, Bob and I were instructed to have sex immediately, and then proceed directly to the doctor's office. Bob thought this idea was AWESOME.

I purchased an ovulation predictor kit, and starting a week after my period, I peed on a dipstick every morning as soon as I woke up. Like, even before coffee, which, let me be clear, is difficult to manage.

On the fifth morning, I saw two blue lines. I woke up Bob. "Honey," I said. "We have to have sex."

There was a lot of faking involved, on my part, but it was really good faking, because, you know, I wanted to make sure he wasn't faking. But screwing in the name of medical research isn't my idea of high romance.

We reported to Dr. Gee's office as instructed. Dr. Gee walked into the examining room smiling, and shook my hand.

"Men just love to have sex in the morning, don't they?" he said. With my feet in the stirrups, Dr. Gee took a sample of Bob's sperm from the place where Bob had deposited them.

"I'll be right back," he said. He took the sample and scrutinized it under a microscope, then returned with the news that Bob's sperm were dead. I had killed them.

The problem was like biological warfare. My body saw Bob—or at least his soldiers—as foreign intruders, and upon invasion, my body released a chemical to destroy them. Dr. Gee said the situation was common, and fixable. The solution was to circumvent the artillery by placing Bob's sperm directly into my uterus using a long thin straw. He explained the procedure thoroughly before he used the term that would reverberate in my head: artificial insemination.

Artificial insemination. It sounded so … artificial. My baby, our love child, would be conceived under the glare of fluorescent lights while I stared at a Mary Engelbreit print on the ceiling. Perhaps this was a sign—the fact that my body assassinated Bob's sperm might be nature's way of preventing us from making a baby. Maybe our gene pools shouldn't mix. And because I'm prone to irrational thought, I wondered if maybe Bob and I weren't even meant to be married. Could two people really be in love if they were chemically incompatible? I imagined my white blood cells feverishly sending urgent messages to my brain: FLEE! DANGER! ALERT, ALERT!

Bob wanted to move forward with Dr. Gee. His father was a doctor, and he has always been comfortable with the miracles of modern medicine. Artificial insemination is no more unnatural than taking antibiotics, he said.

A week after my next period, I resumed daily dipstick-peeing, again waiting for ovulation time. When I suspected the day was near, we were to refrain from having sex so Bob's little dude supply could build up. On the right day, we would report to the office; Bob would visit the bathroom and have sex with himself, and Dr. Gee would place the resulting deposit inside of me.

It was a little exciting the first time. When we arrived, I signed in and sat down. The nurse called my husband up to the window, handed him a glass jar inside of a paper bag, and pointed him toward the men's room. He returned in five minutes (maybe ten?) and handed the bag to the nurse. He looked sheepish. He sat down next to me and looked around the waiting room.

"Did you use a magazine?" I asked.

"No," he said. "I just thought of you."

While we sat in the waiting room, the sperm went through some sort of washing machine to clean it and cull out the weaklings. We held hands and tried not to stare at all the pregnant women going in and out. I flipped through the magazine *Fit Pregnancy*.

After about an hour, we were called in, and I undressed and reclined on the table. Dr. Gee came in and patted my shoulder. "I bet Mama never told you about this part of having babies," he said.

Dr. Gee used a thin tube to send the sperm directly to the uterus, where it would hopefully meet up with one of my eggs. The procedure was over in about a minute. I remained on the table for ten more minutes, and tried to think positive thoughts so Bob's sperm would feel welcome in my lush uterus.

That was it. We went home and waited.

And waited. It would be two weeks before I could take a pregnancy test. I had already bought a pregnancy book, and every day I read the section on possible signs of conception. I poked and prodded my boobs. I felt nauseous nearly every day, and though I knew morning sickness wouldn't hit so soon, it heightened my hopes. Every twinge in my body seemed to mean something was happening. I drove myself insane. After ten days, I began calling clinics to find one offering early pregnancy tests.

The Women's Health Center provided abortions and frequently was the site of protests. Graffiti marred the outside of the building, and the carpets inside smelled like dirty socks. It was crowded with young women—emphasis on young—some with their mothers, others with friends or sisters. One with a boyfriend. The receptionist sat behind a sticky counter snapping her gum and reading *Cosmopolitan*. When I approached, she glanced up and raised her eyebrows at me expectantly.

"I'd like to take the early pregnancy test," I said.

"Ten dollars cash," she replied.

By now I was so adept at peeing on command that my urethra muscles had acquired superior strength. In the clinic bathroom, I peed into a small plastic container like the ones used to serve catsup in restaurants. The receptionist had taped my name on it. The bathroom had a little window in the wall, and inside the window was a ledge. It reminded me of a confessional booth. I slid my urine sample onto the ledge, returned to the waiting room and tried to find a rhythmic beat in the receptionist's gum-snapping.

The woman who called my name a few minutes later looked about 19 years old, a heavyset blond wearing stretch pants and too much lipstick. I watched her face for clues. She smiled at me encouragingly and my heart leaped up into my throat.

She led me into a little room and we sat down, and she looked into my eyes and smiled again, breathing a heavy sigh. "You're not pregnant," she said, and I realized suddenly that we were viewing the situation from opposite shores. I could practically read her mind—*No abortion! Your life is still your own! Nothing to explain to your parents!*

"Okay. Thank you," I said, and I didn't start crying until I was locked inside my car with the air conditioning vents blasting into my face.

My body's cycle decided that the second insemination would occur on a Sunday. For the first time, we had no trouble finding a space in the hospital parking lot. Dr. Hay was on call for the weekend. He was a handsome man with enormous biceps, like a graying Tom Selleck in a surgical suit. I apologized for dragging him in on a Sunday, but he brushed aside my concerns with enthusiasm. He acted thrilled to be doing a sperm transfer.

Bob trotted off to the bathroom, paper bag in hand. I wondered if they ever brought in new magazines. Mission accomplished, Bob returned to sit next to me. Again, we waited until the nurse called us in. When we were settled in the examining room, Dr. Hay burst through the door with excitement, and clapped Bob on the shoulder. "That is the most amazing sperm sample I've ever seen, man!" he exclaimed. "Come see!"

I remained prone on the table, legs splayed, covered by a blue paper sheet, staring at the ceiling while the men went to study my husband's virility. Dr. Hay called my husband the Sperminator. "The nurses are afraid they'll get pregnant just looking at him!" said Dr. Hay. Bob tried not to act proud of himself.

That Sunday I went home with extra hope. Of course it didn't happen the first time, I told myself. We were going to be pregnant—I just knew it. With so many sperm floating around, who wouldn't be? But none of them took.

The third insemination attempt occurred on a weekend as well. This time we were joined by another couple going through the same process, except they were trying for a second pregnancy. Their first child, also conceived through artificial insemination, was two years old.

Since we were the only patients, the nurse introduced us, and we chatted awkwardly while waiting. The husband was scrawny, with sallow skin and a pockmarked face. A thin line of bristly hair rested unconvincingly on his upper lip. He stared at his lap, clearly mortified to be outed as a man incapable of knocking up his wife.

We went through the routine simultaneously, and sat together while the sperm took a spin in the washing machine.

As we sat there, I was struck with a terrible thought. What if the nurse mixed up the two sperm samples? My stomach lurched, and panic rose in me. I thought I might vomit. I turned to Bob.

"What if she mixes up the samples?" I whispered in his ear. He smiled at me, thinking I was joking.

"I'm serious!" I said, and this time my voice was shaking. He looked surprised.

"They do this all the time," he said. "I'm sure they're careful."

I shook my head, and soon became inconsolable. The more I thought about it, the more likely it seemed. A few minutes later, the nurse called us into the examining room, and I spoke up.

"Are you sure you have the right sperm?" I asked.

She laughed. She thought I was joking, too. "Don't worry!" she said.

But I suffered through the procedure with a growing sense of dread.

In the days that followed, I became convinced that the mix-up had occurred. The thought of carrying that wormy man's child was more than I could bear, and I finally resorted to praying that I wasn't pregnant.

I wasn't.

THREE

I grew up just outside of New Orleans in a storybook family: a mom and a dad and four kids with two cars, a dog, and a house in the suburbs, and weeks filled with after-school activities and Girl Scout meetings. But weekends and summers, we lived in Goodbee, Louisiana. Dad had always wanted a place in the country, and had purchased a dilapidated old shell of a house on 60 overgrown acres. The first time he took us to see it, he made us wait on the porch while he chased the bats out with a broom.

But it became a respite from our hurried lives. On Saturday nights, Dad often built enormous bonfires, and invited anybody over to drink beer and watch the orange flames arc up toward the stars.

Everyone looked forward to the bonfires. My sisters and I collected brush until the pile looked like a teepee, and watched the sun crawl down into the tree line, anxious for dusk to arrive.

The third year of the bonfire, I was ten years old, and old enough to start poking holes into the weave of my life.

Dad had spent the whole day getting ready, using the tractor to haul limbs to the fire site and icing down cases of beer. We helped him fill buckets of water to keep handy in case the flames overstepped their boundaries.

By early evening, the cars and trucks started pulling in, and I appointed myself parking attendant, jumping up and down to show drivers where to go.

The rest of the evening passed in a blur of hot dogs and laughter and mosquito bites; I can't remember what time it was when people began drifting away. The fire had died down to burning embers, and Dad wet them good until a gray smoky pillar rose up to the treetops.

"Let's walk up front and close the gate," he called to me when everything was done.

I looked toward the lights of the house, where my sisters were already in their pajamas, then turned to peer into the darkness. The front gate was about a quarter-mile away, with a narrow unpaved road that twisted around the oak trees.

"It's too dark," I said.

"You afraid to go with your ol' Dad? C'mon."

I was so scared my chin quivered and I could hardly lift my feet to make them move. The frogs croaked in an amplified symphony, and an owl's hoot sounded like a clear warning to stay away. Dad put his arm around my shoulders and we plunged into the black night. I took tentative steps, unable to see even the path beneath my feet. The gravel crunched under my shoes and echoed into the dark, alerting my imagined attackers to our presence. My heart beat against my ribcage, and I felt hot tears pushing their way out.

"I'm scared, Dad!" I started crying, and stopped walking.

"Oh, baloney," he said, impatiently. "Nothing to be afraid of." We continued.

I looked up to see his face, and saw only the shape of his head high above me. I watched as he lifted the beer in his hand to his mouth; I saw the shadow of his chin point up as he swallowed. For the first time ever, my father wasn't saving me from my fear. He was by my side, as he always would be, but I suddenly knew he couldn't keep me safe from the dark. The dangers ahead, the dangers behind, all were obscured by the murkiness of the night, and exaggerated by my very inability to define them. All I could do was hold onto him, and move forward.

Bob and I tried artificial insemination a total of six times before meeting with the reproductive endocrinologist. Dr. Owns was a nice-looking man, tall and tan with sandy brown hair and an athlete's gait. I wondered if he was married or had children. I'm still mystified that a guy who looks at vaginas all day can still get turned on by vaginas. I don't get men at all.

Dr. Owns spent a minute going over my records. "I think your tubes are blocked," he said. He speculated that I was ovulating, but my eggs had nowhere to go. I had already undergone surgery to have my tubes cleared; subsequently, I had been diagnosed with endometriosis, but the doctor had cleaned out the accompanying scarring from my reproductive parts. Apparently, though, the scarring had returned.

"I recommend in vitro," he said. The in vitro process, in the simplest of explanations, entails inducing a woman, through drugs, to produce as many as 30 eggs in one month—the usual number is one—then extracting the eggs, making embryos using the man's sperm, and finally transferring the embryos to the woman's uterus and hoping one of them survives.

Bob and I had spent hours and hours discussing our apparent infertility, and the impact this fact could have on our life together. Repeatedly, we spoke of our good fortune, of how lucky we were to have each other, a nice home, and a great dog. It was the truth; aside from irritations like my husband blowing his nose on my bath towel and me suffering from crippling bouts of depression, we had lives filled with friends, travel, and relative privilege. If infertility became our cross to bear, well, it's something we could endure. We could take our nieces and nephews on extravagant trips, and return them when they got mean.

I felt ambivalent about in vitro, both morally and practically. The dilemma of multiple births festered in my mind like a splinter. Conceiving more than two children presented an unimaginable choice: abort one or more of the fetuses, or take a chance on the health of all of them. Again, Bob felt more comfortable with the concept. His faith in medicine has always towered over mine.

I bought books and pored over them, cringing at stories of women who had finally conceived through in vitro on the seventh or eighth try. In the end, I worried we'd regret not trying it. We decided to do it once. If it didn't work the first time, we'd abandon the journey and set off in a new, childless direction, and we'd still be happy. We didn't realize at the time that "trying it once" was like having a head-on collision just once, or only once having a skin graft. And even so, we'd try it twice.

For a long time after it was all over, I kept the leftover hypodermic needles in the bathroom closet, along with some extra doses of the medication. I don't know why. I knew we'd never do it again, but I couldn't just throw it all out. Even now, we have four embryos frozen. Dr. Owns charges us storage fees every year, but we never pay. I fucking hate him.

Years later, I retrieved my medical records from Dr. Owns' office, and was stunned at the sterile, academic way in which our journey had been recorded. "The patient had previously emptied her bladder and was placed in the exaggerated dorsolithotomy Trendelenburg position," reads one report. "The anterior lip of the cervix was grasped with a single-tooth tenaculum. A Frydman catheter was inserted to a depth of approximately 6.5 cm. Embryo transfer was performed. The patient remained in the exaggerated dorsolithotomy Trendelenburg position for 90 minutes following the transfer."

It's the language of medicine, I know. But it seems so far from accurate. A more truthful accounting might be: "Patient shaking badly due to fear. Nurse helps her lay back on the surgical table at an awkward incline, so head is closest to floor. Doctor tells her not to worry. Patient stares at doctor's unruly eyebrows peeking out from mask, suppresses a giggle, then realizes she's hysterical with anxiety. Four embryos (which could very well grow into human beings) placed in patient's uterus. Patient placed in a row with other patients, all of whom lay in awkward reclining positions, and all of whom have been recently implanted with newly-formed embryos they hope will turn into children."

But that bit came later. In hindsight, it was almost the easy part.

Before we could begin the process, Dr. Owns wanted to perform a hysteroscopy, in which a long thin scope is inserted through the vagina and used to check out the uterus. It's a relatively minor procedure, but it did, at least in my case, require general anesthesia, and it took place in the hospital.

Dr. Owns found a polyp in my uterus, which he removed. He saw evidence of fibroid tumors. But besides the polyp, he told us afterwards, my reproductive organs were in fine condition, with no indication they would be unable to protect a fetus for nine months. "Vulva is unremarkable," he wrote in a report. "Cervical and vaginal mucosa is unremarkable." I tried not to be insulted.

When I had recovered from surgery, Bob and I met with the in vitro nurse. She sat us down to watch a video about the process, which consisted mainly of close-up shots of a woman's butt with sharp needles, held lovingly by a husband, hovering above the flesh menacingly.

"Can you do that?" I asked Bob. "Can you give me shots?"

"Oh, yeah," he said, a little too eagerly.

Note: Women who are uncomfortable discussing or demonstrating various bodily functions in front of their partners might have trouble with in vitro. During this process, I discussed and freaked out about everything in front of my husband. I described the exact location of every cramp. We had long discussions about discharge. And of course he had to look at the cheeks of my ass twice a day, pinching them to find a good fatty part in which to stick a needle.

We talked a lot about menstruation. I was supposed to take ovary-stimulating medicine within a certain number of days of my period starting. My period, in those days, started oddly: some spotting, then nothing, then virtual gushing. "When do you think my period really starts?" I asked Bob. Like he would know.

"I don't know," he said. "Doesn't it just ... start?" Men know nothing.

I finally called the nurse.

"Well, Dr. Owns likes you to call at 'First Blood,'" she said.

We received prescriptions for $800 worth of meds and several dozen hypodermic needles. The medication was so rare and sophisticated that only one pharmacy in our area carried it, and I had to call ahead to order it.

It looked a lot like crack cocaine. The medicine came in little sealed vials, each one with a white powdery rock. Another set of vials held the solution needed to liquidate the rocks.

Bob had always thought he would have made a good doctor, and so being cast in the role of chief administrator of this project thrilled him. Each morning, at exactly 6:45 am—it was important to give the injections at the same time each morning and evening —he stood in the kitchen and measured the solution into the needle, injected it into the medicine vial, then sucked it back out. He held the needle aloft and tapped the plastic, trying to eliminate air bubbles.

In preparation, I sprawled on my stomach half-naked. He handed me the needle while he used alcohol wipes to clean a patch of skin. And then, with vigor, he plunged the instrument into my butt.

It wasn't a quick shot. It took him a few seconds to fully inject me. Sometimes he hit the right spot. Sometimes he hit a nerve, and I screamed, causing the dog to leap up and lick my face. Sometimes I stayed on the bed for ten minutes, crying about the ache and the humiliation and the sheer absurdity of it all. Bob always curled up behind me and cried with me until I was ready to start the day.

For weeks, I received the shots twice daily. It made for some scheduling conflicts, since the meds had to be given at precise intervals. Once Bob injected me in the bathroom of a community center, once during a dinner party at a friend's house.

But mostly we did it in our home. The kitchen cabinet where we normally kept glasses had been cleared out and restocked with dozens of vials of meds, needles wrapped in sterile plastic, and used needles securely stashed away in an old spaghetti sauce jar.

In addition to the shots, I had to wear hormone patches to increase the level of something-or-other. At first it was one patch. Then two. Then four. Eventually, I wore eight—so many I ran out of room on my body. Although they were designed to stick to skin through swimming, bathing and sweating, they didn't. I bought waterproof bandages and stuck them over the patches, and still they fell off, leaving sticky residue on my skin.

I tried wearing them on my rear and on my stomach. I tried wearing them on my thighs. When they did stick, they itched. When they didn't, they slipped off, leaving me terrified I wasn't getting some substance crucial to the success of implantation. I developed a habit of feeling my ass to see if they were there.

Adding to the stress were my daily restrictions. Dr. Owns had ordered me to stop taking Prozac, to refrain from vigorous exercise, and to avoid alcohol and caffeine. So as I waited for the joy of pregnancy, I was depressed, inactive, sober, and sluggish.

And fat ... the eggs made my stomach swell. Twice people asked me if I was pregnant. I would have preferred being in a drug-induced coma.

All of the medications were supposed to hyper-stimulate my ovaries to produce lots and lots of eggs. As the weeks passed and we came closer to my ovulation time, Dr. Owns began checking me every few days, then every other day, then daily. Upon arrival at the office, my blood was drawn. My blood was drawn so often, the insides of my elbows were perennially blue. I have bad veins, anyway, and sometimes the nurse drew blood from the back of my hand.

Dr. Owns checked my progress with an ultrasound machine, counting the number of eggs attached to my ovaries. I apparently made an excellent hen—as the date drew closer, he counted a dozen ... 17 ... 22 eggs.

I could feel my body changing, too. My abdomen felt sore and bloated; I was sure I could actually feel my ovaries when I pressed my lower belly. The hormones were causing mood swings and some nausea. When my blood levels and the size of the eggs indicated it was time to extract them, I underwent yet another surgical procedure. Exactly 36 hours earlier, I had received an injection that would cause the eggs to drop off of the ovaries. At the appointed time, I was given a sedative. Dr. Owns, with an embryologist close at hand, extracted the eggs—28 of them! In the meantime, Bob made yet another trip to the masturbatorium.

The next day, I started on progesterone, which is what pregnant women naturally produce to help line the uterus so that the fetus will have a nice comfy place to live. I only needed one progesterone shot per day, but it was enormous, and just looking at the needles made me queasy. The progesterone was thick and viscous, and injecting it was like forcing Jell-O through a pinhole. After just a few days, my ass looked like an abstract rainbow-colored painting.

Three days after the eggs were removed, I returned for the implantation. The embryologist had combined my eggs and Bob's sperm into microscopic baby seeds, which would be planted in me and encouraged to grow.

The implantation was physically quite easy, no more uncomfortable than a pelvic exam. But the enormity of what we were doing felt overwhelming.

Dr. Owns advised implanting five embryos, mainly because of my age (I was 35). The older a woman is, the lower the chances of conception—implanting five embryos rather than three or four dramatically increased the probability of becoming pregnant. But I wasn't comfortable with this number. Numerous in vitro cases had been in the news lately. I didn't want to be pregnant with five children, but I didn't think I'd have the emotional strength for "selective reproduction"—aborting two or more of them. Dr. Owns felt certain that five was the right number for us. The chances of more than two of the embryos surviving were very low, he said, and implanting any fewer than five would significantly reduce our chances of success. He couldn't understand my concern. "What are you *worried* about?" he asked, like I was wasting his time, and I wanted to hit him.

I consented to five, though I don't know why. A friend had recently consented to three, and had conceived triplets. She miscarried one of them; the other two were born early, and with a myriad of problems.

As I reclined on a table, Dr. Owns used a long thin tube to transfer the embryos from a petri dish into my uterus. It only took a couple of minutes.

Afterwards, I was wheeled into a recovery room. A nurse drew a curtain around me. For the next 90 minutes, I remained on a gurney, a pillow elevating my lower body so that gravity would keep the embryos in place, at least for a while.

Dr. Owns came to check on me. "I'm pregnant, right?" I asked him. He looked at me oddly.

"I mean, technically, right now, I'm pregnant, right? I have five human embryos in my uterus?"

He laughed, or sort of scoffed. "I guess you could say that." *Asshole*, I thought. I wasn't trying to be funny. I couldn't see around this fact, that for 90 minutes, I was pregnant, albeit with more microscopic children than I ever wanted to have. The minutes ticked away as I considered my new status. I closed my eyes and imagined the babies inside of me, swimming around, blindly searching for a patch of uterus in which to hide, finding nourishment in nothing more than my unbridled desire to give it to them.

I was ordered on bed rest for the rest of the day. Bob took me home and propped me up in bed, putting so many pillows beneath my lower body that I felt unreasonably contorted. "Don't want 'em to roll out!" he joked with me. But he was clearly excited, and so anxious to feel a part of it, of me, of this day when our baby, conceived in a petri dish, may have come home for the first time.

The real pregnancy test seemed a long time away. According to Dr. Owns' schedule, exactly two weeks after the implantation, I would go into the doctor's office for a pregnancy test. It would be a blood test. A nurse would call me later in the day with the results.

The intervening time was so volatile I could barely function. I had read women often feel an embryo taking root in the uterus a few days after implantation; for days, I waited for a telltale cramp. Some days I *knew* I was pregnant. Other days I knew I wasn't, and just wanted the ordeal to be over. Again I constantly pushed on my boobs to see if they were sore; again, after enough pushing, they were.

I wasn't tempted this time to go to the abortion clinic for a urine test. Dr. Owns had told me that only a blood test could accurately predict whether I was pregnant, though I didn't believe him. The real reason I didn't go back, I think, was to preserve the hope.

My pregnancy test was scheduled for a Friday, the same day Bob was supposed to be at a conference in Memphis. He didn't want to go to the conference. That's silly, I told him. I'll be fine. Go. But he asked my mother to come stay with me so I wouldn't be alone to hear the news, and she did.

That day, before heading into work, I went early to Dr. Owns' office and gave more blood. I felt short of breath, giddy, and terrified. "Someone will call you this afternoon around three," the nurse told me. I plowed through the day, willing the hours to pass yet fearing the loss of possibility. As long as I didn't know, I was free to daydream, to wonder whether we should name a girl after my mother or my grandmother, or whether we could afford a full-time nanny if we had twins.

I called home every hour to check my answering machine in case the nurse had called. That's right—this was so long ago I didn't have a cell phone. I told my mother not to answer the phone. I wanted to hear it first myself.

Late in the afternoon, as I sat waiting on the living room couch with my mom, the phone rang. And as soon as I heard the nurse's voice, I knew. I could hear the slight drag of her words, the low monotone she must reserve for just these types of calls. "You're not pregnant," she said.

My mother held me as I cried. She stroked my hair and kissed my face, and my despair overwhelmed me, not just because of my sudden emptiness, but also because my mother cried with me. And I fathomed, absolutely, that she had for me a love I might never pass on. She had, I saw, a mother's love, and the same space inside of me was a hole full of nothing, a useless void.

I had miscarried my babies. Five tiny embryos—were they five tiny human life forms?—had been placed in my body for safekeeping, and they had perished, every single one. I wracked my brain to remember a misstep I might have taken, an injection we might have miscalculated, an extra sip of coffee I had sneaked. Had I failed to eat right? Had I spent too much time on my feet? Not enough? Had I been too pessimistic? Too upbeat? I searched for a reason other than simple fate. I wanted to know how I had failed so that next time, I could be more careful. We started the next series of shots with heavy hearts. I don't know why we did it at all—no living thing could have possibly survived my morose depression. This time, we didn't tell anyone. I didn't even tell my mother.

We didn't have to go through the whole process—several of our embryos had been frozen, and so we just needed to prepare my body to accept them. On the appointed day, the embryologist took four microscopic fertilized eggs from the freezer and thawed them out like chicken thighs. Then the doctor ushered them into place.

Several days later, while walking on the beach, my friend Anne spotted the telltale hormone patches peeking from beneath my swimsuit.

"What's that?" she asked. They were covered with bandages, as though they were covering up an injury.

"It's the patches," I answered. After a moment, I added, "We're trying again."

"Oh, sweetie," she said. She put her arm around me, and I could hear the pity in her voice. I hated myself suddenly, was filled with loathing for the type of person so pathetically discontent that she couldn't be happy with the sun and the sea and a good friend on the beach. I tried to stop the tears but they slid down underneath my sunglasses and I swiped at them, not sad but angry this time, angry with myself and my stupidity and this ridiculous damn quest.

After my breakdown, I didn't follow all of Dr. Owns' rules. I exercised as much as I wanted. I drank an occasional beer or glass of wine. I didn't freak out if we were late with the injections.

We were on vacation when it was time to take the pregnancy test, so I peed on a stick, just like the old days, and with the same result.

More tears, more rage—but this time, some relief, as well. It was over. No more.

The long dark path had been grotesquely illuminated for us, and as sure as we had forged forward despite our fear and misgivings, we now fled from its borders, for it had been a rocky, barren path I could have gone my whole life without seeing. Our new road stretched ahead, still dusky and unfocused, but nonetheless lined with hope and the promise of a more pleasant journey. We moved to the beach and started enjoying life again.

FOUR

After nearly two years of infertility treatments—and four years of trying to get pregnant—I was ready to not have kids. I made a list of things I wanted to do instead:

1. Buy a sportscar
2. Start riding horses again
3. Travel to Europe yearly
4. Take my nieces and nephews on fabulous adventures
5. Read the Sunday *New York Times* cover to cover each week
6. Maybe get another dog

In December 2000, I began to chip away at the list.

We test-drove a BMW 328i sports coupe with a sunroof. I think Bob thought it was better than sex. He grinned uncontrollably as we sped down the highway. "Feel that engine?" he screamed, trying to be heard over the wind/stereo/fifth-gear revving noises.

I loved the BMW, and I believed I deserved it. I had spent a year of my life allowing my husband to shove big syringes into my butt, and the least I deserved was a flashy little sports car.

The next month, I went horseback riding with a friend. On the way to the ranch, I drove down the country roads in my Beemer, sunroof open, Johnny Cash on the stereo. At the barn, I held out an apple piece to my horse and shivered when his rubbery lips grazed my palm. When I threw my leg over the saddle and settled into the stirrups, I leaned my head against his damp, hot neck and felt my heart pounding.

I grew up riding. When I was seven, I counted up the $23 I had managed to save and gave it to my father, asking him to buy me a pony. He did, and for the longest time he let me believe my Junie had cost exactly $23.

We kept Junie—and Dad's horse, Big Red—at the country property, the same place we had the bonfires. She was a beautiful paint pony stained brown and white, with a stocky brown head and a white streak running down her shoulder. Her mane and tail and legs were white, and she had a perfect white star on her forehead. I spent hours roaming trails through the woods around the country cabin, often singing "Home on the Range" at the top of my lungs, or acting out the plot of the latest Roy Rogers rerun I had seen.

I developed into a horsey-girl. I lived and breathed horses. And so when I mounted Buck that day, and felt the same joy and sense of freedom that Junie had once brought me, I reveled in it. This, I thought, this I will have to do again. I'll use the nursery furniture money on this.

And so life was good.

On New Year's Day, 2001, I went for a walk on the beach with my dog. I was alone—not a soul besides me tracked through the sand. I found the most enormous, perfectly-shaped conch shell I had ever seen. Its nubs and curves were smooth, and it was streaked with countless shades of pink and beige and purple. I picked it up and held it to my ear; beneath the whooshing of the sea, I could hear the future beckoning. A week or so later, Bob and I took another long walk on the beach. The sun shimmered off the blue-green water, and the waves splashed onto shore spitting cold salty wisps into our faces. We held hands and watched our dog jumping whitecaps and licking dead fish. It's impossible to be unhappy while watching a dog at the beach.

We talked about our near-perfect lives. With seven years of marriage behind us, our relationship was strong and fun. Life together had become a harmonized melody. We had enough money to be comfortable. We lived a block from the ocean. We made frequent trips to see family. I was excited for an upcoming walking tour of Italy I had planned with my mom. I had come to understand that bearing children isn't a right, and that there was no reason for infertility to define me. If the worst tragedy to befall me was an inability to conceive, I would be a lucky woman. I felt sorry for women who couldn't see past the conventional path carved out by a judgmental society.

In the past, we had talked about adoption. People asked us all the time: Have you considered adoption? It was a question that exasperated me. Of course we'd thought of it. But adoption seemed like a completely different decision. It seemed second-best, like an option that would lead to piteous words of consolation from family and friends. I did not want to adopt a child out of desperation.

As we walked along the beach that day, the subject of adoption hadn't been broached for months. It had been a year and a half since our last failed attempt at conceiving, and it had taken that long to heal. But the wound had closed. Once again, we were content, both with each other and with our lives. Walking on the beach, feeling the sunshine reddening our cheeks and musing lazily about what to cook for supper, I couldn't imagine a place I'd rather be.

So when Bob squeezed my hand and took a deep breath, I assumed he was going to ask me a question no more complicated than, "How about grilled salmon?" or "Should we bathe the dog tonight?"

"What about adoption?" he said.

Silence. Then, "What about it?" I answered, surprised. I had pushed the idea into a cramped corner of my brain—frozen like some long-forgotten casserole dish that may or may not still be edible.

But Bob was feeling old. He was to turn 40 soon. If he was going to have a child, he said, it was time to get started.

He emphasized that he felt fine about not having children, but that if we were going to do it, it had to be soon.

"Why should we adopt?" I asked him. "We're happy. We have everything. I'm finally excited about not having kids."

Obviously we had a lot to give a child: food, shelter, security —and more importantly, lots of love, attention, and family.

But what would an adopted child do for us?

It was selfish, I know, but relevant. I didn't want to adopt a child out of some misguided sense of responsibility, swooping down upon an orphan like a save-the-world hippie do-gooder intent on earning societal brownie points.

Bob admitted to feeling slightly obligated to raise a child. Our values, he said, and our love—we should bestow them on a child.

Bob also was convinced that bringing a baby into our lives would magnify the joy we already had. We would give this child a home; in return, the child would give us a depth and spirit we didn't know existed.

I was not at all convinced, nor did I want to be convinced. Adopting a child would complicate our lives, overextend our hearts, and reduce our freedom by at least half.

I agreed, however, to set up an appointment with a local adoption agency just to discuss it.

There were—are—dozens, perhaps hundreds, of agencies open to helping people find children to adopt. Some are reputable, some not. Particularly when it comes to international adoptions, it's difficult to keep track of what the agency is doing. There was only one local agency at the time; I reasoned I'd have a better idea of how it worked if I was physically nearby.

We met with the owners, a couple, at 11 a.m. on Monday, February 5, the last day of my carefree, comfortable life.

Bunny was a large, comfortable woman with thick brown hair that fell to her waist, enormous brown eyes and a wide smile. She flicked her wall of hair frequently, as though to point out how laborious it is to be host to such a luxurious mane. She and her husband had three biological sons and, when we met them, four adopted children. Over time, they would adopt more and more. Eventually the total reached over seventeen. Bunny had been an elementary school teacher before starting her adoption agency a few years earlier. Tom had been a used car salesman.

Their small, cramped office was filled with pictures of adopted babies and toddlers, all of them beautiful and smiling. Bunny and Tom sat across from us at a table. They smiled broadly and chitchatted, waiting for us to ask for their help.

I started. "We want to explore the possibility of adoption," I said.

I explained that we had been through infertility treatments, but that we had subsequently decided our lives would be quite happy and complete without children.

"We aren't desperate for kids," I said. "We have a great life."

Bunny and Tom smiled at each other, sort of knowingly, like it was time for them to move in to make the sale. I hated how they thought they knew us.

"We just want to explore the possibility," I explained. We wanted to know, for example, how long it would take. How much it would cost. How healthy the children were.

"That depends," said Bunny. "Do you want an infant? Do you want to specify the sex?"

Bob and I looked at each other.

"We want a healthy infant girl," I said. To this day, I don't know where my voice came from at that moment. We had never spoken of the age or sex of the baby, and I'm not sure what prompted my reply. But I remember Bunny's response, and I remember having the dizzy, disorienting sense of time standing still that often accompanies a life-changing decision.

"Then you want to go to Vietnam," she said. And she pulled out a poster board filled with pictures of smiling, lovely, beautiful children adopted from Vietnam.

I don't remember, really, the rest of the conversation. We left a little while later, application in hand, and drove to the beach where we quietly ate sandwiches in the car. The windows were down and the sea-smell wafted in.

"I think we should do it," said Bob.

And just like that, it was decided. We each made a few cursory reference checks, but we both knew that we would use Bunny and Tom simply because we had been there. We looked into other countries, but our hearts already belonged in Vietnam.

I think back on that moment with awe. We're both natural skeptics and trained journalists, and had spent hours researching what car to buy, where to go on vacation, even what kind of mattress is best for sleeping. But we had spent more time investigating refrigerators than we had dedicated to making this monumental choice. I'm not a big believer in fate, or at least I hadn't been, up to that point. But as I drove home from that interview, everything fell into place. My infertility, Bob's patience, even that crucial walk on the beach—the events of my life seemed to line up like arrows all pointing in the same direction.

We filled out the application. One question asked why we wanted to adopt, and we wrote this: *We are not desperate for children, nor do we harbor the illusion that raising a child will be easy. We simply realize that introducing the world to a child, and helping her find her way in it, will teach us to love and live more deeply than ever before.*

FIVE

Every summer, loggerhead turtles crawl up on Atlantic coast beaches to lay eggs. Each nest contains dozens of eggs, sometimes over a hundred.

Sixty days after the mama turtle carefully covers her growing babies with sand and swims back into the sea, they hatch, and it's a spectacular thing to see.

The little turtles are perfectly formed, not even three inches long, and they nose their way out of the broken pieces of shell with inquisitive vigor. Using their flippers, they scale the walls of the sandy nest, and instinctively begin to trudge toward the ocean. It's a long, arduous journey from nest to water; even a footprint in the sand looms like a cavernous valley when you're less than three inches long and have flippers for feet. It's tempting to pick them up and help them along, but you can't. They need the exercise; the exertion helps develop their lungs and muscles to prepare them for the long swim ahead.

Each little turtle journeys alone, stopping for brief moments to rest. When he nears the crashing waves, he pauses and lifts his head, as if to make sure that he's really hearing what he thinks he's hearing, and then, with a renewed sense of purpose, he marches forth, faster and faster, flipping furiously, leaving a crooked, sandy trail in his wake, until finally he's at the water's edge.

The first wave usually knocks him backwards, but he perseveres. His little head bobs up like an olive, once, twice, and then he's gone, a new, miraculous addition to the creatures of the deep. He won't stop swimming until he reaches the Sargasso Sea. Their resolve astounds me, though I realize it's innate, as much a part of them as their eyes.

As we began the adoption process, we felt trapped on the bottom of a sandpit, clawing to be free, struggling to trudge through the sand, ups and downs be damned, just to have the opportunity to embark on an uncertain journey. And goddamn, the process was slow. We trudged through our own stretch of sand, perhaps more leaden than the turtles.

Obstacles sat between a baby and us. We needed to amass a pile of documents worthy of a complicated doctoral thesis.

Dee was our contact throughout the process. She worked for the agency as the Vietnam and China coordinator. Once we were accepted into the program, she sent out a packet of information that could easily have deterred us had she not warned us in advance, "It seems a lot harder than it is."

Dee, like Bunny, was also a serial adopter. She had two biological children, and seven adopted kids from China, Vietnam, Korea, and the former Soviet Union. An eighth waited for her in China. Most of them had special needs, including cleft palates and developmental delays.

Dee was a jovial, friendly woman with an infectious giggle and a weakness for tears (especially mine). She promised to help us through the adoption every step of the way, and she answered our countless questions with patience. She sympathized with our past disappointments, and told us those days were over. "With international adoption, it's not *if* you get a child, but *when*," she said.

Still, the "when" was contingent upon completing an endless list of tasks. The list of requirements read like a bureaucratic scavenger hunt. In order to submit our dossier to Vietnam—a dossier is the term used to refer to the final application that goes to Vietnam—we needed to have: numerous *certified* copies of our birth certificates and marriage certificate; certified copies of Bob's divorce decree; a notarized letter from our doctor testifying to our good health; results from blood tests screening for everything from syphilis to AIDS; police clearance; FBI clearance; permission from Immigration and Naturalization to adopt an overseas orphan; ten letters of reference; notarized letters from our employers; copies of our past three tax returns; a "home study" done by a qualified social worker; clearance from the state Department of Children and Families; an album of pictures of us, our extended family, and every room in our house; and finally, notarized letters signed by both of us giving power of attorney to a Vietnamese man whose name I couldn't even pronounce. The easy part was a 25-page application, which included questions about our marriage, our families, and our reasons for wanting to adopt.

Assembling the dossier became my full-time job. I spent hours on the phone ordering copies of certificates, re-ordering them when they arrived without the all-important seals from the Secretary of State, making dates with traveling notaries, and filling out paperwork.

I obsessed. Suddenly, Vietnam seemed to be everywhere in the news, and we lapped up information insatiably. For Valentine's Day, we bought each other travel books about Vietnam. I began researching and reading Vietnamese literature.

Mostly, though, we frantically assembled the needed documents, often resorting to begging and pleading in order to convince reluctant clerks to expedite our paperwork.

One morning, we woke early to stake out a place at the medical lab to give blood samples. We arrived before 7 am, and there were already seven people in line before us. Most of them appeared to be on parole and being screened for drug use.

An enormous woman sat behind the desk and thrust paperwork at people. The lab tech, a skinny woman with lots of jewelry and chipped nail polish, came into the waiting room to start the coffee maker, a bummer for those of us who had been fasting for the previous 12 hours.

A third employee arrived 20 minutes later, and chatted with the receptionist for a while about the county's upcoming Monster Truck Rally before calling in her first victim.

An hour and a half later, the skinny woman read my name off a chart, and I follow her back to the lab.

"I have terrible veins," I told her. "You might have to stick me in the hand."

She waved away my concerns, and began detailing to her colleague what she had cooked for dinner the night before. As she plunged and re-plunged the needle into the soft tissue of my arm in a fruitless search to locate my vein, she recited a horrific recipe involving fried chicken and Monterey Jack cheese. After bandaging up my right arm, she tackled the left, still rattling on about her culinary prowess.

Another 15 minutes. Finally, she said, "I'm gonna have to stick you in your hand."

After she coaxed four vials of blood from my aching hand, she clotted the needle prick with my fifth bandage of the day, and handed me a cup and tube-shaped vial. In a scripted tone, she said, "Pee in the cup. Pour it in the vial. Cap it. Throw away the cup. Give me the vial." She said it so quickly I asked her to repeat it, unsure of whether to pee in the vial or the cup or both.

In the restroom, there was a sign: *If you sprinkle when you tinkle, please be neat and wipe the seat.* I couldn't find any soap to wash my hands after collecting my sample, which made me leery of opening the door to leave. When I mentioned it to the skinny woman, she told me it was because people being screened for drugs try to use it as an additive. At least, I thought, any diseases I may catch at the lab won't show up on the blood test results.

A few days later, we headed to the Jacksonville office of INS—Immigration and Naturalization Services. We had heard countless nightmare stories about dealing with INS, but couldn't imagine it would be complicated. All we had to do was have our fingerprints taken.

We arrived at 8 a.m. The office didn't open until 8:30, and there were at least 50 people already in line. At 8:40, we filed into the office waiting room, passing through metal detectors to get there.

We appeared to be the only American citizens in the room, which filled up quickly. As soon as all the seats were taken, the guards started refusing entrance to anyone who arrived at the door. They were told to come back another day.

For the next five and a half hours, Bob and I played hangman and watched a little girl sitting near us steal toys from all of the other babies nearby. The room was filled with waiting families, but there were no vending machines in the room or access to food or drink other than a dribbling water fountain. No one was allowed to leave and then come back. Four televisions hung from the corners of the waiting room, and all screens showed a continuously-running video on how to saddle-train a horse, though hardly any of the people in the room spoke English and none appeared to be cowboys.

The fingerprint man periodically came out of his office to say he was running behind, or that the computer was broken, or that someone had incorrectly filled out a form. He barked at anyone who asked him a question.

By the early afternoon, I felt fully qualified to train a horse. I had done the crossword puzzle in the morning's paper. I had written in my journal. I had gone to the bathroom four times, twice just to pass the time. Finally, the fingerprint man called our names.

He blackened our fingers, pressed them down on a piece of paper, and had us sign our names. It took about two minutes. Then he handed me two yellow postcards—comment cards—and told me to fill them out. He watched me as I put pen to paper. I smiled at him. He did not smile back. "Excellent," I checked, for every question asked. "Excellent. Excellent. Excellent." At the bottom, I wrote, "Thanks so much!"

The most stressful part of the dossier was the home study. A single unknown person held the key to our desire to raise a child —she alone prepared the document that analyzed our strengths and weaknesses, our sincerity, our very ability to be good parents. She attained all of this perspective from a one-hour interview. Apparently her $2,000 fee would encourage her to evaluate us in a timely, positive manner.

Foster parents undergo similar screening, a fact that clears up, in my mind, some of the problems with the foster care system. But that's another story.

The social worker assigned to us was named Sue. She called one afternoon to arrange a time to visit, and told me not to worry about cleaning my house or doing any special preparation. *Right*, I thought.

Sue warned us of two questions she would ask that tend to throw people off.

1. What values did your parents instill in you growing up?
2. What are your strengths and weaknesses?

I did not find these to be particularly hard questions. But I passed them along to Bob so that he could mentally prepare.

"So," I asked him. "What are your weaknesses?"

Heavy sigh.

"Can I just say," he answered, "that one of your weaknesses is that you always think about weaknesses first?"

That's true, I thought. To me the glass is always half empty. I tried to quiz Bob, but he refused to answer, accusing me of thinking he was not smart enough to wing it. "It has nothing to do with smartness," I told him.

On the home study day, I watched the clock. I called Bob to make sure he left work when he promised. I wiped the sink 14 times. I wasn't worried about passing some sort of test, really, but more about any unforeseen circumstance that could either make us seem unfit, or alienate us so much that Sue would write bad things about us in revenge. If Bob arrived late, for example, and I was unable to hide my extreme displeasure, would she jot down a little note? (i.e., adoptive mother—sort of a bitch). What if our dog growled at her?

Sue arrived on time, and we showed her the house. While giving her the tour, I made idle conversation, telling her about the macaw that lives at the house behind ours and screeches all day long. She laughed.

"Once," she said, "we were on a trip to Jamaica, and I started talking to this huge macaw at the bar. It looked at me and said, *Fuck off! Fuck off!*"

We settled in on the couches, and Sue began asking us what she called routine questions.

"What color is your hair?" she asked me, looking directly at my head.

"It's red," I said.

She shrugged. "For all I know, you could dye it," she said.

"What color are your eyes?" she asked.

"Blue," I said. This continued until she had all of our basics. I lied about my weight, because why not? Bob told the truth about his.

As we sat there, I recognized the weird dynamic between us: all three of us held a degree of authority here. It was our house, obviously—and in addition, we had paid her to come evaluate us.

And yet we were the ones on trial. We needed her written opinion that we would be fit parents.

In a way, I had looked forward to this. Bob and I knew we'd be good parents, and I was confident in our ability to articulate why. I had carefully thought about her questions, and had practiced answering them aloud while driving my car. I suppose I had expected (hoped for?) some protracted philosophical dialogue through which I could prove my sensitivity and intelligence.

"What values did your family instill in you?" she asked me.

"Well," I said, looking out the window in what I hoped was a thoughtful pose, "my parents really taught me the importance of family. My three sisters and I, we have remained close, and see each other several times a year."

I paused for a breath. I planned to further expound on the topic—I wanted her to know that we talked by phone almost every day, that I had flown across the country to visit my sister when she needed help with her two babies, that my nieces and nephews feel as much a part of me as my limbs. But Sue was done with me.

"And you?" said Sue, addressing Bob.

Bob responded briefly, recognizing that a longer answer wouldn't be appreciated. "My parents taught me a love of learning," he said.

"Very good," said Sue. She seemed to like his answer better, which made me feel inadequate and jealous.

We turned to strengths and weaknesses. For strengths, I spoke about our strong marriage, my sensitivity, and my love of kids.

I had to limit my weaknesses. I could go on forever. "I'm a worrywart," I said. "And a procrastinator. And also, I find that as I get older, I have less tolerance for intolerant people."

Sue looked at me blankly. Finally, a chance to pontificate.

"I mean, it's hard for me to tolerate people who don't respect other people's differences," I explained. "Like, people I meet who seem to be racist. I'd just rather not be around them."

"Oh!" she said, with apparent dawning. "I know what you mean! My father, he uses the n-word a lot. Although I don't say anything because he's old, it bothers me. But I really get on him when he uses the g-damn word."

I took mental notes. The n-word: not so bad. The g-damn word: unacceptable. We moved on. Bob talked about his strengths—patience, intelligence—and his weaknesses—doesn't like confrontation, forgetfulness.

Then, Sue asked us about how we planned to discipline our children.

Bob and I had talked about this at length; ever since witnessing a neighborhood father slap his toddler.

The incident had been on my mind. It was just a spanking— few people would call it abuse—but it seemed so utterly pointless. And so, when Sue asked us about disciplining our child, we were both ready. "No hitting," I said. "We both agree that we don't believe in hitting." We talked about the alternatives, about time-outs and restrictions and loss of privileges. Sue jumped in eagerly in an advisory capacity. "Well," she said. "I spank all three of my children and find it very effective."

I nodded and smiled and inwardly cringed.

"Of course, all children are different," she went on. "My son, I could spank him forever and it wouldn't make a bit of difference. But my daughter, all I have to do is raise my hand to her."

She continued a little longer about the advantages of spanking. I focused instead about this journey of ours—this long, arduous trek toward a child. I imagined seeing my baby's picture for the first time, flying around the world to get her, kissing away her baby tears and rocking her back to sleep after a nightmare.

I thought about protecting her, forever and ever, from people like Sue the social worker, who believe saying *nigger* is better than saying *goddamn*, and think everyone should be aware of the benefits of hitting children. This woman, who would in the next few weeks compile an eight-page report on our fitness as parents, knew less about me than my dental hygienist.

We finished up, and we showed her to the door. Bob and I stood on the porch and watched the car disappear down the road.

"I hate her," I said.

"Me too," said Bob.

SIX

I should have known better than to tell anyone our baby's name too soon. In fact, we shouldn't have told anyone until we had her home and it was a done deal and we wouldn't have to endure the unwelcome advice from self-appointed baby-naming experts. But keeping secrets isn't part of my makeup.

It was Bob's choice: Scout. He had told me years ago that he loves the name—from his favorite book, *To Kill A Mockingbird*—and that he wanted to give it to his daughter. Perfect.

But I had my concerns, chief among them what I called the Demi Moore Factor. Demi Moore and Bruce Willis had named their first child Scout, and I worried people would think we were imitating them, which made me apoplectic.

I tried the name out on some strangers to test their reactions. A clerk at the baby store said, "Oh, just like Demi Moore!" A secretary at the adoption agency said, "Doesn't Demi Moore have a daughter named Scout?" When I looked the name up in a baby book, it said, "Popularized by actors Demi Moore and Bruce Willis." Goddamn it. But I only became more determined. It was unfair that Demi and Bruce could own the name. I discussed the issue with Bob. "What if Scout Willis grows up to be a movie star?" I asked him.

"It'll never happen," he said, which was an excellent point. "And so what if it does?" We agreed, in the beginning, to keep the name to ourselves. And for several months, we did.

One Friday afternoon, my friend Anne and I met for end-of-week cocktails. Anne is one of my dearest friends, and I knew she would play a significant role in my daughter's life. We began talking about how different our lifestyles would be with a baby in the picture.

"I'm totally unprepared for this baby," she told me. I hadn't considered how our baby's life would change the lives of anyone other than us, but here was proof; other people loved her already, too.

In the loving, intimate spirit that often accompanies a beery haze, I had a sudden urge to share with Anne our baby's name. I had promised Bob I wouldn't tell anyone without his permission, so I called him from the bar via cell phone to ask if I could.

"I'm surprised you lasted this long," he sighed. "Go ahead."

I divulged my secret.

"I like it!" she said. "I like it a lot!"

"Really?" I asked, hoping she would continue to lie to me if she didn't. "You don't think it's too weird?"

"No!" she said. "Not at all. I think it's great."

The next day, I felt terribly guilty for telling Anne before telling my sisters.

"Bob," I said. "I have to tell my sisters. It's only fair."

So I called them all and told them, and each pretended to like it.

Then—"Bob," I said. "It's not fair that my sisters know and not my mom."

My mother could not be cavalier about it. "Scout?" she said, doubtfully. "Huh."

My grandmother asked, "How's she ever gonna learn to live with a name like Scout?"

I dreamed sometimes that Scout had been born. I even pictured her mother—her birth mother—and imagined her in labor. In my mind, she was young, maybe 23, and beautiful. Unmarried, living in a rural village amidst farmland.

She lay in a bed, not in a hospital, and pushed, her black hair slick against her sweating forehead, eyes swollen and voice raw. Maybe her mother was there to help her. I hoped so.

And finally when the bloody little bundle came out—that's my daughter, *my daughter*, I would think—she held the baby to her, momentarily unwilling to give away what's so rightfully hers.

I pictured her—the next day? A week later? Carrying my baby to the orphanage, trudging from her small village on dusty roads, stopping every 15 minutes to rest. And when she arrived at the door ... well, I never dreamed past that point. Did she explain why she couldn't keep her dark-eyed infant with ten fingers and ten toes? Did she leave my daughter on the doorstep and flee? Did she hesitate, just a little bit, enough to nuzzle my daughter's neck and whisper how much she loves her?

The women in Vietnam who gave up their babies did so in only the most dire of circumstances. Poverty, according to statistics, was the number one reason. Also, unmarried women feared being shunned for raising children out of wedlock. Waiting for my child became a time of impatient, bittersweet longing. I couldn't bring myself to wish for a mother to give up her child, and yet it was only under such tragic circumstance that my baby would come to me.

Dee, our case manager, kept saying the baby was growing in my heart, not in my stomach. But Scout was growing all through me. I felt her taking over my heart, my brain, my very bones. She was my waking vision and my final thought every single day.

Dee said God had a special baby for me, and that we shouldn't challenge God's plan. If God was involved, I screamed in my head, this adoption would not cost seventeen fucking thousand dollars. And anyway, is this how God plans stuff out? *I know! I'll get this girl pregnant, and I won't let this woman get pregnant, and then I'll make the first girl give her kid to the barren woman. That way, everyone has maximum suffering!* If God was involved in creating such a scenario, I have some serious questions.

I had heard that expecting an adopted baby was just like being pregnant, but it wasn't true. I did not feel pregnant in the least. I worried I was having a hysterical pregnancy, and that people thought I was preparing for a fake baby. Pregnant women don't have that problem. They waddle through the aisles at baby stores with authority and tangible justification, and everyone smiles at them knowingly. Their babies are right there. Their babies are fact.

Mine was ephemeral. An idea. A notion. A dream.

For my husband, it became real in a single moment. He opened up a gift from his mother—a crib mobile decorated with pink and blue bunnies sleeping atop fluffy white clouds. When wound up, it played, "Dream, Dream, Dream," by the Everly Brothers. Bob held it up and burst into tears.

My belief in the process came and went. Even as I prepared for the baby shower my friend Anne was throwing, I worried it would never happen.

"Do you think people will think … you know, that we're not really having a baby?" I asked her.

She looked at me. "What are you talking about?" she said. "Like you're just saying you're having a baby to get baby presents?"

A few weeks earlier, my period had been late, and I had been terrified that I was pregnant. I tried to understand my panic. Why was I so afraid of a longtime dream coming to fruition?

Finally, in tears, I told Bob. "My period's late and I'm afraid I might be pregnant," I said, my voice shaking.

"But why?" he said. "Why would that scare you?"

I couldn't answer, didn't know how. He thought for a while, and then he said, "Well, if you're pregnant, we'll have two babies, and that will be great."

And then I understood. I had been afraid of losing Scout. "Do you promise?" I asked him. "Do you promise we won't give up Scout?"

"I promise," he said. "Don't be silly. We will never give up Scout." My period started soon afterward, and I was actually glad.

Later, as I dressed for the baby shower, I looked in the mirror and saw, for the first time, Scout's mother. I was utterly attached to this nonexistent child. It filled me with both a joy and a dread. I loved her so much, despite the lack of anything to throw my arms around. It was like loving a scent, or a sunset, or a breeze. It consumed me entirely.

Bob's matter-of-fact approach—we are having a baby, and it's going to be great—helped him sleep soundly every night. I lay awake and thought: *Will she be pretty? Will she love us? Will we love her? Will I be a good mother? Will Bob change his fair share of diapers? Will my mother ever get used to the name?*

The other hard part of the waiting was the incessant questioning from people waiting with me. *Any news? When's she coming home? Do you have pictures? Why does it take so long?* More often, people said stupid stuff because they didn't know what to say. A friend told me, "You're so lucky you won't have to deal with the first few months of the baby's life." I smiled while silently stabbing her eyes out. An acquaintance asked if I was adopting because I couldn't have children of my own. "She will be my own," I said, daring her to ask again.

We told our neighbors, John and Jean, a 60-something middle-class white suburban couple. "We're adopting a baby from Vietnam."

"Ooh," said Jean. "You know, I've heard that a lot of people are going foreign these days! You know, to get away from the crack babies over here."

"What's the matter?" said John, chortling. "You didn't want one of those crack babies?"

I was horrified. "I'd love to have a crack baby!" I blurted out. Bob looked at me sideways.

"Now, will you teach her English?" asked Jean. Bob and I explained that she would be a baby, and that since she would be our child, an American child, growing up in America, yes, surely she would speak English.

Jean considered herself an expert on the subject of foreigners. Their daughter had married a Bosnian, she said.

"Oh, is he part of the local Bosnian community?" asked Bob, ever the diplomat. "We know a few people from Bosnia, and there's …"

"Yes, yes," interrupted Jean. "I begged her not to go out on a second date with this guy. Begged her! But she didn't listen. And now they're married, and I have one Bosnian grandchild with another on the way."

"He's a Maaahzlem," said John. "Not muslin. Muslin is a piece of cloth. He's a Maaahzlem." Furthermore, Jean said, sometimes she catches her son-in-law speaking in Bosnian to his daughter, and she has to correct him.

We finally extracted ourselves from the discussion, and walked toward home. "I feel dirty," I said. Later I thought of retorts I should have spouted off: *Foreign models have better warranties. Going foreign is all the rage. More baby for your buck.*

A friend called to congratulate me. "It's such a wonderful thing you're doing," he said.

"We don't think of it that way at all," I told him. "We're being a little bit selfish, actually—we want a family. And it won't be easy for her. We'll be taking her away from her home country, and her birth family. It'll be difficult."

"Oh," he said. "I see. So, in essence, you'll be stealing her away from her culture."

Sigh.

On September 11, 2001 the world burst at the seams, and suddenly it seemed imperative that I have my little family together immediately. The terrorist attacks on the World Trade Center had brought life to a standstill, and I watched with everyone else as the impossible unfolded. I surprised myself with my reaction—I had no personal connection to the victims, yet I shook with rage and grief.

I felt a surge of unlikely patriotism. I usually have lots of bitter rhetoric to spew. But I dug up an old American flag I had found half-buried on the beach, and hung it from our balcony.

"That flag looks like it's been to Afghanistan and back," said Bob. But it meant something to me, tugged at my heart somehow, and perhaps symbolized our country in my mind—battered but still flying.

As the 9/11 crisis evolved, patriotism swelled everywhere. Being an American took on new significance. I faced my own internal questions: What does it mean to be an American citizen? It was a poignant, difficult mystery for me, one I would be foisting upon my daughter.

I love this country because it's what I know. But we watch citizens around the world fight to their deaths for their own countries, even in places without the freedoms and bounty we have here. Scout would grow up loving Vietnam if she lived there. She will be an American because her birth mother couldn't raise her and because strangers yanked her from her roots and transported her 10,000 miles away. She would be an American, but she would always be questioned about where she's from. She will be an American but she will always have that suspicious hyphenation, Vietnamese-American, which sticks out like a conditional citizenship, a red flag, a dubious distinction. She would never be able to be president because she wasn't born here. She would be an American, and we assume that's a good thing. As an adult, she might feel differently.

I cycled through these thoughts as I waited, and the wait grew longer. At the six-month mark, just after the terrorist attacks, I started to panic. We thought sure we'd have a referral by six months. We passed the seven-month mark with no word.

The impatience, the disbelief, is hard to describe. I dreamed of the baby all the time; I woke convinced she'd never come. Even as I wrote thank-you notes for shower gifts, I wondered how to return all the presents since my inner cynic began to prevail.

We questioned our decision to wait for a baby girl. More boys than girls were available, simply because more adoptive parents seek girls. If we had requested a boy, our son would already have been at home, nestled in our arms. Maybe we should have considered a boy at the beginning. But we couldn't at that point, not now with little girl Scout so distinctly etched in our minds and our hearts. Not with Bob so excited to have a daughter. Not with the nursery covered in mermaids and a wardrobe filled with girly clothes and three pink receiving blankets.

Still, Dee dropped hints designed to convince us to rethink our parameters. "Would you consider an older baby?" she asked. I was desperate, a head-banging, tears-of-rage, short-tempered kind of desperate. "Maybe," I said. "I'll talk to Bob."

But I craved a baby's soft form, the way she would fit into my arms. I wanted to run my finger along her smooth gums, rest my cheek against the mere wisps of hair. I wanted to carry her around in the Baby Bjorn and watch people marvel at her. I wanted to be there, her tiny fingers clutching mine, when she took her first step, and to swoon with the scent of her softness, to watch her giggle when I blew raspberries on her belly.

It was a terrible, gnawing feeling and made me feel like a consumer, rejecting an older model in favor of a fresh new one. The faces of orphans haunted me. I often visited a website called Rainbow Kids with photo-listings of international children available for adoption. They stared out at me balefully, and I imagined their thoughts as they plastered on their best smiles for the camera: *Please take me home. Please be my parents. Please, please, please come get me. I'll be a good son. I'll be a good daughter. Aren't I worth something to you? To anyone?*

Looking at their pictures, my throat closed up and I ached to touch their faces, to kiss their foreheads.

But still, I waited for Scout.

On a Wednesday night, 13 days before Christmas, the call came. I had been in an exacerbated state of despondency, unable to contemplate a holiday season without news of a referral. I was probably on my third glass of wine. The phone rang, and I could see from the Caller ID it was Dee. I had no interest in talking to her unless she had news, and so I answered the phone skeptically. "Tricia," she said. "This is ..."

"Do you have news for me?" I blurted out.

"Yes," she said. "I do."

And with those three words, my world view shifted.

She said we were being offered the referral of a baby girl, born October 21 in the province of Bac Giang just north of Hanoi. The baby was so far healthy, and had tested negative for hepatitis and HIV. There was no picture yet—the photo hadn't transferred properly from Vietnam—but one would be forthcoming. She sent us what little paperwork she had, and we spent the evening reading and rereading the details of our daughter's existence.

Scout's birth mother's name was—is—Thi Hai, which is Vietnamese for "blue ocean," a fact I could hardly believe. She was

21 years old, and unmarried. A letter she gave to the orphanage had been translated into words that still feel burned on my skin, like a tattoo only I can see: *I am a young girl; I am unable to control myself in the love area, so I have given birth to my illegitimate child, Phuong. I hereby apply for transfer of my parental rights …*

My daughter's birth name was Nguyen Minh Phuong. Vietnamese names are written backwards, so Nguyen would have been her last name, and Phuong her first. We received varying translations for Minh and Phuong. But a Vietnamese woman sent us this definition via email: *Minh means clear, bright, smart … Phuong (depending on markings) could mean direction as in North, South, East, West or a certain red flower that blooms in the summer. They grow all over Central Vietnam and perhaps in the South. This flower is romanticized and its name is mentioned in many love songs about summer separation.*

It was a strange transformation, from expectant mom to motherhood based on nothing more than a phone call. I didn't want to give Bob the news on his cell phone, and he had already left work for home. So I wrote YOU'RE A FATHER! on a piece of paper and sat in the foyer with the dog to wait for him. When his car pulled into the driveway, I stood against the front door with the sign pressed against the glass, and watched him squint in the darkness. I watched him read the words—twice? Three times? And then I met his eyes.

"We're parents!" I shouted. "We got a referral!" We spent the evening calling friends and relatives and hugging each other and smiling so broadly our cheeks hurt.

By the next morning, I was feeling let down. My *alleged* daughter was 8,835 miles away. Could this possibly be real? The baby's picture didn't arrive that day, which fueled my cynicism. And yet, more snippets of info came, and a mental picture was emerging. At not quite two months old, our daughter weighed 7.92 pounds and was 22 inches long. Her head was 36 centimeters in diameter, her chest 37.5 centimeters. She was underweight for her age. Her respiratory rate was 38, and although I had no idea what it meant, I could close my eyes and envision a tiny heart pounding against the confines of a tiny 37.5-centimeter chest. I could feel her little body in my arms, her delicate weight like a feather against me. I found a tape measure and counted out 22 inches. Here are her toes, I thought, and here is her head. I thought quite a bit about her head. I wanted her to have a lot of hair.

On the third day after receiving the referral, I was glued to the chair in front of my computer, waiting for Dee to call me with news of the photo. I sat there for hours. I cruised dozens of websites offering products ranging from baby clothes and car seats to Vietnamese dolls and travel products. I searched for information about Bac Giang. I gazed at pictures of Asian babies on adoption websites.

Dee finally called to say she was sending the photo. It arrived at 1:14 p.m. I asked Dee to stay on the phone with me as my computer downloaded the image, slowly, pixel by pixel—the longest 10 seconds of my life.

From the top: I first saw a straw mat with a colorful painted border. And then, her hair! Black feathers sticking straight up, locks and locks of them. Brown eyes looking toward the right, not at the camera, wispy eyebrows arched with infantile concern. *Who was she looking at?* Lovely pale skin, pinkish against a pastel-patterned pillow. Full cheeks. Perfectly kissable lips, not smiling, not frowning. Wearing a bright yellow sweater etched in red piping, with a red and green design on the cuffs. Little fingertips peeking out. Tiny sock-covered toes pointed downward, like a ballerina's pose.

So beautiful. *My daughter is beautiful*, I thought.

I shook, and cried without tears. My physical being swelled with an unfamiliar emotion—motherhood, I guess? And I studied the photo again and again, top to bottom, incredulous that this digital configuration existed as a real child, a baby, my baby, our daughter, a family link we didn't even know had been missing.

In order to bring Scout home, we would have to travel to Vietnam twice—once to personally deliver our paperwork, and the second time to formally adopt her. Within days of the referral, we learned we'd be leaving for Vietnam mid-January. We would meet her on this first trip—hold her, even feed her, kiss her— then leave her at the orphanage for three to four months while the Vietnamese government processed our request. I imagined it would be like cutting off my arm, and having it sewn back on at a later date.

We traveled to New Orleans to spend the holidays with my family. For Christmas dinner, Dad set a place for Scout and put out an 8x10 framed photo of her to mark the spot.

SEVEN

The Hanoi airport sits amidst rice paddies. As the plane landed, we saw women in conical hats working in the fields, and water buffalo hauling carts along dirt roads. It was an astounding feeling, being delivered via airplane into this ancient country for the purpose of bringing home a child, and I wondered if I would ever be able to fully make sense of it.

After retrieving our bags, we headed into the airport lobby and waited for something to happen. Within seconds, a tiny energetic Vietnamese woman wearing big round glasses tugged on my arm. "Adoption?" she asked me in fast clipped English. "You here for the adoption?" The woman was Hanh, and she worked for the organization funding the orphanage. The organization, known in country as a facilitator, was tasked with handling the Vietnam portion of the adoption process. Hanh escorted us to the Hang Nga Hotel on the north side of Hanoi, a lovely old building with ornate mahogany beds, clean bathrooms, and a lobby filled with cigarette smoke. Staff greeted us with charming broken English, and the clerks smiled each time we passed the front desk; a restaurant atop the building offered fresh spring rolls, delicious French toast, lukewarm beer, and a 360-degree view of the city.

Hanh was not quite 40 and unmarried. She had worked for the facilitator for a decade, and she lived for the babies, remembering every one of them by their Vietnamese names even years after they'd been adopted. Hanh knew her way around the governmental web like she knew the streets of Hanoi, and we quickly came to see her as our fearless leader. For the next three days she flagged down taxis, dragged us into government offices, told us when to sign our names, when to keep quiet, when to smile, and when to offer a handshake.

In our off time, Bob and I headed out alone. We had spent months preparing for this journey, and not just because we were traveling to meet our daughter. We were also visiting the place of her birth, and we were thirsty for the taste of it. We had pored over guidebooks searching for places to visit and sites to see. We paid our respects at Ho Chi Minh's Mausoleum and toured the Hanoi Hilton—but in the end we found nothing more intoxicating than walking the streets of Hanoi, breathing in this exquisite country. We watched old women making the beef noodle soup called *pho* in cast iron pots on the sidewalks. Customers squatted down on stools next to them and sipped from steaming bowls.

In the park, men tied mirrors to wrought-iron gateposts and set up makeshift barbershops; customers stopped by in the noontime sun for a trim and a shave. Women carried poles across their backs, balanced by straw baskets on either side holding their wares, everything from flowers to rubber sandals. Hundreds of mopeds sped along the streets in no discernible order—no lanes, and no rules, apparently, against weaving wildly and gratuitous horn-blowing.

We had wondered how the Vietnamese people would react to us—representatives from a nation that nearly destroyed them not so very long ago. It was humbling and disconcerting how they welcomed us anyway, greeting us with their arms literally open, showing us their lives, their spirit, their love of children and family. Vietnamese is a tonal language, nearly impossible to learn for the casual observer—the word "ma," for example, has six different meanings—but we managed to communicate through hand motions, smiles, and a sense of adventure.

We ate like bears about to hibernate. Who visits a third world country and gains weight? But the food was so good, and so cheap, that we couldn't help ourselves, and we feasted on fresh seafood and salty noodles and stir-fry dishes.

We visited the orphanage on our fourth day. The trip north to Bac Giang wasn't far, but the highways meandered like poorly-paved back roads. We occasionally slowed down to allow a water buffalo to cross, or veered off the pockmarked asphalt to avoid a head-on collision.

After a 30-minute drive, we arrived in Bac Giang, and Bob and I stepped out of the van and into the rest of our lives.

The Bac Giang orphanage was a small, tidy, peach-colored building with a small fountain out front. It was surrounded by rice paddies, and usually housed fewer than a dozen babies and toddlers. But the facilitator also sponsored a boarding school for deaf children at the site, and so when the van stopped, a dozen children ran toward us and waved furiously.

We walked across the front yard and into the orphanage director's office. He offered us tea—room-temperature light brown water, which we accepted but didn't drink—and we sat, smiling and anxious, while he and Hanh chatted in Vietnamese. I had to restrain myself from screaming, "Oh my god, *shut up! Where is my child?*"

After a few minutes, Hanh and the director stood up and asked if we were ready. I practically jumped into their arms. We walked down the hall to a room, not small but not large, and my eyes searched the beds for Nguyen Minh Phuong.

I didn't see her. And when a young, kind woman with a wide smile placed a tiny bundle in my arms, I still did not see her so much as feel her. A wriggling eight pounds with a shock of black hair sticking straight up in the air. I didn't recognize her from the photo I had carried with me for weeks—it suddenly seemed like such a poor substitute for this living, breathing, baby girl.

Someone grabbed my camera and started shouting instructions at Bob and me—"Smile!" "Look here!" "All together now!"—and though I later enjoyed those pictures, in the moment I thought only of protecting our new little family from the commotion surrounding us. Bob put his arm around me and we turned our backs on everyone. I held Scout before me and gazed into her wide eyes—and she gazed back. Her face had mosquito bites, and I leaned over to kiss them. I kissed her little face over and over. And then—honestly—she smiled at us, a guileless toothless smile I still remember. She stared as though memorizing our faces. The Vietnamese nannies chattered around us; Hanh later said they thought Scout understood we were her parents.

We had brought Scout a little dress and a doll, and a small photo album with pictures of us, her new cousins, and her new home. Our baby's caretaker, the one who had first handed her to us, was named An, and we showed her the photos. An was in her early 20s, and had been working at the orphanage for several years. She lived in a little room adjacent to the orphanage. As we watched, she wrapped the baby in a blanket and snuggled the baby doll next to her head. We posed for pictures, the four of us, but Scout wouldn't look at the camera—she kept twisting her little head around, craning her neck to look at me. I wanted it to be because she knew I was her mother, but it was probably because I seemed like an enormous cartoon next to the petite dark women who cared for her.

Through Hanh we asked questions, and learned that Scout slept with An every night on a tatami mat. We saw the connection between them—this woman loved our baby, we had no doubt. A wave of envy passed through me, and I pushed it away and tried to feel grateful that An was giving our child her first taste of love, a security our daughter would carry with her forever.

The scant 45 minutes flew by, and just as my baby began to feel like an extension of me, it was time to go. I buried my face in her little neck, and smelled formula and spit-up. I could have breathed it in all day.

Back in the van I felt numb, already worried about when we'd be back, how I'd cope with the intervening time, and whether I'd wither up and die or kill someone if this adoption fell apart. Fortunately, our first trip to Vietnam turned out to be longer than most because of changes in Thai Air's flight schedule. Hanh, feeling sorry for us, arranged a rare second visit to the orphanage. On our last day in Hanoi, we made the trek back to Bac Giang, and spent three hours with Scout.

When we arrived, we found Scout asleep in a wicker basket, curled up next to a gorgeous baby boy. As we watched, she woke up, cried, and reached her small arms upward, asking to be held. A caretaker lifted her up and handed her to me. She needed changing—but babies at the orphanage didn't wear diapers. The caretakers wrapped soft old towels like loincloths around the babies' bottoms, then tied the towels in place with strips of cloth. When the babies needed changing, they were held over a small plastic tub of water and the caretakers swiped at their rear ends with washcloths. It seemed wholly unsanitary. But neither Scout nor the other babies had any sign of diaper rash. Briefly, I thought, *We should try that at home!* Then I banished the thought entirely.

When placed in my arms, Scout looked up at me and smiled, and I nearly shouted, "LOOK! LOOK! SHE REMEMBERS ME!" The caretakers grinned at each other, and nodded approvingly. We took Scout outside for a walk around the orphanage compound. It was a gorgeous day with blue skies and a warm breeze; Scout stared up at the trees like she'd never seen them before. She probably hadn't. Bob held her, too, but not for long—he said he liked watching us together.

It was An's day off, but she came over to say hello and invited us into her room for tea. We sat in tiny child-sized chairs while she organized the cups. It was an incredible honor, both for us to be invited and for her to host us as guests. She had no tea; she poured warm tap water into small porcelain cups. We sipped the water, humbled by her gesture. She spoke no English; we spoke no Vietnamese. She pointed at Scout, asleep in my arms, and then at Bob, gesturing that she thought they looked alike. We gave An some of the pictures we had taken earlier in the week, and she nodded her thanks.

Departure time seemed to arrive in a second. We gave final kisses to Scout, and I noticed that her hair was matted at the back of her head. An used scissors to cut off the knotted part; as it fluttered to the ground, Bob grabbed the little black tuft and put it in a film canister to keep. An laughed.

I spent the trip back to Hanoi trying to memorize my baby's face. My shirtsleeve smelled like her from where she had rested in my arms, and I sniffed that spot a hundred times.

"Didn't you just want to give her a bath?" asked one of the other adoptive moms. I did not. Scout had smelled milky and a bit sour, but the scent of her breath seemed like her very spirit and I savored the taste of her skin. A part of her stayed with me, just as a part of me had been left behind.

Back home, I fretted. I called and emailed the agency representatives handling our case almost daily. I was a nightmare client with no patience for the ambiguous, lackadaisical nature of Vietnamese bureaucracies. Finally, during the last week of March, we received a travel date, and on April 12, we boarded a plane for

Hanoi. This time, our bags were packed with diapers and onesies and blankets—and one special dress.

Over a year earlier, just after we decided to adopt a baby girl, I had bought this dress for Scout. It was expensive and, to me, exquisite—a white cotton frock with pastel embroidery on the collar, and matching bloomers. I had hung it in my closet and ran my fingers over it every day, in my mind slipping it over my baby's head and pulling her little arms through the sleeves. I couldn't wait to put it on her for real.

When we arrived in Hanoi, our old friend Hanh greeted us, and broke the news that we wouldn't be going to the orphanages the next day, as anticipated, but rather the day after that. It shouldn't have made any difference. We were there, in Vietnam, just days away from holding our girl, but I was tired, and scared, and fearful of anything that could jeopardize this union, and so I burst into tears. "I can't wait!" I whispered to Bob. "I just can't wait."

"You can wait," he responded. He mostly ignored my drama.

I came up with a plan to pass the time. The nearby Hotel Sofitel had a luxurious workout gym and spa, so Bob decided to lift some weights, and I arranged to have a massage, which did help my anxiety. Afterwards, I noticed the spa offered eyelash tinting. My eyelashes are nearly colorless; without mascara, they're invisible. If I got them tinted, I thought, I could go forego makeup for the rest of the trip. Plus, the process would consume an extra hour.

The eyelash woman washed my face, and motioned for me to close my eyes. I felt something cool and wet on my eyelids, and my eyes start burning a little. They started burning a lot. And then I sat up and screamed like my face was on fire, which I thought it might be. I didn't want to open my eyes because I was afraid whatever was burning them would leak into my eyeballs and render me blind, or even penetrate my brain and kill me. I flailed my arms, and the poor little Vietnamese woman tried to calm me down, shouting back at me, "Is okay! Is okay!" while I yelled back, "IT'S NOT OKAY!" A second woman ran into the room to see if I was dying. She spoke better English, and assured me the burning was normal and would disappear soon. I remained unconvinced, and spent a panicky few minutes thinking it was a good thing I saw Scout on the first trip, since I was about to be blind forever. Then I panicked about whether I could still adopt her considering the new status of my vision, and I started cursing myself for being stupid enough to get an eyelash tint at a random spa in Vietnam.

But the burning did subside, and my eyelashes actually looked quite nice. Best of all, the day passed, and I returned to the hotel exhausted and just one night's sleep away from my darling girl.

The next morning—April 16—I checked and rechecked the diaper bag I'd be using for the very first time: diapers and wipes, two outfits, three baby bottles, formula, a blanket, a camera, bottled water, and the beautiful white dress I had been saving. I wanted her to wear it for the adoption ceremony. We drove to Bac Giang with two other couples meeting their children, excited and nervous, three families about to grow. Upon our arrival at the orphanage, Hanh hopped out of the van and ran inside to let the director know we were there. She arrived back in a few seconds, and pointed at us. "Your birth family is here," she said, and the moment changed completely.

We had known it was a possibility. At the time of Scout's adoption, the provincial government in Vietnam notified birth mothers when their babies were about to be adopted and the women often showed up on adoption day to say goodbye. I had even prepared for the possibility, though I never imagined it would happen—I had a small photo album with pictures of Scout, of us, and of our home.

We found Thi Hai and her sister sitting on a bed, Scout in Thi Hai's arms. *In her mother's arms*, I thought, and my heart sank. I didn't recognize my baby, and this upset me. Her long spiky hair had been cut short, and she appeared slightly bigger, more full in the face. She was wearing the outfit we had brought to her in January, and I knew An had dressed her in it to please us.

Thi Hai looked up as we approached. She was young and lovely, with long, thick dark hair and large chestnut eyes. She wore a hat. She didn't smile, but she wasn't frowning. She appeared to be in shock. Her sister stood and hugged us each, warmly and tightly, and we hugged her back. The four of us stood awkwardly in a circle, Thi Hai still holding her baby. After a moment, the sister took Scout from Thi Hai's arms and handed the baby to me. I stared down at her tiny face and suddenly felt like a stranger, like a misguided knight arriving to whisk this child away from all she knew.

I kissed my baby hello, and looked for recognition in her eyes. Emotion swept through me—love, excitement, envy, and regret. *I am meeting the woman who made Scout*, I told myself. I swallowed the debilitating fear that this whole process was wrong, and that this baby would never love me as much as she could have loved Thi Hai.

Thi Hai looked stricken, unable to move. I handed the baby to Bob so I could embrace her. Kissing her on both cheeks, I put my arms around her, trying to envelope her with a peace I knew she didn't have. I held her away from me and looked at her, trying to find in her face a sign of something. I didn't want to look too happy, knowing it probably compounded her desperation. It seemed clear she hadn't seen Scout since leaving the hospital after giving birth. In October, she gave up a skinny, squirmy mouth to feed. Now, she said goodbye to a smiling, healthy, gorgeous child. I knew in my heart she could not keep this child. But I also knew she wished she could. I gave her the photo album. She took it and bowed her head at me in thanks.

We didn't have much time—Hanh would be ordering us back to the van soon. It had come down to this, I thought: years of waiting for a child, 15 months of dreaming about it, weeks of staring at this child's picture —and here, in a rural Vietnamese village, during a 15-minute exchange, the mantel of motherhood passing from Thi Hai to me. Her heart breaking as mine expanded. For a while, I suspected, we would both be sleepless, me because I'd be caring for Scout, her because she couldn't.

Quickly, I snapped pictures of Thi Hai and her sister with Scout, and Bob took pictures of Thi Hai and me with Scout. I held Thi Hai's hand. On a whim, I removed from my neck the gold locket Bob had given me for my birthday just days after we received the referral. I opened it to show her a tiny picture of Baby Nguyen Minh Phuong, and then I clasped it beneath her thick hair, less a gift to her than a reminder of the gift she bestowed on me. *Wear this,* I wanted her to intuit, *to know how much I love her, and to remember how you loved her enough to let me have her.*

It was time to go. We settled back into the van with our daughter between us. We were in the back seat, and could see Thi Hai and her sister watching us as we prepared to drive away. The sister had her arm around Thi Hai. I held Scout up so Thi Hai could see her baby one last time through the van's back windshield, and instantly realized it was the wrong thing to do. Thi Hai's face crumpled and her body bent like she'd been punched, even broken by my gesture; I wept, stunned by the depth of both my joy and my sadness and by the invisible connection I would forever have with this woman. My everlasting joy, I realized, would only come at the hands of Thi Hai's perpetual pain.

The van carried a driver, six adults, four infants, and no car seats or seat belts. The driver attacked the roads like we were being followed. I held tight to the baby, and Bob held tight to me, and despite the crowded van, we felt alone with Scout for the first time. I rubbed my nose on her cheek; Bob ran his hand through her short silky hair. We examined her face. I ordered Bob to *get this, get that*, out of the diaper bag. Scout didn't seem to mind wearing her first disposable diaper, and she sucked down the bottle I gave her.

I changed her into the little white dress I'd been saving for her all those months. The dress looked ridiculous on her, too frilly, or maybe too white, I don't know, but I understood I was getting a first glimpse of my daughter's personality, and it made me laugh. The dress just wasn't her style.

The final adoption step took place at what was known as a Giving and Receiving ceremony. Adoptive parents often refer to it as "Gotcha Day," and most celebrate it with as much joy and love as their children's birthdays. The procedure itself was short and simple. We sat around a long table in a small, warm room. Some fruit and cans of soft drinks and beer served as a centerpiece. Four families with babies were present—the youngest was four months, the oldest just over a year.

Hanh translated as the provincial minister made a speech. He welcomed us to Bac Giang, congratulated us, and ended with two sentences I will remember forever. "There is no turning back now," he told us, through Hanh. "In the eyes of Vietnam, you are family." For a moment, none of us could speak.

Then, each family thanked the minister, expressed love for their child, and signed the final paperwork. We became a family of three. It seemed every bit as miraculous as birth.

At the hotel, we couldn't stop staring at her. She had a little reddish mark between her eyebrows. "That's an angel kiss," said one of the other moms. Scout also had a birthmark on the back of her neck. "That's a stork bite," said someone else. She had a little cradle cap on her head, and mosquito bites on her legs.

That night, she slept in the bed between us, though Bob and I hardly slept. We watched her little chest rise and fall, and put our hands by her mouth to feel the warm breath. It was the first time she had slept on a real mattress. In the morning, just as the stars faded away and the sun turned the room to a shadowy blue, we both watched as she woke, and pushed herself up to see where she was. She looked at me, and turned to look at Bob. She looked at me again, and at Bob. And then she grinned hugely, still turning her head back and forth between us, and we laughed together, all three of us, sharing our first family moment.

The first few days passed slowly—it was harder than we thought to get used to being parents, to being solely responsible for this 13-pound bundle. And I stressed myself out. I had noticed that Thi Hai had strabismus—a wandering eye—and I worried Scout would have one, too. I worried she missed An. I worried because she seemed so agreeable, so willing to let anyone hold her. I worried I wasn't special enough to her. In general, I guess, I worried everything wasn't perfect, even though it was.

At breakfast one morning, as I gave her a bottle, I expressed my worst fear to Bob.

"I don't think I love her enough," I said.

"Why would you say that?" he asked. "What do you mean?"

"Well, I do love her. I feel like I'd do anything for her. And I don't like being away from her."

"It sounds to me like you love her enough," he said. We were quiet for a moment.

"I think," he said finally, "that you're waiting for lightning to strike, like this big Eureka moment to hit you." He was right. I wanted the arrow in the heart, the fireworks bursting before me.

"It doesn't work like that," said my wise husband. "Scout's going to be with us for the rest of our lives. You have plenty of time to love her even more than you already do."

Our second trip to Vietnam lasted two weeks. There is lots to tell, but none of it very interesting to anyone who's ever loved a child. We spent most of our time in the hotel room, falling in love with our daughter. She slept between us at night, took her bottle while we sipped coffee in the morning. One early morning she rolled off the bed while I wasn't looking, and I thought I would have a heart attack. I screamed and rushed her to a room down the hall where an agency staff person—a woman who worked in the orphanages—was staying. Scout was fine; she stopped crying within minutes. I was a wreck. But in hindsight, it was a defining moment for me. When I heard that thump, turned and saw the baby lying prone on the ground, quiet for an instant while she gathered her strength for a mighty wail, the pain I felt was physical and scarring. And later, after I had calmed down, I knew I had really become her mother.

We spent the last few days of the trip in Ho Chi Minh City finalizing Scout's visa, and from there we flew home. When she was a little bit older, I would tell her a story that she asked me to repeat again and again: *Once upon a time there was a mother and a father who lived in a big green house by the sea, but they didn't have a baby to love. And halfway around the world in a place called Vietnam there was a baby who needed a mommy and a daddy. So the mother and father flew to Vietnam to meet her, and they all decided to love each other forever and ever and always in the big green house by the sea.*

EIGHT

When Scout was a baby, I often took her to story hour at the neighborhood library. There were two children's librarians—the exuberant, spirited Miss Lisa, who had a nose-ring, and timid, plain Miss Marcia, who wore corduroy pants and button-down shirts. Scout loved "Story Time." As soon as she could crawl, she positioned herself up front, and she listened intently to each story.

Not long after she started talking, she invented a game she called "Library." She played the cool, hip Miss Lisa; naturally, I was boring Miss Marcia. At first, the game consisted of us setting up book displays and reading to each other. Then I weirdly became Miss Marcia all the time, and she insisted I call her Miss Lisa. When she called me in the middle of the night, she cried out, "MISS MARCIA! MISS MARCIA! I NEED YOU!" I would snuggle her back into bed, whispering, "It's okay, Miss Lisa. I'm right here. I love you, Miss Lisa." Bob became jealous of our special world, so we gave him the name Butterfly.

Life became a series of wonderful, hilarious, unpredictable anecdotes. I was so enamored with my little girl I sometimes felt sorry for anyone unable to adopt a baby from Vietnam. I carried Scout everywhere in a Baby Bjorn, and everywhere we attracted attention. It always surprised me when people instantly surmised she was adopted— could human beings really look so different from each other? Did my zillion freckles not blend together into a skin color near that of my child? Apparently not.

"What's she mixed with?" asked the Winn-Dixie checkout girl.

"Where'd you get her?" people asked all the time. Like, every day.

And, every once in a while, the Big One: "Do you know anything about her parents?"

"I am her mother," I sometimes replied. "What do you want to know?" Or "Do you mean her *birth* parents?"

I usually managed to tolerate imposing questions from strangers. After all, in the game of life, I was winning. I had this gorgeous, awesome baby, a great husband, and a big green house by the sea. Still the inference that she wasn't really my child bothered me. "I hate when people don't get that she's mine," I frequently complained to Bob.

"Well, she's not really ours," he once told me. "I think of us as her caretakers. I mean, we're her parents, but we don't own her. We just have to do the best we can to raise her, then set her loose in the world."

It was a noble, selfless sentiment, and it endlessly annoyed me. "Whatever," I said. "I disagree. She'll always be my own."

Soon after Scout settled into her role as our daughter, Bob stepped into a mid-life crisis. At the time, he was editor of a popular alternative weekly news magazine, and he was very good at his job. Under his guidance, the paper had won national awards and become a major player in local politics. It was the region's most adept investigative news organization. When we were kid-less, his long hours weren't an issue. He always had weekends off, and on late nights I could always find something to do. But now, with his baby girl at home, he was missing out. Often, Scout was asleep when he left in the morning and asleep by the time he came home.

He decided he wanted to become a consultant. "What do you want to consult about?" I asked. He didn't know, but he would aim for a six-figure salary. I didn't think his plan would work. But something else was percolating in his man-brain.

Soon after we moved to our beach house, Bob had joined a community volunteer fire station. At the time, the volunteers were first responders to any area emergencies, whether medical or fire-related. He took a couple of courses to qualify, and soon enough he was answering pages in the middle of the night and roaring off in the station's old engine. He loved it.

Around the time he started thinking about leaving Folio, the neighbor who had convinced him to become a volunteer took a paid position with the fire department. The man, a good friend, was ten years older than Bob, who was 42 at the time, and it gave Bob permission to dream something crazy. *If he can do it*, Bob thought, *so can I.*

"I know what I want to do," he said one night over dinner. The sun was setting over the Intracoastal Waterway, and we could smell low tide. Scout sat in her high chair making a mess. "I want to become a full-time firefighter."

I silently tried it on for size: my husband, the firefighter. *Damn*, I love a man in uniform. The idea seemed so organic— such a simple way to return to life's basics. Paperwork, newsroom politics, the drudgery of business meetings—it all seemed so trivial compared to putting out fires and saving lives.

"Let's do it," I said.

Bob had been inspired not by 9/11, but by Pat Tillman, the professional football player who gave up a multi-million dollar contract in order to join the military in the wake of the Trade Center attacks. He died in Afghanistan. Tillman said he joined because he wanted his life to mean something more than carrying a ball across the field. "Passion is what makes life interesting, what ignites our soul, fuels our love and carries our friendships, stimulates our intellect, and pushes our limits," Tillman said. "A passion for life is contagious and uplifting. Passion cuts both ways. Those that make you feel on top of the world are equally able to turn it upside down … In my life I want to create passion in my own life and with those I care for. I want to feel, experience, and live every emotion. I will suffer through the bad for the heights of the good."

In hindsight, Bob had been working up to this for decades. His father had been a doctor, and his mother a nurse. After college, Bob joined the Peace Corps and spent three years in the former Zaire, now the Democratic Republic of Congo, as a health worker. He organized the building of outpost medical clinics, and helped eradicate intestinal worms in several small villages.

He had stumbled into journalism by accident; when he returned from Africa, he needed a job, and the editor of a local newspaper hired him because he could play softball. He couldn't even type at the time. Though certainly his stint in journalism had been worthwhile, he was ready for a change. Within a week he had given notice at his job and enrolled in firefighter school. Boom. People told us we were crazy. My parents worried about how we would support ourselves. Friends assumed it was a phase.

Strangely, I wasn't worried at all. I didn't know it, but this change was the first in many, many steps we would take to simplify our lives. At that moment, however, it just made sense to encourage my husband to follow his heart and simultaneously spend more time with his daughter. It was the type of midlife crisis I could actually embrace.

NINE

It's a little known fact about adoption that prospective parents overwhelmingly ask for girls. People assume the opposite because of China, where thousands of baby girls have been abandoned by their birth parents due to China's one-child policy and the financial advantage of having a son. But in other countries, adoptive people *request* girls, which has left a preponderance of baby boys to languish in orphanages. Many are never adopted, and grow up in institutions.

In the beginning, we were no different, though I don't know why. I guess I had my heart set on a girl, and once I had decided, I couldn't change my thinking on it. And in the beginning, I wasn't aware of the overwhelming number of baby boys needing homes. Our request seemed reasonable at best, and at the very worst, simply random. Once Scout was ours, I never regretted having asked for her. But a little twinge of guilt remained stuck in a corner of my gut. We had requested a healthy infant girl. It was like ordering out of catalogue, really. *Baby girls are out of stock right now ... Would you take a boy? Maybe an older girl? No? We should be getting a new shipment soon ....*

As Scout toddled her way from infant to little girl, Bob started talking about another child. I routinely rolled my eyes and changed the subject. Our lives seemed pretty awesome: I had a hot firefighter husband, a beautiful baby girl, and a part-time job teaching at the local university. Why mess it up with another kid?

Bob's not a big talker. Sometimes it takes a while for him to put thoughts into words. But when it comes out, it's worth absorbing. "I feel like we have more love to give," he finally said. I wasn't sure. Seriously, I wasn't sure I had more love. Scout was so perfect; what if the next child was a pain in the ass? My normally easygoing husband persisted, and since he honestly asks so little of me, I finally agreed. So we started the whole thing over again.

For a moment, fast forward ten years: *Bob's at the fire station, it's dinnertime, and my son, Nico, is upset because I don't have the right brand of macaroni and cheese for him. The kind he wants is a frozen dinner—he calls it freezer mac and cheese. "I WANT FREEZER MAC AND CHEESE," he shouts, over and over. He's not listening to anything I say, so I purposefully ignore him. It's the latest incarnation of the myriad plans of action we've received from professionals over the years: planned ignoring.*

He follows me to the kitchen and pulls on my shirt. "FREEZER MAC AND CHEESE. GO GET ME SOME. THAT'S THE ONLY THING THAT WILL END THIS. I WANT FREEZER MAC AND CHEESE." He pulls on my shirt, my pants, and my arm. I deflect and pull away, and he grabs again. He punches me.

I grab both his arms and pull him into my bedroom, where I sit on my bed, pull him into my lap, cross his arms in front of his body and restrain him. He's screaming incessantly now, a guttural, low-pitched wailing noise full of bitterness and rage.

"LET ME GO! LET ME GO!"

"Stop fighting me and I will let you go," I say. He throws his head back into my face and I wonder if today he will finally break my nose. I let him go for a minute and he turns around and punches me with both fists, hard. I push him onto the bed and lay on top of him. He kicks his heels at my back and tries to bite my arms. After a few minutes, he stops fighting and I

loosen my grip. Immediately, he jumps up and runs to the bathroom door to try to lock himself in, but I get there first and block the door. He kicks me and punches the side of my head. In a calm, robotic voice, he speaks: "I'm strong now. Do you see how strong I'm getting? And I'm going to keep getting stronger. Dad will still be a challenge, but I'll be able to handle you."

Scout comes into the room, sees her brother's emotional state, and starts crying. At this point I've been fighting him for nearly 45 minutes; I'm exhausted. I instruct Scout to get the neighbor to come over and help.

Kay arrives five minutes later; when Nico sees her, he stops fighting me and stands completely still. She reaches her hand out to him. "Nico?" she says. "Can I give you a hug?" For a moment he just stares at her; it's as though he's trying to break free of a spell. He takes her hand and she envelops him in her arms, and the three of us sit on the side of the bed in silence for a full ten minutes.

"Can I hug you?" I ask him. His face crumples into sobs and he climbs into my lap. I tell Kay it's over, and she leaves.

Nico weeps as I hold him. And then this: "It's never going to change, Mom. The fighting. Nobody can stop it. We've tried everything. All those doctors. Nobody can make it stop. There's no point. It's all pointless. I'm never going to change. It's no use."

I have never heard such despair in his voice. My 10-year-old son had glimpsed into the future and seen a bleak, violent desert of disappointment and pain. "We'll figure it out, honey," I say. "It's okay. We'll get through this. We'll find a way to make it better. Mom's always here. We'll always love you. We'll figure this out."

I fetch his pajamas and he stands to put them on. Suddenly, he grasps my arms and squeezes gently, then moves to my waist and legs. I ask what he's doing. "I'm making sure you're not hurt," he whispers, crying. "Did I hurt you? I never want to hurt you, Mommy. I'm sorry! I'm sorry!" The fear in his eyes nearly slays me.

"No, honey. I'm fine. Don't worry." I reassure him twice more before tucking him into bed. I brush back his thick hair, and kiss his sweaty brow. I

comfort him the way a mother soothes an infant. It's what he craves. It's what he missed. It took us a decade to figure that out.

I used to wonder if, had we known such episodes were even possible, we would have moved forward with growing our family. If, upon placing a handsome baby boy in our arms, some voice from above had whispered, "This child will one day punch you in anger. He will use a golf club to try to break down a door. He will wrap a scarf around your neck while you're driving and try to jump out of the car." If we had been forewarned, would we have taken him home?

But I stopped torturing myself a long time ago, because in the end, we were the ones who found the cure for what ailed him. Where in the world would he be without us? More importantly, though, this boy, this child of my heart—he held the cure for what was ailing us, a condition we didn't even know we had.

Of course I had more love to give. Without this boy, I never would have known it.

TEN

An ancient Afghani folk tale describes the existence of a "div," a horned ogre, which steals children at night and takes them away forever. In the story, one bereft father tracks down the div to find his son, and discovers the monster has kept all of the kidnapped children in a magical kingdom where they are educated, fed, and raised with joy and hope. The father must decide whether to reclaim his child and return him to a life of poverty, or trek home empty-handed, but with the knowledge that his son is happy.

In the novel *And the Mountains Echoed*, writer Khaled Hosseini recounts the tale through the character Saboor, who tells it to his children as he journeys to Kabul to sell his daughter, both to give her a better life and to help lift his family out of indigence. I read Hosseini's phenomenal book ten years after I first held my son. It's a brilliant piece of fiction that illustrates many of the painful truths inherent in how we became a family. We are a magical tribe, the five of us, in a magical place with joy and hope. But buried deep, like roots, their first lives—the ones into which my children were born—form the bases of who they are.

Around the time we brought Scout home, Vietnam closed its adoption program. Countries around the world were struggling to comply with the Hague Convention, a worldwide effort to streamline the international adoption process in order to fight corruption and impropriety. Often, in order to change, countries found it necessary to shut down their programs completely to reorganize them. The agency we had worked with in Vietnam had begun working in Guatemala while waiting for Vietnam to reopen.

The Guatemala adoption program was quite different. It featured private attorneys who arranged adoptions between birth mothers and adoptive parents. While the new parents waited for required paperwork to be approved, they could visit their prospective children in country, and even take care of them in hotels. Guatemala's government involvement pretty much was limited to paperwork approval, but due to corruption, the paperwork—both from the Guatemalan government and the U.S.—was extensive. In addition, prior to being approved, adoption applications had to include DNA proof that the birth mother and child matched.

Here's what I have been told about the circumstances of my son's birth: his young mother worked at a factory, and had a young child. She was widowed. On the way home from work one night, she was assaulted by two men, and became pregnant. The story may or may not be true: Guatemalan women giving their babies up for adoption often lied about the circumstances of their pregnancies to avoid involving the birth father in the process.

She gave birth, and named her son Estuardo. A few days later, she brought him to the orphanage of Luca Suasa, a Guatemalan adoption attorney who owned an orphanage and had legal custody of the dozens of children who lived there.

In a picture, the birth mother sits in a chair holding her infant son, who will soon be my son. Another son, maybe four or five, sits next to her, his head against her shoulder, looking up at the camera. After the picture was taken, the birth mother gave her baby to the orphanage workers. Luca Suasa, or one of her representatives, almost certainly gave her some money—I don't know how much—with the promise of more money after she showed up for the required DNA testing. I didn't know about the money back then.

And then this tiny baby was placed in a crib. A few times a day, a worker propped a bottle up next to him so he could eat. His diaper was changed on schedule. I suppose he was bathed, but I don't know how often.

Ten days after he was born—like with Scout, it was just before Christmas—I received a phone call. Scout and I were in the baby section of Target, and it was the day before my birthday. Scout was 3 years old.

"You have a son," an agency representative said in my ear.

I rushed home to see the picture on my computer, and stared for a very long time at the tiny face. He was a little baby with eyes scrunched closed and smooth dark hair. Six weeks later, I boarded a plane bound for Guatemala to meet our second child. We named him after my great-grandfather, Henry, often called Enrique by his Cajun co-workers. His nickname had been Rico, which Bob couldn't stomach because of the R.I.C.O. Act. We compromised with Nico. Our son, Nico.

The Guatemala airport sits in a decent area of town, and it's possible to think, when being driven around by a careful cabbie, that the country isn't burdened by squalor and desperation. But it is.

I didn't want to believe the circumstances of my son's adoption were any different than my daughter's. But from the beginning, it was clearly more complicated and worrisome.

I traveled on the first trip alone, and went straight to the orphanage. I found our son, known then as Estuardo, in a long narrow room lined with bassinets. Each bassinet held a tiny infant—some crying, some sleeping, and some just staring into space. Several had bottles propped up against their mouths with formula leaking down their necks. An adjoining room had an area cordoned off for crawling babies to roam around while a nanny sat in a rocking chair and watched.

The place was relatively clean and seemed to have staff and supplies. But it seemed so soulless, like a dystopian version of a day care center. Not someplace I would have left Scout for an hour, much less for the first months of her life. It smelled like disinfectant and looked like an underfunded daycare.

I took our tiny eight-pound boy back to the hotel. He was seven weeks old, and I was almost scared to hold him. Looking back on that trip, it's sort of shocking. The attorney, who had legal custody of this infant, allowed him to go to a hotel on a weekend trip with a stranger, about whom she knew virtually nothing. It makes me so mad even as I'm writing this that I could stab her eyes out. *What were you thinking?* But it wasn't just me; each month, dozens, if not hundreds, of prospective parents descended on Guatemala City to spend time with the children they had applied to adopt.

Luckily, I'm me and fairly responsible. Nico was so small; I bundled him up in a blanket and made a crib for him in a drawer. During the first night, when he cried, I gave him a bottle and he started choking so violently I thought I might have killed him. I held him for the next 24 hours straight, and cried for an hour when I brought him back to the orphanage. Comparatively, it had been almost pleasant to think of Scout in her Vietnam home, being spoiled by An while a breeze drifted over the rice paddies. Imagining Nico in a virtual baby factory nearly broke my heart.

Three months later, Bob, Scout, and I returned to Guatemala to visit him again. He stayed in the hotel with us for four days. Scout spent hours stretched out on the bed next to him, stroking his cheek and kissing his belly. She adored him. I tried to cut his long fingernails and snipped off a tiny piece of one finger, and he bled like I had sliced an artery. "I told you so," said Bob, who was a paramedic by then. He rolled his eyes and staunched the bleeding.

Leaving him in the orphanage after that second trip remains one of the hardest moments of my life. The smell of that place—diapers, formula, sweat, disinfectant—paled in comparison to the stifling cloud of loneliness smothering its many rooms. Nico's room was still lined with cribs—maybe a dozen of them—and the babies just lay in them, staring at the ceiling. I sobbed as I handed him to the nanny, sobbed as we got into the taxi. Hugged Scout to my chest, told her I was fine, but sobbed into her hair. Had I known then what that place was doing to him, I simply would not have left.

In July 2005, when he was seven months old, Nico Robert DeLeon Snell came home for good, and we were thrilled with our happy, healthy boy. Scout became a model big sister—fetched me diapers and wipes, helped make his bottles—and he was such a good baby. He went to sleep easily at night and stayed in his crib for hours. Some mornings I'd go to check on him and find him awake, content, just looking around the room like he couldn't believe his luck. I know now his life so far had taught him that crying does no good. He had spent months waiting for someone to notice him. A little more waiting, his infant brain fathomed, was probably in order.

Life with two children—a near-perfect 3-year-old and a quiet, affable infant—was exhilarating. It was so wonderful, in fact, that I immediately decided we needed one more child. Maybe I was sleep-deprived? High from smelling too many baby wipes? It just seemed like the right thing to do.

Bob was certain I had lost my mind. "No," he said. "No. Just no." But the same characteristic that makes Bob a great husband makes him a terrible negotiator—he finds it difficult to deny me anything. It's like my superpower.

I secretly began researching the possibility of adopting from Ethiopia. I loved the idea of making Africa part of our family. Also, the process in Ethiopia was moving pretty quickly —adoptive parents were reporting mere weeks between being accepting a referral and bringing a child home. And time had become a critical factor. The months we had waited between meeting our first two children and bringing them home were tantamount, I would guess, to weeks and weeks of giving birth. The thought of the babies languishing in institutional settings while we waited for some official somewhere to stamp a piece of paper was maddening. I regularly experienced nausea, moodiness, and exhaustion. And weight gain, now that I think about it. Yet another hysterical pregnancy.

So the idea of a quick adoption appealed to me, and it made sense because I knew the need was great. Thousands of children in Ethiopia had been orphaned or abandoned due to illness and poverty.

Finally, Bob sat me down for a come-to-Yahweh meeting. "Look," he said. "If we do this, then this is going to be your thing."

"Okay. What does that mean?"

"It means we will have three kids. And the main thing you're going to do for the foreseeable future is have three kids."

I thought about this for at least 10 or 15 minutes. It was a fair point. Bob worked full-time as a firefighter—24 hours on, 48 hours off. I maintained my spotty employment schedule— freelance writing, and teaching the occasional college course. If we had three kids, I would have to be the Chief Domestic Engineer, primarily in charge of the childcare.

I wanted to write a book. But I'm a procrastinator by nature. Somehow, having another child seemed easier than writing a book.

And anyway, I had become slightly obsessed about expanding our family. I could squeeze in some writing along the way, I decided.

"Let's do it," I said. I spent the next few weeks putting together yet a third dossier, and Googling pictures of Ethiopian children.

But for several muddled reasons, Ethiopia didn't work out. In the meantime, while we debated going with another agency, Dee called. Dee, the agency rep who had helped us bring home both Scout and Nico, had remained in contact with us and knew we were looking to bring home a third child. "This hardly ever happens," she said, "but I have this baby girl in Guatemala and I don't have anyone waiting to adopt her. Do you want her?" She emailed me a picture of the baby with her birth mother.

I was pretty committed to Ethiopia, and partially because of the *WOW!* factor. Three kids from three different continents? Way cool. I felt torn. My mother happened to be visiting at the time, though, and bestowed upon me a different perspective and an experienced mother's eminent wisdom. "It seems to me," she said, "that you're waiting for a baby to need you in Ethiopia, and here's a baby in Guatemala who needs you now."

I looked at the picture again, and knew she was right. The birth mother gazed sorrowfully at the camera, her tiny baby like a cloud in her arms. The picture awoke in me some sort of global responsibility; I realized I *needed* to be this child's mother. How could I complain because I had imagined a child with darker skin? We wanted a third child for our family, and here was a child in need of a family. The end.

But as with all aspects of adoption, it turned out to be much more complicated than we expected.

ELEVEN

Nico transitioned from baby to toddler, oblivious of our plans to make him a middle child. At age one, he was a big healthy boy but toddled nowhere. He preferred to crawl or be carried. I worriedly asked the doctor about why he wouldn't walk. "He just doesn't want to," he said, laughing.

In April 2006—Nico was 18 months old—we visited an Orlando hotel where the carpet was so damp and dank Nico finally gave up crawling. We rejoiced in his newfound mobility; it was also the first sign of our son's sensitivity to gross textures.

As he neared his second birthday, Nico started talking more in a soft, hoarse voice; he also developed a frequent screech capable of shattering my eardrums. He sounded like a Pterodactyl.

Boys are different, Bob and I told each other. *He'll grow out of the screaming meanies.*

We decided to name our third child Neale, after Florida writer Zora Neale Hurston, a prominent African-American writer during the first part of the 20th century and author of *Their Eyes Were Watching God*, one of my all-time favorite novels. Despite Scout wanting to name her Cleopatra and Nico campaigning for Lucas, we stuck with Neale, and I flew back to Guatemala to meet her in January 2007. Bob stayed home with Scout and Nico.

I was in the lobby of the Guatemala City Marriott when my third child was placed in my arms; it was like being handed a breath. A shock ran through me, some sort of current, so real and distinct I looked around to see if anyone else had noticed. I looked at the woman who had given her to me to see if it was static electricity, but she had already turned away and I was standing alone. From that moment on, this baby and I were connected, and I knew she was meant to be mine. After spending a few days with her, though, I was worried: she had a fragility about her that made me uneasy, and I couldn't quite define it. She was so, so tiny—at three months old, she weighed just eight pounds, and seemed to be running a low-grade fever. More concerning to me, though, was her countenance. She didn't cry much, but neither were there any funny gurgling sounds, no cooing, no reaching for toes. She was beautiful, yes. Gorgeous. But surly.

I talked to Dee about it. "All babies are different," she said. "Maybe that's just her personality." This seemed far-fetched. What the hell? My baby's main personality trait, at just a few weeks old, was *morose*?

The same attorney, Luca Suasa, was handling Neale's adoption. She was so successful by this point—had facilitated so many adoptions—that she had built a new state-of-the-art facility to house all her children, which numbered in the dozens. She herself had adopted a couple of the children, two little girls; when she went out of town or on vacation, she put them back in the orphanage until she returned.

After a few days, I traveled with Neale to the *hogar*—the Spanish word for orphanage—to drop her off. The new place was clean and spacious, which allowed for more children. Dozens of them were school-aged, and they ran around the small yard with dirty bare feet and smiles, tugging at my shirt, motioning for me to take their pictures. Cheerful bright paint decorated the inside walls; the supply room was stacked with diapers, formula, and canned food. But again, the institutional setting of the place made my heart sink. I instantly realized the nannies had less time to spend on each child, and were probably less likely to dote on a quiet, surly baby. Again, I said a tearful goodbye to one of my children in the confines of an orphanage, and yet again I thought about how fucked up the world must be for this whole damn situation to even be a thing.

Back home, I started researching baby development milestones and symptoms. Since the dawn of the Internet, this has been a favorite pastime of mine—alarmist research and self-diagnosis. I'm remarkably good at it, especially the alarmist part. But in this case, I knew I was onto something. After a few days of obsessing, I decided Neale had *failure to thrive*, an ambiguous condition with a myriad of causes, which can lead to poor physical and mental development. Living in an institution housing dozens of children, having minimal human contact, with a revolving sea of faces providing her with basic care—recast quite simply, Neale was depressed.

Bob and I made plans to visit Neale again the next month, and to take her to a private pediatrician in Guatemala City for an evaluation. We spoke to Dee about our plan, and she said Luca Suasa, the attorney, wasn't happy about it. A doctor visited the orphanage regularly, she said, and Neale's health was fine. We rephrased our rationale, saying we *knew* she was fine, but just wanted to see if there was anything extra we could help provide for her, at our expense. We were lying, but we were learning that in order to work with Luca, we had to pretend to adore her, and more importantly, to trust her.

We found Dr. Hadney Sagen through one of the many adoption support groups I perused. He was a tall man with sandy brown hair and excellent English, and he took his time with us. He examined our girl top to bottom; he felt the little lump on the back of her head we had noticed, and tried unsuccessfully to get her to laugh. He listened to her lungs, and held her up to estimate her leg strength.

Finally, he put her back in my arms, leaned against his desk, and sighed. "She is not doing well at the orphanage," he said. The lump on the back of her skull was from a type of self-stimulation —she was rubbing her head back and forth just to feel something. And she wasn't smiling because she wasn't happy. *Failure to thrive.* Shit. I was right. And then Dr. Sagen uttered nine words I'd remember forever: "If I were you, I would not leave her."

I'm not sure he could have said anything else as shocking to us. Bob and I stared at him, and then at each other. I felt sick to my stomach. "But Dr. Sagen," I said. "What are we supposed to do? Our adoption isn't final."

He didn't back down. "I'm just telling you what I think. If she was my child, I wouldn't bring her back to the orphanage."

We told him we had two other children at home in the U.S.

"We have schools, here, too, you know," he said.

I was probably crying by then, because I cry all the time anyway, and certainly this was good reason to cry. I know I must have been slack-jawed. We were in Guatemala City, 2,500 miles away from two of our children, and being told the life of the third depended on moving to a third world country, at least temporarily. We thanked Dr. Sagen for his time; he told us to contact him again if we needed him.

We returned to our hotel; instead of staying at the usual adoption headquarters hotel, we had opted for a smaller boutique hotel with beautiful gardens and a luxurious quiet about it. I packed Neale in a Baby Bjorn and we walked and talked. Our options seemed limited: we could either bring the baby back to the orphanage and hope for the best, or stay in Guatemala to take care of her. So really, in our minds, we had one option. We had to save our daughter.

We decided the kids and I would move to Guatemala until the adoption was finalized. Bob could take some limited sick time, but mostly he would commute back and forth every few weeks. We could easily and affordably rent a house in Antigua, a lovely and safe village just outside of Guatemala City. School wasn't too big of a deal—Scout would miss the last two months or so of kindergarten, and Nico was just in preschool.

We called Dee to tell her of our plans; she said she would speak to Luca Suasa about it. A few minutes later she called back to say Luca had nixed our plan. We were shocked. "But why? Why wouldn't she want us to do that?" I cried. But apparently she was adamant. We called her directly.

"No, no, no, can you imagine if all the mothers wanted to do that?" she asked. "No, we will take care of the baby. We will give her one-on-one care, I promise, she will be fine. We will have a special program just for her. Tricia, Tricia, you have to trust me." She pronounced my name *Ter-eeza, Ter-eeza*. We were beginning to hate her.

We had no choice. We did not have legal custody of Neale —for the time being, Luca was her guardian. Through Dee, we came to a second-best agreement—Neale would return to the orphanage, but I would fly back every month to check on her. Luca reluctantly consented. "If that's what you want, fine," she said.

Two days later, still in our custody, Neale's condition worsened. Her body burned with fever, and she vomited again and again. Her cough kept all three of us up all night. She stared into space, her eyes glazed and sad, and I whispered into the curves of her tiny ear. It was the weekend, so we couldn't call Dr. Sagen; reluctantly, we called Luca, and she told us to bring Neale back to the *hogar* to receive medical attention. We weren't scheduled to bring her back for another day, but we were worried she needed antibiotics, so back to the orphanage we went. Standing in the *hogar*, I could barely let go of her; once she was out of my arms, I sobbed. I wanted to explain everything to the nannies, but no one spoke English. Neale whimpered as they carried her away. I felt paralyzed.

Emotional subtlety has never been one of my strengths. In my imagination, I resembled the star of a Lifetime movie, wracked with tears and still standing only due to the sheer strength of my husband's arm and my determination. In reality, I'm sure I was a psychotic mess with streaky mascara and snot flowing down my face. Bob poured me into a cab and we returned to the hotel, where I wept some more, then drank myself to sleep. We flew home the next day.

For the next few weeks, I mapped out my next trip and sent frequent emails to Dee asking her to check on Neale. I received occasional vague updates. *Her fever is gone! She's gaining weight, she's happy!* None of which I really believed. At Luca's instruction, the nannies had kept her in the infant room rather than promote her up to the room with babies her age, assuming I'd be happy with that. But I wasn't—I knew she'd be getting even less stimulation than was appropriate for her age, and practically no time out of her crib. As long as she wasn't crying, she'd be left alone. And she didn't cry much.

One month later, I flew back to Guatemala City, and this time my mother-in-law met me there. A retired nurse with a flair for adventure, CJ was anxious to meet and assess her newest granddaughter, and excited to visit Central America. We went straight from the airport to the orphanage to get my girly, and my heart sank when I saw her. Glazed eyes, pale skin, blotchy face—I could tell something was terribly wrong. But I didn't let the nannies know. "Oh, she looks beautiful!" I exclaimed. "So healthy and happy!" Her neck and ears had dirty grey streaks. She smelled spoiled.

Back at the hotel, I gave her a bath and snuggled her into a blanket. The little lump on the back of her head had been spliced open, and had turned into an enormous oozing cyst. She had a fever of 102. I tried to give her a bottle but she wouldn't take more than a tiny sip. She was miserable, and I couldn't put her down for even a second without causing big fat tears. Her breathing sounded wheezy and forced.

That night, I sat up in bed with her for hours. She cried and cried; I wept with her. CJ, staying in the room next door, heard the crying and came over to help. But this child was inconsolable. The next morning, with her fever still high, I realized she had not peed even once since I had picked her up. I called Dr. Sagen and we brought her in that afternoon.

Dr. Sagen was shocked at the baby we presented to him. She had lost two pounds since our last visit, and, at five months old, weighed 11 pounds. The cyst on the back of her head was now infected. He wanted to do X-rays because she sounded like she had pneumonia; and the inside of her mouth was covered in thrush, a painful rash, which discouraged her from eating.

"This baby belongs in a hospital," he said, incredulous. Six more words I would never forget. I asked him what he thought I should do. "She's not mine yet," I said. He thought about my dilemma, and then volunteered to call Luca Suasa and intervene. He phoned her from his office. I don't speak Spanish, but I understand anger in any language, and Dr. Sagen was angry.

After a few minutes, he came back, shaking his head. "She says you should bring the baby back to the orphanage."

Not this time. "I can't do that," I told him. "Morally, ethically, I can't do that. She's my child. I just can't. I won't."

He looked at me; he appeared to be assessing me. After a few minutes, he said he had maneuvered Suasa into opening a small window of opportunity. "She said you could take her to the hospital if you are willing to take *total responsibility for her.*"

He emphasized those last words, and I understood immediately. She wanted me to pay for everything. "Fine," I said. "Tell me what to do."

Dr. Sagen sent us to the best private hospital in Guatemala City, the one with which he was affiliated, and he walked us through the preliminary check-in and helped administer the various blood tests and x-rays. By the time we were admitted, he had confirmed viral pneumonia in both of Neale's lungs; she also had a staph infection on the back of her head, and was showing signs of malnourishment. She was severely dehydrated, and the thrush had caused white painful blisters all over the inside of her mouth.

For five days, I shared a single hospital bed with my daughter, and carefully kept the IV lines from getting tangled up in the oxygen tubes. With one hand, she held tightly to a colorful cloth rattle I had brought her, and with the other hand she clutched my thumb. All night I held her close; she cried if I tried to remove my hand from hers to change position or go to the bathroom. During the day, CJ sat with her while I returned to the hotel and slept for a few hours.

I didn't speak to Luca Suasa during those first few days. Dee was our go-between, and through her, we conveyed that we would not be returning our daughter to the orphanage. Dee reported back to us that Luca was questioning our suitability as parents because of our perceived histrionics, and was thinking of pulling the referral away from us—in other words, taking Neale back. And thus began an uneasy truce between Luca and us: she feared us talking publicly about how sick our child had become in her care, and we feared she would try to take Neale away from us.

She came once to visit Neale and me in the hospital. She walked into our room and saw my tiny baby hooked up to an oxygen mask and two I.V.s. "The baby looks good!" she exclaimed. I silently killed her.

The hospital wasn't unpleasant. It was not air conditioned, but the open windows provided cool breezes, the linens were clean, and the coffee was hot. The night doctor spoke English, and he helped me understand Neale's medical issues. The nurses stayed with her while I took breaks to grab food or make phone calls. I felt comfortable and safe.

After a few days in the hospital, I began to worry about the hospital bill. I knew I would be asked to pay it before we could be released, and I had no idea how much it would cost to care for an infant in the intensive care unit of a private Guatemalan hospital. I asked Bob to up our credit card limit as high as he could, which wasn't very high; I asked CJ if she could possibly extend hers as well, and she received approval to charge as much as $65,000. The potential debt concerned me, but it seemed pointless to worry much about it. We didn't see any other options.

On the day of our release, I reported to accounts payable, and the clerk passed a piece of paper under a window transom. The number at the bottom was $1,500. I looked at the clerk, and pointed to the number. "Is that right?" I asked. She nodded and smiled. I was terrified there had been some mistake. Perhaps that was the first payment due. "That's the total?" She nodded again. "U.S. dollars?" I asked. She nodded vigorously, clearly annoyed. "Si! Si!" she answered. With my hands shaking, I pulled out my credit card. Even with our paltry credit limit, we could handle $1,500. I controlled the urge to run out of the hospital before someone tried to charge me more.

I was elated. We had been able to help our daughter without bankrupting ourselves. But I was enraged, too, at how little money it would have taken to prevent her from getting sick in the first place. Adoption was big business, we were learning. Neale had been a widget in line to be shipped. But, not any more.

With Luca Suasa's reluctant permission, CJ and I found a furnished apartment in a hotel-like setting in downtown

Guatemala City. At the time, we thought Neale's case would be cleared within a couple of weeks. We didn't know then that Luca Suasa had filed a lawsuit against the president of Guatemala, and had pretty much alienated herself from every judicial figure that could have expedited our case. The judges, in fact, were routinely avoiding any paperwork stamped with her name. Nobody wanted to help her, or even deal with her.

I regularly called Dee in the U.S. to complain, but she steadfastly defended Suasa. "She is trying to save the children of Guatemala!" she told me. "She's a hero!"

"My daughter was dying," I said.

"She wasn't *dying*," Dee said. "Don't be so melodramatic. I've seen babies *dying*." Suasa, she insisted, was trying to support a revolution by forcing the Guatemalan government to change the way it handles foreign adoptions.

"I'm sorry," I said, "but I'm a mom now, and I don't care about the revolution. I care about the health and safety of my kid."

"In every revolution, there must be sacrifices," she said. Honestly, I don't remember how I responded. But it wasn't kind, and it wasn't patient. I'm not sure we ever spoke to each other again.

Our new apartment was bright and clean; just down the street were luxury hotels, eateries, and boutiques. We set up house there, and scheduled our days around Neale's eating, sleeping, medication doses, and doctor's appointments. We shopped for groceries at a little store around the corner, and occasionally ventured out to the taco cafe down the block for dinner and a cold beer. After a week or so, CJ flew home and I was left alone with Neale.

As the baby healed, she became stronger and happier. She opened her eyes with wonder each morning, and stared at me for long precious moments. I kissed her little lips a hundred times a day and blew on her belly every time I changed her diaper. I read book after book as she napped, and together we watched old movies with English subtitles in the early evenings.

As the days turned into weeks, Bob began to sound as desperate as I felt. Nico wasn't doing well without me, he said. At age 2 1/2, my little boy couldn't understand where I had gone, and my voice on the phone only confused him. And Bob wasn't doing well without me, either. He had taken time off, but wasn't used to taking care of both children all the time, especially when one of them periodically turned into a screeching pint-sized hellion—which was happening more and more frequently.

Around the time we learned of Neale's existence, Nico had begun having what we assumed were night terrors. He had just switched from a crib to a toddler bed, and we were trying to prepare him for the arrival of a sister. About an hour or two after falling asleep, he would wake up screaming. Sometimes it started with a whimper, and I'd wait to see if he lulled himself back into slumber, but that rarely happened. More often, I rushed to his room and found an upright flailing boy, screeching with panic, eyes squeezed shut, wet, sweaty hair plastered against his skull.

I was the only one who could comfort him, and the relief never happened instantly. For long minutes, I rubbed his arms and back, kept him tightly embraced, spoke soothingly with my mouth against his ear. If you've ever witnessed a child having a night terror, you know the insanity; it's like watching a horror movie and not being able to find the exit door. While I watched helplessly, my kid's brain made him think he was in terrible danger from some nameless, intangible being. Or maybe he saw a describable threat—a horned devil with gnashing teeth or a yellow-eyed bogeyman carrying sharp knives. He couldn't fathom that I was there, right outside his consciousness, ready to pulverize the scary thing into oblivion and rescue him from his own messed up head.

Recently, I told him about these episodes; I said he might have been having bad dreams, which seemed to jog his memory.

He said: *You know, I have the same nightmare over and over again. Well, it's not really a nightmare, just a bad dream I keep having. I'm stuck in one of those games? Where the person pulls a handle and makes a ball go into the machine?*

Me: *A pinball machine?*

Him: *Yes! I'm stuck in a pinball machine, and someone keeps shooting balls trying to hit me, and I can't get away.*

I needed to return home to see Nico and Scout. We came up with a plan for Bob to fly to Guatemala to stay with Neale while I flew back to spend time with the kids. My parents volunteered to be home base for the summer and to take care of the kids while we managed Neale's care.

Bob flew to Guatemala, and I spent a day explaining Neale's meds and schedule before flying to New Orleans to be with the kids.

It was a bittersweet reunion; at the airport, I enveloped them in my arms, and cried to hug them again. Scout's smiles and kisses —she was five at that point—they brought me to tears. But my little boy looked at me shyly, almost tentatively. He hung onto my mother for a long minute before coming to me.

Over the next few days, I spent every waking moment with Scout and Nico. We went swimming, we played on the levee, we went to the aquarium. And it was hard work; for every loving, adoring, gorgeous glance my daughter gave me, my son screamed as though I had ripped out his heart. His first hugs were all "tight-tight"—that's what we called them, those hugs when he squeezed with all his might. When he wouldn't let go, I gently tried to pry loose his arms—he first clung to me, then flailed to get away, then rushed back sobbing my name over and over, finally screaming NONONO and crying uncontrollably.

But again, he was two. *The terrible twos*, I thought. And I had spent nearly two years with this boy, day in and day out. It didn't occur to me that he could be feeling abandoned, especially when he was with his father or my parents while I was gone.

After five days, I returned to Guatemala. I missed the children and was sad to leave them—but it was with some relief that I returned to my quiet little temporary life with my quiet little baby girl. I was ready for it to be over, for sure—I didn't relish being away from any of my kids—but Neale's easy predictable nature brought me some peace.

Bob needed to get back to his job in Florida. With my mother's help, he found a young woman who could return to our home and be a nanny to the kids so he could return to work. Laura was a friendly, enthusiastic girl in between college semesters. She relished spending a few weeks near the beach.

I called her nearly every day to ask about the children, and she always told me how helpful Scout was, how much fun they had at the pool or beach or wherever they had gone. Scout spoke to me happily and asked about baby Neale; Nico liked to have the phone held to his ear, but he never spoke. He was having trouble getting to sleep, Lauren told me. He had frequent temper tantrums, according to Bob.

I spent the remainder of that summer living in Guatemala. The days blended together. I wasn't comfortable traveling much further than the immediate area; I didn't even have the proper paperwork allowing me to be Neale's guardian. Through friends, I met a woman who sometimes stayed with Neale while I went to a gym to work out, or to go grocery shopping. But mostly, we hung out in the apartment.

Our file was allegedly stuck in the final stage of court approval for no apparent reason. One day, Luca Suasa called and requested my presence at a meeting with a judge. She insisted I bring Neale and have her stay at the orphanage while we attended the meeting. I didn't want Luca to know I had someone else who knew about our situation, so on the appointed day, a cab driver drove the baby and me back to the orphanage. I choked back nausea as I handed her to a nanny, and closed my eyes as we left. Luca drove. We crossed over a bridge spanning the infamous garbage slums of the city. "I wish these people would take better care of their homes," she said. "It looks terrible."

At the courthouse, we met with the judge. Afterwards, Luca told me I had done a good job acting desperate, so maybe the judge would sign the files. But I had seen the way the judge looked at Luca, and I knew she had been unimpressed by my pleading voice and tears, none of which had been an act.

We returned to the orphanage for Neale. I had dropped off a smiling, clean baby; the child who clung to me two hours later was wide-eyed, pale, and hungry. She needed her diaper changed. The moment rests indelibly in my mind—my baby had recognized the orphanage (the smell? the chaos?) and she was scared. I never brought her back there again. But that afternoon, while she slept soundly, I sank to my knees and sobbed uncontrollably to a God I no longer worshipped. I begged Him to let me bring my baby home. I chastised Him for acting like a good and just God while babies suffered, and cursed Him for keeping me away from my other children. If someone had told me to burn a lock of Neale's hair along with a taco shell and feed the ashes to a stray dog, I swear I would have done it. Only once before had I felt so desperately in need of divine intervention—that day, decades earlier, when I had prayed and prayed I wasn't pregnant.

By the end of the summer, our case was still mired in bureaucratic spaghetti. "You need to come home," Bob told me. "The kids need you." I knew that. I needed them, too. But again, I didn't know then how badly my absence was affecting our son. Abandoned by his birth mother, ignored as an infant, now left for weeks on end by his mom, he was charging through his third year of life with a quick temper and frequent tears. Bob was unable to appease him in his frequent rages. Laura had been a tremendous help, but she needed to go back to school. And Scout—my poor angel Scout—she was such a good and happy child; it didn't even occur to me how much she must have missed me. Her summer days were monopolized by a frazzled dad, a miserable brother, and a nanny she barely knew.

We decided to find a foster family to care for Neale.

The majority of adoptable kids from Guatemala lived in private foster homes until they were cleared to go home with their new parents. The foster families mostly consisted of poor people needing the small stipend they received for caring for a child, plus whatever money the adoptive parents gave them when visiting. And while many of the homes were safe and loving, they were still a cog in the adoption machine, and I didn't want my kid to get caught there.

I started questioning everyone I knew about connections they might have in Guatemala, and the frantic search led us to my sister's high school friend's former nanny's brother. I understand if you have to read that twice.

George and Maria lived in an upper middle class neighborhood outside the chaos of Guatemala City with their three children, and they agreed to keep Neale until we could bring her home. I instantly felt at home with them; their house was neat and clean and full of life. The children hugged me, and appeared loved and happy. I liked them all immediately, and I knew they would love my Neale.

George and Maria and Neale and I took a quick trip through the Central American version of Babies-R-Us, and with a heavy heart I handed my child to a family of loving strangers and flew home.

At the airport, Scout flew into my arms and molded herself to me like a sweater I didn't know I needed. I never wanted to let her go. After a few long seconds, I pulled her to one side of me and opened my other arm to Nico.

I still remember his stance, how he leaned against Bob about ten feet away, his weight on one leg and the other foot tucked behind his ankle. He had one hand near his mouth, chewing on his fingers, the other hand still by his side. I squatted down and called him to me; he didn't come, just stared at me, not smiling, not unhappy. A lump rose in my throat.

"He's confused," Bob said. "Give him time."

Maybe, in that moment, maybe I understood. Maybe for a nanosecond I realized how deep my son's emotional injuries went, and how long they would last. Maybe I suddenly intuited how painful my absence had been, in light of his precarious start in life; maybe I knew then the treacherous nature of the journey ahead of us. But if I did, I put it all out of my head. Because really, I must have thought, what in the world could we do about it?

For the next four months, I returned to Guatemala every two to three weeks to check on Neale. George and Maria and their children loved Neale from the first minute—I couldn't have picked better people to care for her. They sent me frequent email updates with pictures: Neale crawling, Neale playing with a toy I had sent, Neale smiling. Every photo tore at my heart. Finally, in October of 2007, three weeks after her first birthday, the last piece of paper was signed; Neale came home to Florida, to our big green house by the sea, and our family was complete.

We talked excitedly about settling into life with three kids, playing a lot of board games, and putting money into a really nice retirement fund. But of course, that's not what happened. Not at all.

One evening, not long after the homecoming, Bob and I spent a couple of hours getting all three kids to bed, and then we stood facing each other in the kitchen, too tired to even clean up the dinner dishes. "I've ruined everyone's life," I said. Bob didn't disagree. The chaos had begun.

PART II

TWELVE

The summer before my senior year in college, I worked as a manager of a snowball stand at the 1984 World's Fair in New Orleans. One night, after hours, a fellow manager and I got a tiny bit smashed and set sail on the original African Queen, which was docked on display in a manmade pond. Once the security guard spotted us, we paddled with our hands to the opposite shore and disembarked and made our escape, though the guard wasn't trying too hard to catch us, as he probably had no idea what to do with us.

Anyway, the next day I was off and hungover and decided to lay low, which is why I was sound asleep in my bed the night I woke up to a stranger screaming somewhere in the house.

I launched myself out of bed and ran toward the noise. When I reached the foyer, I stopped and stared at my father in his boxer shorts sitting on top of a naked black woman. Naked. Except for high-top sneakers. Dad was sitting on her stomach holding her arms down. She was screaming and kicking. We lived in a wealthy New Orleans suburb with little to zero diversity; it was unusual to see black people in the neighborhood; naked, screaming, black women were even scarcer.

Dad saw me staring and said, "Get me a blanket, goddammit!" like, of course, I was supposed to know that he needed a blanket, *goddammit*.

As I ran to the linen closet, I passed my mother in the kitchen on the phone with the police. I found a blanket and returned to the foyer. We tried to cover the naked woman but she started screaming that we were burning off all of her skin. "GET AWAY FROM ME, YOU WHITE BITCH!" she shrieked. So we just hung out for the ten minutes or so that it took for the police to arrive, and watched the woman spitting and screaming at us, me and Mom in our pajamas, and Dad sitting there atop the naked woman.

When the police arrived, they asked my father for a tee shirt to cover the woman, and he gave them one. They offered to return it later, but he said he didn't need it back. Dad explained how he and my mom had been in bed when they were awakened by the sound of glass breaking. Dad ran to the front of the house and spotted the woman on the front porch with our sprinkler. She was systematically smashing in the living room windows, one by one. My father was afraid she was hurt, or running away from someone. So he opened the door, grabbed her and pulled her inside, and locked the door.

She didn't like that. The police told us they thought she was on drugs. We later learned she also had broken into a neighbor's house and assaulted a woman. Her clothes were strewn along the street. The police handcuffed her and took her away. Dad said he didn't want to press charges. After the excitement, Mom was a nervous wreck. "I need a bowl of cereal!" she exclaimed. Dad and I each had a beer.

I've thought about the woman a thousand times since that night. Maybe she was on drugs. Maybe she had been raped. Or maybe she just had a touch of the devil in her, and she needed to get away from herself. It's a scary feeling, I'll bet. I've always been a little afraid of it.

Nico was just about three years old when Neale came home, and the first pictures of them together are predictably adorable. But even in photos, especially when I look at them now, I can see the wariness in his gaze, the suspicion inherent in his hugs. She was 13 months old—old enough to steal his toys, cute enough to steal everyone's attention, and—most importantly—still young enough to steal my time. He had no patience for her needs. When I was changing her diaper, he wanted something to eat. When I was rocking her to sleep, he wanted a hug. If I smiled at her, it was a smile she had taken from him.

I had expected life to be a little more challenging. What I hadn't anticipated was the all-consuming, beastly task of keeping three young children alive and healthy. At the time, we still lived in the green house by the sea—in a beach community about 20 miles from everything—so I spent a good bit of time schlepping everyone from place to place. Scout was in kindergarten, but there was no bus. Nico was in preschool three days a week, and though he loved school, he hated being dropped off. At times I had to pry his little fingers from around my arms while he wailed and screamed. His teachers saved us; on those tearful days, after I dropped him off, I sat in my car and cried until they called to tell me he was fine. And he was always fine—when he wasn't with me. But I inspired in him some sort of psychotic mania.

One day I was at the gym with Nico and Neale in the gym's "Kidcare" program. I ran into Fara, an acquaintance with whom I often worked out. I knew she had three young children. "I don't know how you do it," I told her. "You always seem so calm, and I feel like I'm losing my mind."

"Well," she said. "It's hard. When I had my fourth ..."

"You have four?" I cried, and fell apart right there by the ellipticals. I felt tears pushing their way out of my eyeballs, and whimpered, "I'm sorry. Excuse me."

I ran to the bathroom, mortified. Fara followed me, gave me a hug and asked what was happening. Sobbing, I told her I just couldn't do it—the three-kid family had been a huge mistake, and I didn't know what I was going to do. "I can't even shower," I told her. "My son won't leave me alone. He hates the baby. It's like I can't even take care of her because it makes him so mad."

"You're exhausted," she said. "Listen. I'm going to take Nico to my house right now. You and Neale go home, and take a shower, and nap. We'll be fine, and you'll feel much better." I tried to object, but she insisted. Together, we got the kids out of Kidcare and I walked them to Fara's car. Her daughter was the same age as Nico, and I told him he was going to her house to play.

A thought occurred to me, and I started crying again. "I don't even know your last name!" I whimpered. Fara laughed and gave me her last name, address, and cell phone number. "Take as long as you need," she said. "Don't worry, I'll take good care of him." I knew that she would, and she did. I wasn't worried about her. I was worried about me.

It was such a relief to have Neale home from Guatemala. But with her adoption complete, it was time to worry about Nico. His angry outbursts had continued to intensify, and Neale's arrival made him even more demanding. We couldn't leave the house without Blue Puppy. Then it had to be Blue Puppy and Blankie. Then Blue Puppy, and Blankie, and a Thomas book. Any efforts to curb his requests resulted in tantrums that became increasingly physical.

He's a boy, we again told ourselves. *Boys are different. He's just a high maintenance kid.*

Shortly after Neale turned two—Nico was four, and Scout was seven—we moved from the beach house we loved to a large suburban home closer to schools, the grocery store, and the rat race. I cried to leave that house, where I could fall asleep listening to the waves crash and cook dinner watching the sun set over the Intracoastal Waterway. Pelicans flew so close to the balcony we could look into their eyes. It was the place that had healed me after the failed infertility efforts, and brought me closer than I'd ever been to intertwining my life with the natural wonders around me. Our living area was on the second floor, giving the effect of living in a tree house. I watched storms roll in and over me like I was part of the landscape.

But the 15-mile trip to Scout's elementary school on a two-lane highway was wearing me down. I often made the trip twice each day, and knew, as the kids grew older, play dates and extracurricular activities would pose a hardship.

So we joined the masses. We moved into a large suburban house close to everything. "It's perfect," I told Bob, even though it immediately seemed like a mistake.

Life continued. I drove less, but spent more time managing our big new house. There were no kids in the neighborhood, so our children spent lots of time playing by themselves in the driveway.

Nico struggled. He had a crush on his preschool teacher. While taking a bath one night, he told me, "I want my hair to be all clean, so Miss Rachel will say, *ooh, that smells good.*"

I'm not sure how much hair-smelling Miss Rachel did, but I knew she was luckier than the previous year's teacher, who had big boobs. At the end of the year, she said, "We love our Nico. I call him our little perv." Each time the teacher offered him a hug or a snuggle, she'd feel his little hand sneaking under her blouse toward her breast.

My 3-year-old son, copping a feel off his pre-school teacher. I thought he only did that to me. But there was something heartbreaking about his desire to please. It was a fear, really—he worried incessantly about displeasing his teachers, and obsessed about how much he loved them.

And he kept screaming. Like, all the time. The year before, I had taken him to the pediatrician because his temper tantrums had come to resemble volcanic explosions, complete with rumbling and the spewing of liquid in the form of spit. He was unreasonable, even for a youngster, and occasionally downright mean. His little voice was so raspy it pained me. The doctor examined him from head to toe. "Well," he said. "He's hoarse and raspy because he screams so much. And he screams so much because he's 2."

But the terrible twos had morphed into the terrible threes and the formidable fours, and my boy still suffered from the Screaming Meanies. I didn't love him any less. But I often preferred not to be around him. Having children is a constant battle of contradictions. Your heart expands impossibly, and sometimes feels like it might explode into a millions shards of love. It can be painful. I remember biking over a bridge when Scout was a baby, and suddenly becoming paralyzed with the fear of Scout falling off that bridge one day.

Yet the love, ever-present, can be tempered by ... resentment? No, let's call it extreme frustration and exhaustion. One day, I left the house to walk the dog, and tiny Neale pressed her little nose to the living room window and threw me kisses goodbye. She smiled her best smile, and did a little dance and waved at me, never taking her eyes from mine. As I walked the dog, I was struck with the possibility of being hit by a car and never seeing her again, and my love for her surged like blood in my veins, running through my body and nourishing it with life. Ten minutes later I found her naked, eating lipstick and throwing dollhouse furniture at her brother, and I suddenly needed a long solitary nap. It's the part of motherhood no one tells you about: Your 7-year-old will say "whatever," when you ask her about her day. Your son will learn to incorporate the words *poopy*, *wiener*, and *pee-pee* into every lullaby he knows. Your toddler will climb up on the counter, open the medicine cabinet and help herself to some Tums. Your children will learn to play a violent rendition of musical chairs to Lady GaGa's Poker Face while you're on the phone, and the baby will beat a lizard to death with a diving stick.

Actually, though, I could handle that stuff. I could power through the normal peaks and valleys of motherhood. But as Nico's foul temperament grew more constant, Bob and I knew something was not normal. We sensed Nico's emotional core had been somehow compromised. As a result, he was pretty much wrecking everything.

One night, we took the trolley down the beach, and Nico, obsessed with all things that move, was beside himself with excitement. "Look, Mom! I see a lake!" he shouted as we passed a retention pond. His sense of wonder made me weak with joy. Later, at a restaurant, he stole his sister's crayon, threw his lemonade on the floor, drew all over Scout's picture, and locked everyone out of his room when we got home.

Other times, he was hilarious. Often at dinner, he launched into what we called his Stevie Wonder impression—eyes squeezed shut, head swaying side to side, for no apparent reason. And he was a sponge. He threw back my phrases and admonitions daily, making me feel like a shrew. "Mind your business!" he yelled at his sister. "You take care of your own self!"

He measured his love for people with numbers; those closest to him, he loved "five." Sometimes he even loved me "ten." When he was mad, he loved me one.

He mostly loved Neale zero, since she had ruined his life. One night when he wouldn't go to bed, I resorted to yelling at him, and he yelled back. "You go to jail, Mom! Go to jail!" I said fine, I'd go to jail if he went to bed, and he agreed. But he snuck out of bed to see where I was, and when he found me on the couch, he yelled, "That's not jail!" And so I had a heated discussion about why it's inappropriate to send mothers to jail. Finally, I wore him out, and tucked him in for the final time. "Give me a kiss," I said, and he did. "That makes Mommy so happy," I said. He pulled my face close to his, looked into my eyes, and whispered, "I don't want you to be happy."

Neale was too young to understand her brother's moods and tantrums, but they tormented Scout. She sometimes cried herself to sleep as Bob and I struggled to contain Nico both physically and emotionally. If she thought I was being mean to him, she screamed at me to stop, bringing us both to tears.

Despite the "episodes," as we began calling them, we settled into the soccer-mom routine—metaphorically, though, since we never really played soccer—with days planned around school, play dates, and trips to the grocery. I became really agitated by all the mother-of-the-year types who waxed poetic about *how it all goes so fast!* Even old ladies in the grocery store were in on the conspiracy: *Enjoy it now! It goes so fast!*

"You think so?" I always responded. "Because really, I'm not finding that."

I guess the years pass quickly. But the days! The hours! The minutes till bedtime! A fucking grind on the good days. With one in first grade and two in pre-school, my life had turned Sisyphean. The kitchen was clean every morning for two minutes, and then suddenly my checkbook was stuck to the counter with maple syrup glue. All of the Tupperware was organized, and then the containers were being used as hospital beds for tiny Webkinz toys. I finally fixed the hinge on the leather ottoman, and then

Nico drew a blue ghost on it that honestly looked like a smiling penis. If Neale pooped in her underpants one more time, I was ready to dose her with Imodium. If the boy didn't stop calling me Pee-Pee-Head, I was going to give him a soapy mouth.

I woke up each morning, had coffee, and counted the hours until naptimes, then counted the hours until I could have wine, then counted the hours until bedtime. I really, madly, desperately loved my kids … but I still hailed bedtime as something akin to the Rapture.

I had never really yelled at kids before, but suddenly I became a yeller. Twice I wrecked my car *in my own driveway* after backing up in a hurry while simultaneously yelling at Nico. One time in particular, it was because he wouldn't stop naming objects for me to retrieve for the ride to school. "Blue Puppy!" I found Blue Puppy. "Blankie!" I got Blankie. "BOPPY!" I fetched him some milk. By the time I finally was able to back out of the driveway, I was a stewing, shaking, raging mess. "If your teacher wants to know why you're late," I yelled at Scout, who had done nothing wrong, "you tell her it's because your little brother is NAUGHTY, NAUGHTY, NAUGHTY!" I must have sounded like a monster. Behind me in his car seat, my son sniveled and wept, and sucked from his sippy cup.

The kids sent me not-subtle signals that my parenting style needed some tweaking. One day I screamed at them, "What did I just say? *Speak nicely to each other!*" and little Neale pointed her finger at me and said, "No! Stop it! Don't do dat, Mom!" and the Pterodactyl did his eye-blinking thing which means he's about to cry. But honestly, they constantly gave me shit to yell about. At least twice a day I had to tell Nico to stop grabbing my boobs or refrain from sticking his finger in my ear. He *touched* me constantly, without boundary. He found perennial joy in tormenting Neale —he might accuse her of having poopy ears until she was finally convinced, and ran to me screaming and holding her ears. But if I held her, he wanted to be held, too.

Neale was turning into a tyrant. More than once I had to remind her that she could not wash her hair with body lotion or paint her walls with lip gloss. One day, I found a stick of butter in her closet.

But mainly, I knew in my heart, it was Nico causing the household to implode. I worried I was screwing up; I found a shrink to help me parent my son, and a different shrink to help me deal with the fact that I needed a shrink to deal with my son. The first shrink told me to figure out my "moment," the signal to myself that I needed to take a few deep breaths and regroup. For her, she said by way of example, she could feel her heart rate speeding up. I knew exactly what she meant. For me, it was when a little voice inside my head started chanting, "*Shut the fuck up. Shut the fuck up.*" It happened every single day. The therapist's parenting advice included lots of charts and schedules and routines, none of which really rang right for us. I occasionally wrote lists for Nico; he tore them up. His schedule was limited by the compartments of his brain.

And yet—this boy was my enigmatic everything. We shared moments of such profound intimacy they shattered my heart. Sometimes, he snuggled in his bed, pulled my face to his and locked lips with me for what he called a cricket kiss. Other times, he screeched, "Get me a BOPPY!" and kicked me in the ribs as I tried to say good night. He loved to stroke his big sister's hair and tell her how beautiful she looked. He also liked to throw his little sister's beloved Teddy against the wall. While in timeout once, he leaned over and repeatedly deposited globs of saliva on the floor until there was a puddle. Then he rubbed his fuzzy blanket on his upper lip and fell asleep in the fetal position. One night, around 2:00 am, he woke me up to show me how he had flushed his nightlight down the toilet, where it lodged so perfectly that I had to replace the whole fucking toilet. He was so proud.

This boy was kicking my ass. There were times I thought I might die of love for him, when tears stung my eyes just thinking about his toothy grin and sticky-uppy hair and the way he loved to have his ears cleaned. I felt desperate to rid him of his middle-child syndrome—that's what I thought it must be—and to convince him of our forever love for him. "I wish Neale wasn't in our family!" he told me all the time. "I told you we shouldn't have buyed another baby!"

Nico tortured her mercilessly until she grew up enough to fight back. By then, they had turned into two little magnets spiked with explosives. They couldn't stay away from each other, but nearly every contact ended badly. He tried so hard to love her, he really did. When she woke up, he often gently approached her and touched her hair, saying, "Good morning!" in his sweetest voice. But Neale, wary after two years of abuse, usually responded with a quick right hook and a growl, and so hurt my poor little boy's feelings that he dissolved into sobs.

One night, after Neale had called him *Weiner butt! Weiner butt! Wiener butt!* for several long minutes, I pulled him into my lap and whispered, "Let's go for a bike ride. I want to take you someplace special, just you and me." Normally he argued about alone time with Bob or me because he was afraid he was being left out of something. But that night, beleaguered, he agreed.

He rode in the bike carrier behind me and I pedaled through the quiet neighborhood. Soon, I pulled over in front of a lake surrounded by tree canopy. Hanging in front of us was an old-fashioned swing, fastened by ropes to a high oak branch. We had to descend the bank slightly to get on the swing. I pulled him into my lap. I walked backwards as far as I could, then let go, and in a magical swoosh, we soared through the air and peaked over the water. I believed I felt my boy's heart flying upward with mine right then, like together we were lifting ourselves above a world filled with pesky little sisters and cranky mothers and wiener butts, and at least for a moment, we became part of the very air beneath us. We kept swinging. We watched little turtle heads pop up in the lake and water bugs making circles, and we listened to the crickets chirp. I nuzzled his neck with kisses and nibbled his ear, which was one of his most favorite things in the world besides airplanes. "Mom. It's peace out here," he said.

We swung and swung. I got vertigo and felt nauseated. I threw up a little in my mouth, and felt a headache looming. But I could not break this fairy spell, this rare moment when my boy internalized, more than learned, the meaning of peace.

"Could you take a picture of us so we can remember this?" he asked. I didn't have my camera. Of course I would remember it, I told him. But I knew what he meant. Memories morph into blurry versions of reality, particularly for little children who struggle so hard to understand the complexities of a grown-up world. He was the one who needed the photo, or some other tangible proof of my love—something he could turn to the next time he found himself on the wrong side of trouble.

Finally, the sun started setting and tiny no-see-ums buzzed into our noses and mouths, and he said he was ready to go. We rode home without talking, but I could feel his contentment. When we walked back into the house, the usual chaos reigned. Scout had taken a shower with Neale, who was screaming she had soap in her eyes. The bathroom floor was flooded. It was nearing 9:00 p.m. and no one seemed interested in going to bed. My husband sat on the couch watching preseason football as though bandits had told him he'd be killed if he moved. Nico joined the fray, and within minutes, all three kids were involved in a fracas worthy of reality television.

But later, after the household had settled for the evening and I lay in bed mentally steeling myself for the next day, I thought about the secret swing, my beautiful boy, and the way he looked at me when he crawled into my lap to soar into the sky. And I thought about his favorite moment of the excursion, when, as he flew over the grassy slope over the calm clear water, I heard a little noise followed by inexorable giggles and this most important announcement: "I gassed!"

THIRTEEN

I have three sisters with blonde hair and blue eyes. They all look like beauty queens. As a young girl and later as a teenager, I thought myself the ugly duckling of the family. I'm 5'10", with curly red hair and freckles; I like to think of myself as tall and lean, but in reality I think I've always been tall and muscular with plenty of padding, if you know what I mean. One day—I was 18 years old—as I ate lunch in a restaurant with my family, the waitress complimented my parents on their beautiful daughters. I remember internalizing her comment to mean: *You have three beautiful daughters! Too bad about the fourth.* I immediately went to the restroom and threw up, thus beginning a battle with bulimia that would last two years.

I'm happy now with the way I look, but my experiences have given me insights into the potential pitfalls my children face. My children, who inexplicably look like biological siblings, have beautiful caramel skin and dark brown eyes. Scout and Neale have thick, straight, black hair, and Nico's is dark brown and long, like a surfer's shag. He hates haircuts. I think it's a Mayan thing. Mayans really value their hair. Also, they used human hair to sew sutures, so it's handy as well.

On a dark night and with some pointed squinting, the children bear a slight resemblance to my short, Italian husband. The only physical similarity they have to me is that we all have human organs. People rarely approached us with comments when we were all together. But when I'm alone with the kids, verbal speculation abounds.

"What's she mixed with?" asked a grocery store clerk, eyeing Scout when she was a baby.

"You're like Angelina Jolie!" gasped an acquaintance, seeing us all together.

"Are they siblings?" people have asked again and again, right after I've introduced them all as my children.

The list of inappropriate comments is endless. *Could you not have children of your own? Where you'd get them? I want one! What happened to their parents? I know someone from China!* And my favorite, *I can ask you about this, because my grandson is a mulatto.*

Misconceptions about adoption abound, but seem especially prevalent in areas lacking racial diversity, like the suburb where I live. Because I am raising brown children, I have more reason to notice the area's innate *whiteness.* Curiosity regarding my kids' origins is to be expected, I suppose. But people often feel entitled to question me about our familial history based on one factor: race. My children have been examined from afar for the entirety of their lives simply because they have brown skin and I don't. From the beginning, I fought against it, and rebuffed attempts by strangers to extract my family's story with a Miss Manners-approved polite, weary, smile and an incredulous look that discouraged further questioning. I have always been proud of my children's heritage, and proud of how our family came to be. I happily talk about adoption in the appropriate setting, and can blather on endlessly about our diverse household and our allegiance to multiculturalism. But asking me specifics about how my child came to be an orphan—*in front of my child*—well, just go away. Or tell me how and when your own child was conceived, and whether you had an orgasm that night. Really, it's that offensive.

As the days, weeks, months went by, I began to anticipate what people would say and when they would say it; I could manage it. What was more difficult to handle, though, were the unpredictable moments that arose with unnerving frequency.

One rainy Sunday, Bob was working and I suggested we pile onto my bed to watch a movie on the Disney Channel. The movie playing that morning, as described in the on-screen blurb, was about a boy who starts turning into a fish on his 13th birthday. That seemed a bit quirky, but innocuous enough, and it does seem that children transform themselves as they enter the teen years. We started watching. And listen: it turns out the boy was *adopted*, and his birth mother was a mermaid who abandoned him on a shrimp boat when he was a baby. The shrimp boat captain and his wife found him and raised him. His only remarkable feature was his tremendous propensity for swimming. At age 13, his true heritage began to, um, swim to the surface. Every time he touched water, he grew scales and fins. Seriously. This caused him to lose some popularity points at school. He began to see his "real mom" whenever he happened by the harbor. She swam around waiting for him, gracefully flopping her silvery tail. You see, it was time for him to join her and fully transform into a "merman."

Eventually his adoptive parents understood that a merman's got to do what a merman's got to do, and they let him go. The plan was for him to spend a year with his "real mom" swimming around the ocean. Then, somehow, he would be prepared to come back ashore and be part human again.

Scout and I were riveted: me out of horror and Scout, I think, out of sheer perplexity and perhaps some slight concern regarding her love of the water. But I couldn't turn it off because I was afraid it would be like saying to my adopted daughter "We are absolutely not going to watch a movie about some adopted kid." Listen, I'm all for openness and candor when discussing adoption with my children. So thank you, Disney, for helping viewers understand that children who were adopted are so weird and unnatural they very likely will morph into different species as they age.

Of course, my children have birth mothers, and I'm eternally grateful to those women for entrusting me with these gifts of life. But am I not their real mother? Who fed them Cheez-Its for breakfast? Who let them skip brushing their teeth at night? Who taught them the words to "McDonald's is your kind of place/ hamburgers in your face?" Who told them homework is stupid, peace signs are cool, and peanut butter spoons can make a meal? Me. I don't think they'll grow fins and scales, but if they do, they won't be swimming out to sea without me. We'll just move to the Caribbean, I guess, and live on a houseboat and I'll learn how to scuba dive, and together we'll brave whatever the tide brings in.

As Nico transitioned from preschooler to little boy, he often seemed to be morphing into something alien. He terrorized us. His screech contained a decibel level that penetrated the brain. He also had some kind of built-in radar instructing him how to drive me wild—emptying a basket of clean folded laundry, scribbling on his sister's favorite artwork, throwing a pencil at me because I didn't draw an airplane the way he envisioned it. Stabbing a freshly baked cake with a fork. Tearing up a birthday card. Throwing my shoes in the trash.

He had a feminine side as a result of having two sisters, but it was bitchy. At age four, he loved to play dress-up with the girls, mainly so he could take what was theirs. One day, he wanted his little sister's purse, her pink shiny purse with the enormous heart-shaped rhinestone buckle. She carried it everywhere. It usually contained her Teddy, an old remote control she used as a cell phone, and something ridiculously inappropriate like a screwdriver.

"That's hers," I told him. "Do you want a purse? I'll find you a purse." But he wanted the one SHE had. That's how he thought of Neale—SHE—as in *SHE'S the one who came into this family and took my rightful spot as the most adorable child on the planet, thereby destroying the universe.*

When Neale understood the problem, she offered to give her brother the pink shiny purse. She could be very helpful when she wasn't throwing shoes at my head. But her generosity ruined the purse for him. He no longer wanted it. He still wanted something, but it had become indefinable, an intangible void he needed to fill. Eventually, he settled on demanding a piece of raw cookie dough, which I gave him, thinking about the eating disorder therapy bills we'd have to pay when he started filling all emotional voids with junk food.

Ten minutes later, we were on the road headed to preschool with the kids harmonizing to "Boom Boom Pow" by the Black-Eyed Peas (*Them chickens jackin' my style*) and I started thinking about how funny it all was, because if I didn't think it was funny, I would cry. I was crying anyway, in fact. And I knew these issues weren't the result of Nico's *boy-ness*. He wasn't morphing into anything as otherworldly as a merman, but as sure as I was of my love for him, I was equally certain his status as an adopted child had somehow changed who he was.

Back in those days, I cried so much my eyelids felt perpetually heavy and droopy. I didn't think my little boy was capable of breathing for a whole day without me, and the thought filled me with despair. I often reported a day's events with humor, so friends didn't understand my worries. When I spoke with loved ones, I gave upbeat reports: we were happy, life was good. A truer report might have been: "Well, this morning Nico told me I was going to get my butt kicked, then he used a fork to stab holes in the leftover pumpkin still hanging around the kitchen. He calmed down after I locked him out on the back porch for a few minutes, and to celebrate we taped his life-sized scarecrow up on the front door and carved the pumpkin. Then he ate raw cookie dough and a hot dog for breakfast and is currently spreading pumpkin seeds all over the house. Neale is screaming because she can't color in the butterfly on her iPad, and because the dog ate her raw cookie. She visits me every few minutes to hand me boogers. She says she is NOT going to school today, so I'm glad it's Saturday. Scout is perfect, as usual, except that she's freezing, bored, hungry and her ankle hurts. She ate noodles for breakfast and is watching "So You Think You Can Dance" reruns and staring very hard at the Victoria's Secret commercials. I'm fine, but I had sushi last night, which always makes me gain about five pounds in water weight. I have five baskets of unfolded laundry in the living room and countless piles of dog shit to remove from the front yard. How's it going with you?"

Sometimes, it just wasn't funny.

FOURTEEN

Nico turned five in December 2009. His teachers proclaimed him the sweetest, most disciplined child to ever walk the earth; we were grateful he could hold himself together during the day at school. Nearly every afternoon, though, he turned into a Category 5 hurricane the minute he walked through the door.

I listened almost indiscriminately to advice from friends and family, always hoping the next trick might be the one that fixed our son. Most of them thought Nico was just a sensitive, undisciplined kid. I wanted them to be right. If Nico could be healed by more stringent discipline, I was ready. We installed a lock on his door to enforce time-outs. He threw himself against the door a hundred times until the doorframe broke. We took away his toys; he emptied out all of his drawers, tipped over the dresser, and scribbled on the wall.

One day, my friend, Sammy, and I took our combined five kids to a craft fair where they could make their own art projects, like painted shell necklaces and bandana bracelets. Nico chose to paint rocks first—he picked a huge rock, which he colored green. Then he wiped all the paint off and painted it brown. Then he wiped all the paint off again and painted it blue, and decided it was Pluto. That was the last cute thing he did for quite some time. Leaving the paint station, he freaked out because the cotton candy was pink instead of blue. He took the Diet Coke out of my hand, poured it onto the grass and stomped on the can. He ran away from me into the crowd three times. He told me I was a *bad, bad mama* and he hated me. He screeched it, actually. He threw trash on the ground. He begged me to hold him, then threw himself to the ground when I tried to pick him up. I wish I could say that went on for a good 20 minutes. But it was more like an hour and a half.

Finally, exhausted, he collapsed under a tree that happened to be next to a kiosk where some community cheerleaders were helping children decorate sugar cookies. He dragged himself over, slathered an enormous cookie with an inch of icing, and ate every bit of it.

Within a minute, the devil-child disappeared. Totally. Sammy and I were left slack-jawed. He held his little sister's hand. He kissed me. He thanked people.

"I bet he's hypoglycemic," Sammy said. Or … maybe I hadn't been feeding him, which sounds bad. But listen, Scout could go three days on a spoonful of peanut butter and a bag of Cheetos. And when hungry, she just rummaged in the pantry and inhaled stuff for a few minutes. Neale grazed on power bars, Goldfish and whatever candy she found at the bottom of my purse. So when I thought about it, we might have gotten into a habit of skipping meals, which is probably contraindicated for 5-year-old boys.

For the two days following the craft fair, I force-fed the boy every two hours. He sucked down food like a vacuum. Yogurt, smoothies, chips, rice and beans, pasta, waffles, popcorn, eggs, watermelon—it was like he hadn't really eaten for weeks. And for two days, he did not have a tantrum. That's not to say his behavior was stellar. He doesn't like any brown spots on his omelet so I had to surreptitiously turn his bites of egg inside out so he would eat them. When I told him he was doing a great job on his cartwheels, he insisted I reword it so that I said his cartwheels were great. He still whacked his little sister on the head whenever it was convenient. But when he ripped out yet another padlock Bob had molly-bolted onto his bedroom door, he simply smirked about his accomplishment and returned to his room to serve his time-out sentence. I was so thrilled about the tantrums disappearing I didn't think maybe my behavior standards had slipped too low. It was stuff I could handle, particularly if it meant I had my darling boy back. One night, when I was snuggling with him, he started singing Britney Spears' "Womanizer" and was giggling so hard he almost fell out of bed. And I thought gleefully, *I'm so glad I started feeding him again.* Case closed, I told Bob. The problem had been his accidental starvation diet.

But the tantrums had not disappeared. A few weeks later, on my 46th birthday, he made me a beautiful card with the number 46 written across it six times, but he tore it up into pieces because he regretted using the word "great" to describe me. Later, after attending classroom Christmas parties, I took him and his sister to Starbucks. In retrospect they were a little too hyped for public interaction, but I really wanted a latte. So we went in and I bought them some cookies and they sat down. Neale dropped her cookies. Nico picked them up, which infuriated Neale. She hurled the cookies across the store and beaned the Starbucks manager in the butt. Nico rushed to grab the thrown cookies. Neale tackled him. They landed on a mop. Neale rolled over on the ground with her legs in the air. She wasn't wearing any underpants.

For a full five seconds, I sipped my coffee and pretended to wonder whose kids they could possibly be. Then I dragged them out to the motorized landfill, which doubled as my van, strapped them into their car seats, looked around to make sure no one was watching me, and popped every one of their Christmas party balloons. We rode home in silence, and it was the most peaceful part of the day.

"That's a mom's birthday," said my sister. I guess. Still, I perpetually sipped from the half-empty glass, worried I was ruining my children. What was I doing wrong? George Bernard Shaw said, *There may be some doubt as to who are the best people to have charge of children, but there can be no doubt that parents are the worst.* Truth. Ten times a day I wondered, "Who thought it was a good idea to make me the boss of these little people? Who thought I could do this?" Me, of course. The whole damn thing had been my idea, and I worried it would end in disaster.

That year, we managed to sustain some festive holiday magic. We took sunset bike rides to look at holiday lights, and baked cookies. We played holiday music and wrote letters to Santa. On Christmas Eve, everyone went to bed early because they knew Santa wouldn't come otherwise. Bob was working overnight, so I was relieved to be able to organize the Santa presents early. It took me over an hour to drag the loot over from the neighbor's garage, divvy it up, and artfully arrange it all. Then I covered each pile with a sheet so the kids wouldn't be able to see it until their dad came home from work the next morning.

When I was done, I settled into bed to wrap some presents and watch *A Christmas Story*. Near midnight, a sleepy Scout came in, and the moment at which I saw her seemed to last a hundred years. I thought maybe she hadn't recognized the sheets as piles of presents because I often store clean sheets on the furniture before folding them—a habit I knew would come in handy one day. I decided to play dumb. "Hi, honey," I said, pulling her into my lap. "You'd better get back to sleep so Santa can come."

"He came already, Mom!" she said, but I couldn't read her expression.

"He did?"

"Yes! But he covered everything up!"

"That's weird."

"And he left a note saying we should wait for Daddy before we open our presents."

"Wow! That's so exciting!"

We sat in silence for a minute. Then I said, "I have a confession. I left the sheets for Santa and asked him to cover everything up."

"Mom! I can't believe you!" But she seemed pleased, like what I did offered some sort of proof.

I kept on. "I can't believe Santa came while I was here in my bed and I didn't even hear him!"

More silence. "I know," she finally said. I carried her back to her bed and tucked her in. She said she wouldn't be able to sleep. So I pretended to peek at her pile and told her she had gotten a Life board game, and she felt better.

I went to sleep thinking that either my 8-year-old daughter was not as brilliantly astute as I thought she was, or she was desperate to cling to what remained of her girlhood. It was probably the latter, and frankly that's the sadder of the two, but I embraced it like a favorite thinning tee shirt I knew I wouldn't be able to wear for much longer.

The next morning went perfectly. Nico enjoyed his electric train, although we were all bummed when he washed the locomotive in the sink. Then he used his remote-controlled fart machine to fill the house with gas every 15 minutes. We all stayed in our pajamas until 5:00 p.m., except Neale, who wore her new pink tutu all day. Even then, we only dressed in sweats to walk around the block. Scout practiced putting her new earrings in and taking them out, and played an entire game of Life with her new doll, Callista. "That way I sort of get to take every turn!" she said. That girl.

I made my grandmother's housekeeper's famous Brown Spaghetti and Meatballs for dinner, and did it right. No one mentioned television all day. Bob gave me a beautiful tabletop water fountain and a Flip video recorder. But the best present I received was the day itself, nearly perfect because of—not in spite of—its imperfections. No fancy food demanded accolades, no schedule insisted on time limitations. Most importantly, no meltdowns. We were limited only by our tolerance for one another, and our ability to understand that we were all we needed.

Two days later, the Christmas magic ran out. Nico had become infatuated with the Tyrant's play kitchen, somehow convincing himself it was far better than his awesome electric train. A bop on his sister's head, a stolen plastic ice cream cone, a glass-breaking screech: it all led to a time-out.

While in his room for time-out, he eyed the locomotive, the one for which Bob had diligently shopped, the one we both imagined he'd cherish forever and gift to his own children one day. Nico was in love with trains, and we watched programs and read books about them constantly. While emotionally a bit stunted, his ability to understand how things worked seemed uncanny; Bob, nearly desperate to connect with his small son, had traveled across town to an independent hobby store dealing in electric trains, and found a set that would have pleased any child, or even any grown-up, for that matter. It had realistic whistles and bells, and noisy tracks and bridges. It was perfect.

Nico, angry and frustrated, alone in his room, grabbed the locomotive and ripped off the wheels. He dismantled the engine. He pulled out wires. He systematically destroyed it. Then he quietly brought the resulting pile of junk to his father.

My husband has held the hands of dying people. He has pulled broken bodies from car wreckage. But this broke his heart. His eyes welled up, and he couldn't speak. Nico saw the impact he had made, and stood silently watching the both of us. Together we picked up the remainder of the tracks and the train cars, and put them in a box. We explained to Nico that he had broken his very special train, and it couldn't run without the locomotive. We didn't yell or punish him or get angry. Then we left him in his room.

Bob cried. Nico cried. I cried. Nico pleaded through his tears. "I want my train! I want my favorite train!" Later he wrote on his chalkboard, "DAD FIX IT." Bob had trouble recovering. He had been so proud of this, his first significant gift to his son, and though his son was just 5 years old, the rejection felt calculated and symbolic. It hurt.

After that day, Nico never mentioned his train. "Let me buy him another train and talk to him about it," my mother said. But I didn't know if it was the right thing to do. I only knew a seminal moment had passed, an event father and son might never speak of again, but one which would shape them both. It was the first time we had tried to make our kid's dream come true. But in hindsight, I think we had taken his dream and morphed it into our own. We gave him the moon when the light from a star would have done nicely. More significantly, we had crossed a line. Something, we finally knew for certain, was just not right.

We plodded on for a while. The pediatrician told us he was fine. Teachers loved him. Life became a series of inane anecdotes. Nico's need for me was so constant, I joked that he wanted to crawl down my throat and live in my boob. We had joked about his obsession with boobs, but it made me a little uncomfortable because it seemed a clear sign of his emotional insecurity. When he was a baby, he often had tried to latch on to my breast as I rocked him to sleep, even though, to my knowledge, he had never been breastfed. Could he possibly be subconsciously craving that connection? He wanted me touching him all the time. Ear cleaning remained a regular method of bringing calm to a situation—he loved when I used a cotton swab dipped in baby oil to rub around the delicate curves of his ear. It lulled him into a peaceful complacency.

One evening, after a long afternoon of *I hate you* and *you're the worst mother ever* declarations, I snuggled Nico in my bed to watch television. "Mom," he said. "Draw a heart on my hand and write M + N in it." The M was for Mommy, the N for Nico. I did it with a purple Sharpie. He held his hand up, palm out. "It's upside down," he said. I found some toner and scrubbed it off and drew another one, right side up. "Draw one on your hand," he said. I did. "I need something else to remember you," he said. I retrieved a gold elephant broach with a red eye. "Give me your bracelet with the hearts," he said. I did. He gave it back. "Give me the one with the flowers," he said. I did. He gave it back. "Give me the one with the hearts," he said. I did.

I wanted so badly to give him what he needed. But I had no earthly idea what that was.

FIFTEEN

The city of New Orleans rests just south of Lake Pontchartrain, and the longest continuous over-water bridge in the world—24 miles—stretches across that great inland sea. On weekends, when I was a girl, the bridge seemed endless; I would rest my head against the window and count off the mile markers as we sped by them. One day, as we drove on the bridge toward our country cabin, I watched the sky open up to a mesmerizing vision of castles and turrets, all built with pastel clouds. Its skyline appeared to me like a paradise, and my heart felt full and content by simply knowing this place existed. I looked for a road, or a path to take; just as instantly as it appeared, it was gone.

"Mom!" I whispered. "Mom. I just saw heaven."

"Wow," she answered blithely. "That's wonderful." I'm sure she assumed I'd been dreaming. And maybe I was. Still, I'm glad I saw it.

One evening at dusk, Nico approached me shyly and whispered, "Would you like to visit The Beautiful Place of Peace and Crickets?" Well, who wouldn't? Nico had been puttering around on the back deck in his bright yellow shark pajamas and a pair of his sister's sparkly high heels. I thought The Beautiful Place of Peace and Crickets sounded like an innocent version of shooting up heroin; I stepped outside.

"First, we have this," he said. He picked up a broken Japanese fish kite by the string and swung it around in a circle. One of his heels got stuck in a splintered 2x4 but he soldiered on.

"Next, we have the throwing of the number 7 Frisbee." He tossed an angle ruler across the deck. "Now, a roll of the dice," he said, and dropped a Mega Lego at my feet. He deemed it a perfect roll.

"The broom is next." He swept the bristles back and forth in an even rhythm.

"And finally, the brush." He took a push broom and finessed it across the wood with a flourish. "That's all," he said, and clopped inside, adorably adept in heels, leaving me alone, dazed and weepy, and grateful to be in a peaceful place adorned by the music of crickets and invented by a complicated, mysterious boy.

The next night, he used a sword to punch a hole in the wall while screaming about how much he hated me.

My fears about Nico became all consuming. I worried he suffered from fetal alcohol syndrome, or some form of autism. I couldn't conceive of how we'd be able to usher him into adulthood. I Googled things incessantly, and diagnosed him with dozens of incurable afflictions.

I researched who could help us, and ended up at a local psychological center specializing in children's disorders. We were assigned to a psychologist and a behavior analyst; together, they did a $1,000 analysis of our son based on two hours of testing and pretty much concluded we were parenting Nico all wrong. The problem, said the doctor, was a lack of discipline. I swallowed my sense of déjà vu and reminded myself that they were the experts. We needed more timeouts, more consequences, the doctor told us. "Also, and I rarely say this to parents," he said to me, "but I think you need to hug him less." I looked at him in disbelief.

"That's why he's throwing the tantrums. Afterwards, you hold him and hug him, and that feels really good."

"Like makeup sex?" I asked.

He squirmed. "Yes, I suppose you could say that."

We pondered this for a moment. "How are we supposed to keep him in timeout?"

He rambled on for a few minutes with the basic message of, "you just do."

But we had tried it a thousand times. We had even put a lock on the outside of his bedroom door. He broke it within a week. Anyway, when he was locked away from me, he reacted like a caged animal, enraged and freakishly strong. He smashed whatever was handy, and beat the walls and doors until they were pockmarked. I was worried he would escalate to hurting himself.

"You need a place to put him where he can't do any damage," said the doctor.

"But how do we keep him there?" I asked again. We were done with useless advice. If professionals wanted to help, they would have to be explicit in their instructions. We were not at all unwilling to share blame in Nico's behavior patterns. We had started our first meeting, in fact, by saying the situation could be a parenting issue. But we needed someone to tell us what to do. When our son morphs into a human tornado intent on destruction, what's the plan? Because calmly instructing him to *Change that tone, mister!* Or, *Stay in that chair for five minutes!* was like spitting in the wind. The doctor asked us to think of a "safe" place in our home.

"I guess we could put him in the laundry room," I offered.

"Should we put a lock on the door to keep him from getting out?" asked Bob.

Pregnant pause.

"I can't really recommend that, as a therapist," said the expert.

"Well, what's your recommendation?" I asked.

"I can see how that would be an option, though."

"So you do think we should do that."

"I can't suggest that to you," he said carefully.

I sighed. "Okay, are you telling us that maybe we should put locks on the laundry room door, but you're not allowed to tell us to do that?"

He declined to answer the question.

So let me be clear here: the doctor did not explicitly tell us to put reverse locks on the laundry room doors to create a punishment room for our son. But that's totally what he wanted us to do.

The handyman we called reserved judgment, too, at least audibly, on why we wanted the ability to keep our washer and dryer from escaping. But he easily installed reverse locks and deadbolts on the doors.

Was this the answer? Would we be able to stabilize our chaotic home with the simple click of a deadbolt? Was our son on the verge of transforming into a mild-mannered child who smiled pleasantly when his pathetic mother left some of the crust on his sandwich?

The first time I dragged him into the laundry room, shoved him in and locked the door, the desperate pleading in his voice stained my brain; he begged me like he was in solitary confinement with a bunch of snakes and spiders. His panic was a terrible cloud seeping under the door. I don't think I'll ever forget it, and I don't think he will, either. I set the timer for five minutes, and ignored him until it beeped. When I opened the door, he flew at me like a bat, flailing and screaming. Back into the room he went, me trying to ignore that awful despair. Another five minutes. I opened the door, and the same wild child flew at me. I held him down, and we struggled for a while. As I dragged him back to the laundry room, he begged me not to put him there. "Is it over?" I asked him. "If it's over, I won't." It wasn't over, so he went back in.

It was around this time we began using the phrase "Is it over?" to define the end of a tantrum, kind of a tacit understanding among us all that these episodes were definitive slices in time, entities with beginnings, middles, and endings. The laundry room locks did nothing to stave them off. The episodes still ended physically and awfully, with our little boy finally giving up out of sheer exhaustion and me cradling him with armfuls of remorse and comfort, trying to will him into understanding that *if you could just act reasonably,* none of this would happen, and him full of fears and emotions I couldn't intuit. *I would if I could. Don't you know that?*

I tried to avoid hugging him so much, per the doctor's advice, but this advice was counterintuitive to every parenting instinct I had. The doctor essentially was telling me to avoid giving my son love exactly when he needed it the most. It was unbearable. Nico's pain was as visible as a landscape; to see it and not respond to it was simply impossible for me. His need for me was a thirst.

His emotional pain gave him empathy, which occasionally astounded us. One day I told Bob that if he cleared our backyard, we could have a view of the tidal creek and pretend we lived on a waterfront property. He spent the next six hours cutting a swath back to the creek with a machete.

Nico was utterly uninterested in this process until he understood a machete was involved. I found him a pair of garden shears and showed him how to find small branches to cut. As I tromped through the leaves and vines, I noticed a little bitty tree. Not even a tree. A sapling. A scrawny little sapling about the diameter of my finger, or maybe my thumb. I pointed it out to him. "Look here! This is the perfect kind of thing to cut!" I broke it in half.

"Mom!" he cried. "You hurt it!"

"What?" I said. "No! Honey! It's fine! It was nothing! That needed to come down! It wasn't getting enough sunlight!" I tried to sound light and breezy and non-murderous.

"Put it back together!" he yelled. "I'm going to put it back together!" He picked up the piece I had amputated and tried to rejoin it. It wasn't a clean cut—I hadn't snapped it so much as bent and twisted it off, so jagged layers of bark and wood reached out like tendrils. Frustrated, Nico ran inside and returned a few minutes later with a roll of Scotch tape. For the next 15 minutes, he methodically operated on the sapling. When he was done, the little tree stood tall again, and my son called me over to see. "I told you I could fix it, Mom," he said. He was so proud. He stood there next to his tree like it had grown from a magic bean; my heart soared for his love of this scrawny branch.

The next day we hit another rough patch, the boy and me, which peaked with him locked in the laundry room, screaming at me: *You're an idiot! I don't want to live here any more. I'm breaking off the ears of this rat thing in here!*

The rat thing was a painted wooden armadillo that Bob weirdly had given me for Christmas one year. I loved it even though it was an armadillo.

For the next five minutes, he raged in the laundry room, me listening to the destruction and wondering how much damage he could do in five minutes.

When time was up, I opened the door. He stood there heaving, big tears running down his cheeks. "Here's your rat thing!" he said, handing it to me. The ears were gone. My sympathy dissolved, my rage imploded into a physical bubble inhabiting my brain, and I wanted him to learn a lesson. If he didn't want to live here, maybe he should explore other options.

"Do you really not want to live here any more?" I asked, and he nodded.

"Okay," I said. "I'll go pack you a bag."

I went into his room and put a change of clothes, a toy airplane, some pajamas, Blue Puppy, and Blankie in his Thomas the Tank Engine duffel. "C'mon," I said. We walked outside into the driveway. "You know, I'll always be your mom, and if you leave, I'll cry every day all day until you come home." I was crying already, in fact. "But if you need to live somewhere else, I understand." I told him I'd take him to the neighbor's house until he decided where he wanted to go.

Again, not a stellar maternal moment. But I didn't know what to do. Day after day of trying to keep this child from hurting his sister, damaging the house, ruining fun—it was wearing on me. It's not like I could research, "What to do when your 6-year-old calls you an idiot and breaks the ears off your armadillo." I did Google it, actually, found a link to a site called CRAZYTHOUGHTS. COM.

Scout started crying and begging her brother not to go. I tried to telepathically let her know I wasn't sending him away for real. When your 6-year-old is a nightmare and your 9-year-old is near perfect, you tend to think 9-year-olds are practically adults.

"Let's go," I said brusquely, and yanked him outside. When we reached the driveway, he pulled me to a stop and said, "Wait. Mom. *Why are you so mean to me every day? Why do I have to go to timeout in that room and nobody else does? I don't understand it every day! Why are you mean to me? Why are you like that?*" Then he melted. My strong-willed child wilted into my arms, and his eyes could hardly stay open to let the flow of tears out. I felt, more than understood, his loneliness, his confusion, and his sense of rejection. It was true—he alone got locked in the laundry room, he alone had to be restrained when he was naughty. And for good reason—but they were reasons he didn't understand.

I pulled him to me and we sat there in the driveway and cried together, my little boy's arms warm around my neck and his tear-stained cheeks wetting my shoulder. I wanted to explain to him why he went to timeout more often, why pulling his sister's hair warranted greater punishment than not eating peas, why his refusal to leave the park made me so irritable. But I couldn't because I knew he wouldn't get it. We just held each other and cried, and after a bit he asked if he could go inside and unpack. We walked back inside. Then he used the rest of the Scotch tape to put the rat thing's ears back on, and he went to bed.

I sat on the back porch and stared out at the newly cleared yard. Rising above the mulch was a strange little sapling, which had been accidentally broken, but made whole again, at least for a while, by a sudden infusion of hope and charity from a scared little boy who felt pretty broken himself.

We needed new help. In addition to me feeling increasingly irrational, the physical nature of the altercations really bothered me. I often thought of how we had told the social worker, prior to our first adoption, that we didn't believe in spanking, and remembered our vow to never ever hit our children. But then came Nico, transformed at times into a writhing, thrashing mess. If I ignored him, he found ways to force my attention—grabbing something breakable to hurl across the room, or using a bat-like object to stab holes in the wall. One time, he punched a hole in the wall, ran to the kitchen and grabbed all of my stainless spoons, and threw them into the hole. They're still there. We later sold them with the house.

If I restrained him, he'd fight back—hard. He was only a little boy, but even at six he was strong, and when he hit me with all his might, it hurt. I learned how to hold him in my lap with his arms crossed in front of him—he learned how to throw his head back into my face and smash my nose. Sometimes I lay on top of him; then he kicked me in the back. Often he drew blood with his nails.

It was hard to remain calm during these episodes, and I usually didn't. I started off measured, but as the minutes ticked by, my patience waned, my brain became scrambled, and I often resorted to hitting him. I slapped his butt if I could reach it, or his legs. I squeezed his hands. Each time, he screamed and screamed at me to stop. "Is it over?" I would ask. If he said yes, I'd let him go; if the flailing and hitting continued, I'd hit him again.

Eventually, defeated, he would collapse, but often not before wrestling some meaningless capitulation from me. One night at bedtime, he insisted I fix the computer. But I couldn't fix the computer, just like I can't explain how electricity works. (Magic! It's one of my favorite words.)

And so began his tantrum—a huge, loud, frightening tantrum, which involved throwing, threatening, screaming, and tears. His words were so visceral and alien I half-expected his head to spin.

It lasted a solid 25 minutes. I sat inside his room against his bedroom door so he couldn't get out; he was determined to engage me, and eventually, when he began throwing toys at my head, I grabbed him and held him down. We fought each other hard, him hurting me and me lashing back with swift slaps or revised holding tactics. He said terrible things—*I hate you. I want a new mother.* My language wasn't great; I cursed. Who wouldn't? I uttered phrases I worry are etched in his psyche forever. *Goddamn it, what is wrong with you? Shit. You want to live somewhere else? Go ahead. You're so mean. You're being a mean, mean boy.*

Finally, he picked up a five-foot plush sword he caught one year at a Mardi Gras parade and a steel mesh trash can. He pointed the sword at me and shouted, "This will not end until you put this trash can on your head!"

"No," I responded. "I'm not going to put a trash can on my head."

He thrust the sword at me again and restated his demands. This time I squinted at him as though to say, *Really, son? This is what you want?* But I saw something different in his eyes. It was like the alien who inhabited my son's brain was giving me a glimpse of the real boy, and I saw the need in his face and the pleading in the downturned corners of his mouth. *I got it.* He needed closure as surely as a gate needs to be latched. He had mapped out this exit strategy, and if we didn't follow the route, he would be lost.

"Okay," I said. "Can I scrape the gum off the bottom?"

"YES."

I pulled the gum off, and slipped the metal can on my head while he stood there, an armed inmate holding the prison guard at his mercy. Then he put down the sword, helped me lift the trash can off my head, and slipped into my lap. He buried his head in my shoulder, and silently shook. "It's over," he whispered. "I'm sorry." After a few minutes, I carried him to bed. The next day, I started researching new therapists.

SIXTEEN

When Nico was 18 months old, I had a hysterectomy, which was one of the best days of my life. My uterus had served me no purpose and I was glad to be rid of it. I had a genetic predisposition to endometriosis, and the years of fertility treatment had exacerbated it; by the time of my surgery, thick scarring covered my ovaries, my fallopian tubes, and my bowels. It had taken over the inside as well as the outside of my uterus. Menstrual pain had become debilitating—for about two weeks every month, cramps dominated my body. The whole menstruation process is a major design flaw, from my perspective. I can see why creationists believed in the subservience of women; if a god had actually planned for women to bleed from their vaginas for a week every month, he obviously didn't like them very much. Once I had healed from my surgery, I was anxious to resume exercising. I had always been active, and am convinced to this day that I could have had a professional basketball career with the proper coaching. (I'm learning to let that go.)

At our local YMCA, I found a personal trainer who also was a heavily-tattooed Mixed Martial Arts fighter. We were a perfect match. He's a total alpha male, and built like a meticulously piled stack of bricks and mortar—a short young fireplug of a guy, with a blocky head covered by a short blond buzz cut and some scruffy cheek growth. One of his tattoos reads "sinner" if you look at it from one direction and "saint" if you read it upside down. Don't ask me how this works but it does.

It's a strange sort of intimacy that develops between trainer and trainee—this man, after all, was slavishly devoted to my body for two hours every week. He knew how much I weighed, which of my muscles was strongest, and whether my calves had gotten bigger. He knew whether I'd shaved my legs.

I grew freakishly strong. I could do deep squats with 135 pounds on my back, and real pushups. I could run a half-mile in 3.5 minutes. Me—a middle-aged mother of three, with spider veins and reading glasses—I could do 20-inch weighted box jumps. My trainer wasn't a kind, gentle, trainer. His version of verbal encouragement included, "Pain is weakness leaving the body" and "Can't never could" and "It's always easy when it's done."

Workouts became my therapy, and as I grew fitter, I discovered that my physical abilities carried me through the bleakest of days. When my spirit sagged wearily and the kids were sucking the life right out of me, my stamina powered me up. My physical strength became my mental strength.

On one off-training day, I wandered into what I thought was a step aerobics class. But it was a women's boxing class, and after throwing my first punch, I was hooked. Since my trainer was one of those nutso ultimate fighters who can kill a man with his bare hands, he became my boxing coach, and we incorporated boxing into my workouts. How anyone ever stepped into a real fighting cage with him is beyond my comprehension. Sometimes, as he demonstrated a punch to me and I saw his fist coming at my face, I peed a little.

There's nothing like feeling a punch connect, even if it's connecting with a thick padded mitt. It's a rush, and it's addicting, not just because of the power but because I was unexpectedly excelling at something so improbable.

My trainer suggested—I don't think he was joking—that I try sparring with someone for real. I told him I'd be terrified. "But that's why you do it," he said. "If you weren't terrified, what would be the challenge?" It became the unwanted motto for my life.

Eventually, I took over the boxing program at the Y and began teaching the class, and through boxing I met the woman who introduced me to the therapist who finally agreed with us that yes, there was something not quite right about Nico.

Life had become one day of crisis management after another for me. If there's another aspect of motherhood nobody warns you about, it's the constant ON-ness of it all. It's not even multitasking; it's more like one part of your brain must be constantly diverted to child-related drama while the other half just reminds you to breathe and sip coffee and cocktails.

When Bob was off from work, he struggled to help—and he did, around the house and with the girls—but Nico only wanted me. Bedtimes were excruciating. The child was exhausted, we could see that—but the idea of going to sleep seemed akin to being skinned alive. I became prone to saying things like, "Oh my god, this is fucking unbearable!" through clenched teeth so nobody understood the *fucking* part, except Bob. Each evening, as the minutes ticked, Nico's demands increased. Evenings progressed like this:

Nico: *Carry me to bed!*

Bob: I'll carry you.

Nico: *Noooo! Mama! Mama! Mama! I want you. I want you. I want you.*

Me: Fine. I'll carry you.

Nico: *Noooo! Start over! Don't walk that way! Put me down!*

Me: No, we're already almost to your bed.

Nico: *No! No! No! I won't go to bed! Put me on the couch! I wanna watch tv! I'm hungry! Carry me like a baby!*

Me: *For god sakes, get it together! This is ridiculous!*

Eventually, after standing my ground for long stupid minutes, I caved in to whatever he wanted. I would walk back into the kitchen, pick him up, carry him to the couch, pick him up again, carry him to bed, cover him, lay next to him, sing him songs, and rub his back until he was asleep. If I tried to leave too early, he followed me, and we'd have to start the whole CARRY ME thing again. It's why I had to keep working out; I needed my strength every single day.

Bob and I had always been best friends and easy lovers, but the constant struggle to keep Nico in check was taking its toll. We argued frequently; we both resented Nico's tortuous attachment to me, and his refusal to let his father parent him.

We dutifully reported the episodes and our feelings to the new therapist, Betty, and when I sensed she, too, failed to comprehend the situation's severity, I began videotaping. She watched one episode and we saw her jaw drop. "No," she said. "You're right. That's not normal." Finally, we had found someone who could help us.

Betty met with us first, and then with Nico. She was warm and inviting, and listened carefully. She asked the right questions. Nico loved her. Within a month she thought she had solved the mystery behind Nico's bedtime trauma.

"I just don't want the day to end," Nico confided in her. Our poor boy was so grateful each night to have made it through the day that he dreaded having to do it again. To him, each day represented a new set of challenges and events, and I don't mean in a good way. Imagine if you had to start a new job every day. Each morning you start anew, and by evening, you've figured out how everything works, but you're told you'll be given a new assignment the next morning. That's a little like how he viewed his life. "It's part of something called an attachment disorder," Betty said. "And that's what I think Nico has."

According to renowned 20th century psychoanalyst Erik Erikson, whose work led to groundbreaking understanding of how children develop, a child's first year of life is when he learns to trust his parents to meet his basic needs. If a child's basic needs aren't properly met at this age, he could learn to mistrust the world, or lose hope that life will ever get better.

So what happens when a child's basic needs—not just nourishment, but love, LOVE, love, love—aren't met?

Sometimes, the child grows up with an attachment disorder, which manifests itself differently depending on the child. In Nico's case, it was not that he couldn't attach to us; the opposite, in fact, was true. He was overwhelmingly attached to us—to me, in particular—because he had no faith that without us present, all would be well. I had always resisted the notion that my children were adversely affected by being adopted. But it made sense.

For years, I worried I hadn't given my middle child enough attention. But Betty explained how his thirst for my love was unquenchable. He knew I loved him when I held him in my lap —but he had trouble understanding I loved him still when I was at the grocery, or if he got taller, or after he learned to ride a bike. It was like he was on a train traveling from Toddlerville to LittleBoyLand, but the engine derailed and he was stuck; he didn't mind being stuck because who knew what kind of food they served in LittleBoyLand? What if there was no bologna, and what if the mothers there wouldn't let him play with Barbies? It was best to stay in familiar territory.

I had heard of attachment disorders before, mostly in reference to children adopted from Russia who spent years in orphanages and were too damaged to form emotional bonds with their adoptive parents. I was immediately dubious that this could possibly be Nico's problem, even as the evidence mounted. I wanted something chemical, a black and white ailment we could cure with a pill. But fix the inside of his head? The intangible reaches of his heart? It terrified me. I'm a problem-solver by nature; in some ways, I'm not a great listener because I'm always thinking of ways to make a situation better. This had been my approach so far with our son.

"Mom, my shirt is itchy," he said. And I fixed it; I cut out the tag.

"I don't like my haircut." I introduced him to hair gel.

"I can't find my Pokémon cards." I found them.

Soon after Betty's diagnosis, Nico lost a tooth, and the Tooth Fairy brought him five dollars because the Tooth Fairy didn't have any ones. He was so excited and proud; but after a few days, he put his arms around my neck and whispered, "I want you to put my tooth back in." That's what he said, but thanks to Betty's perspective, I knew what he meant: *Mom, my big grown-up tooth is coming in, and it looks different, and I'm scared. I'm learning to read and I'm afraid you won't read books in bed with me. I'm getting too big for you to carry me like a little tiny baby, which might mean you don't love me as much.*

"I want you to put my tooth back in," he said. It killed me that I couldn't.

Betty told us the first step in healing Nico was to solve the bedtime routine because it was wearing everyone out, and when I'm chronically tired, I might as well be dead. Betty suggested we homeopathically drug him, and I wasn't against the idea.

We had tried melatonin before, and it worked so well that Scout called it The Poison. "We can't tell them what it is this time," said Bob. So he scraped off the label and wrote NIGHTTIME VITAMINS on the pill bottle. Then he told the kids our pediatrician had called and instructed us to give them special vitamins before bed every night. The first night we gave them Nighttime Vitamins, it was like the closing scene in Blue Lagoon—you know, when Brooke Shields and what's-his-name are floating in the boat after eating the poison berries. I had never seen Scout unable to finish a chapter. Nico still didn't want to go to bed, so he decided to just lie down and rest for a minute. Zonk. After a few days and nights of good rest, we started thinking more clearly.

We began seeing Betty once a week. Nico resisted going; but once he was there, he loved her. They played games and talked, and afterwards she gave us ever-deepening glimpses into his psyche. We still sometimes videotaped his tantrums at home; she watched them in awe, and it gave her a better understanding of the more violent episodes we *hadn't* recorded.

She also recognized the toll Nico's behavior had taken on Bob, me, and the girls. I was living in a perpetual state of fear, exacerbated by my inability to convince anyone that my son had problems. At school, he acted like Little Lord Fauntleroy. He followed the rules and "excelled in all areas." One day, while at a birthday party, he was all "please," "thank you," and "this is the best day ever!" Later, when we went to a restaurant, he didn't want to leave after dinner. I dragged him to the car, where he banged his head into my face a few times then dialed 911 on my cell phone. I hung up as soon as I saw what he had done; Sergeant Efficiency called back and said, "We just received an emergency call from this number, ma'am. Is everything all right?" And I had to say in a calm, breezy voice, "Oh, yes, ha ha. I'm so sorry, ha ha, my son dialed you by accident," while hoping Sergeant Efficiency didn't hear my son screaming, "*I'm sending you to jail!*" After I hung up, Nico exited the car and pulled the windshield wiper off the back of the van.

Betty began counseling me, too. I was not the same person I used to be. Prior to adopting the children, I had spent years working hard to stabilize my clinical depression, but had begun to lose that battle. I yelled all the time, and could feel myself on edge whenever Nico was in the room.

One night, Nico refused to get out of my bed. As 11:00 pm approached, I watched the remainder of my patience slide through my fingers like sand. I yelled; I tried sarcasm. I dragged him out of my bed and across the floor. He escaped my grasp and ran back. Finally, exhausted, I convinced him to move to his bed by promising him new Pokémon cards if he cooperated. Bribery was always my failsafe Plan B. He let me carry him to his bed, and I quickly tucked him in.

"I'm hot," he said. I took off his blanket.

"This sheet is scratchy," he said. I took off the sheet.

"My pillowcase is sweaty," he said. We ditched the pillow.

And together we lay on the bare mattress pad, him soaking his spot with tears and me thinking I'd buy him $100 worth of Pokémon cards if he'd just let me go to bed. After five minutes, he pulled my ear to his lips and whispered, "I want to start over." So we remade the bed, and walked out of his bedroom and I carried him again to his bed and we pretended the previous half-hour hadn't existed. It was nearly midnight by the time I finally crawled under my own covers. I fell asleep thinking about how much I love my children even when I'm not feeling love for my children. I suppose it's like remembering how awesome thunderstorms can be when you're not stuck outside in the middle of one. But love was not conquering all. My maternal instincts seemed to be dissolving in the face of this increasingly impossible child.

Betty could see me losing hope, and losing my ability to feel joy on a regular basis. She enlisted Bob's help for me.

Bob wanted more than anything to help—he longed to be able to soothe his own son. But Nico wanted only me. It was my job—my job only—to soothe the boy when he was acting infantile, because, in a nutshell, that's what this attachment disorder business is about—him needing to recover the baby snuggling time he missed while languishing in an orphanage. It was Bob's job, according to Betty, to soothe me. "Why?" I asked. "Because I'm acting like a big, fat baby, too?"

Pretty much, she said. Bob nodded in agreement.

Well. I couldn't deny it. But I was taking care of everyone in the family, and no one was taking care of me. If it would have been at all appropriate, I might have hired someone to visit me twice a week just to stroke my head, tuck me in, and bring me buttered toast.

Instead, I forged my way through the weeds. Bob went to work at the fire station every two days, but I was the one dousing fires. Nico needed the swing on the left precisely when his sister sat down on it. Nico insisted he be the only one allowed to hand me the remote control. When Nico wanted to help with dinner, no one else could come in the kitchen.

I realize a lot of this seems like normal kid shit. But at the risk of sounding self-absorbed, it was different. Change wasn't just a disappointment to Nico; it was a complete fracturing of his limited world. Having dinner on the porch, when he thought we were dining inside, was like canceling a trip to Disney World and going to the dry cleaners instead—irreparably crushing. And when he was crushed—well, you might as well pull the head off a puppy before his very eyes. He was traumatized.

In fact, some aspects of attachment disorder are similar to post-traumatic stress disorder, and it was impossible for Nico to calm himself after reaching DEFCON 5. If I ignored him and his bad behavior, I was further detaching from him; the key was to spend more time soothing him, reacting calmly to his tantrums and refraining from losing my temper.

I tried. When he told me to pack my bags and leave the house *"this instance,"* I held him in my arms and whispered, "Shhhh, shhhh, Mommy's here, I'm not going anywhere," and when he screamed that I was *the worst mother*, my instructions from Betty were to sit with him as long as it took for him to calm down. Sometimes I tried to distract him; once I started fake crying in his face, which made him laugh, and another time I used his Mexican marionette to start a conversation about how he was feeling.

At first we had limited success. And a random interaction reinforced the validity of Betty's diagnosis. One day on a whim, I picked up a couple of sippy cups. About a year earlier, I had rid the house of sippy cups, because sippy cups are a pain in the butt and I longed for the day when everybody drank their beverages all civilized-like, you know? The problem with sippy cups was twofold: one, they need to be assembled and disassembled using rubber stoppers, which tend to grow mold when left unwashed for more than, say, two days, especially if they've been left in closets, under car seats, and in the far reaches of the front yard. And mold is hard to clean from tiny rubbery crevices.

Secondly, children tend to chew on the cup lips, so the plastic starts to chip, and before you know it the kids are consuming microscopic bits of plastic and you're reading an article about the many ways in which plastic causes cancer in mice.

So I threw out the sippy cups, and Nico announced that to protest the end of this era, he would stop drinking milk, which he did.

But when I saw sippy cups on sale that day, I wondered if maybe I had been too hasty. Who cared how long he used a sippy cup? When I showed him what I had bought, he was so excited he asked for some milk in it right away. A moment later, Bob pulled his son into his lap, and cuddled him like a baby while he drank his milk. And I can't really describe what happened next, but those five minutes infused our boy with an energy, or lightness, I had not seen in his face for days. He laughed all afternoon and played with his sister; he cooperated with bedtime routines. He happily went to bed on time.

I knew we had a long road ahead of us. But this had been a little breakthrough. I had a small tool in my parenting arsenal that could help me occasionally grease a squeaky wheel. I was learning how to *soothe*.

SEVENTEEN

At age 6, Nico was a captivating, enigmatic soul with a gentle yet fiercely protective spirit. He was up and down like the moon. He would be skipping along the street, whistling—he was always an excellent whistler—and then his sister made a mean face, or he missed pressing an elevator button, a leaf fell in Times Square, and suddenly he fractured into a million pieces that took hours to reassemble.

The summer after we started seeing Betty, Scout flew to Chicago by herself to visit her cousins. My neighbor said, "Well, hopefully having one less will make things easier for a while."

"Are you kidding me?" I said. "She is the only child who comes close to pulling her weight around here." *She* isn't the one who draws pictures on her wall using lipstick (Neale) or writes I M PEPE AND POOP on his sister's door (Nico). So no, it would not be helpful to have her gone. In fact, the only being who would miss her more than me was her brother, who launched a campaign of unfettered grief. The night before she left, he sat in my lap for an hour to talk me out of sending her. His comments ranged from, "I won't let her go" and "if she goes, I go" to "she will always be in my heart," and "I'm going to make you buy me the most expensive thing they have at Target." Finally, he fell asleep. The next morning, as Scout prepared to leave for the airport, Nico began drumming the sadness out of his system using his own personal 12-step program.

1. He wrote sister a letter telling her to HAV A NISE TIYM and reminding her he would MIS MIS MIS HER 900.

2. He pinned down Neale and bent her fingers back.

3. He refused to tell Scout goodbye, then clutched her and wouldn't let her go.

4. He got furious at Neale for making a face, and pulled her hair.

5. Pulled her hair again.

6. Pulled her hair again.

7. Tried to sell Neale.

8. Started the washing machine.

9. Broke a door.

10. Mixed a potion made of hand sanitizer, pepper, lemon juice, shampoo and conditioner, dish soap, Benefiber and parmesan cheese.

11. Watched The Backyardigans.

12. Ate some ice cream.

I hoped he had worked out his frustration. But the next day, he ran away from home as fast as he could after I fussed at him for yanking Neale's toy away from her. I ran out the door behind him, down a half block, with the dog following behind me and Neale following behind the dog. I rang the doorbell of a neighbor, and when she answered, I explained the situation in a torrent of words.

"Hi!" I said brightly. "I'm so sorry to visit you for the first time like this, but I can't find my son, and my dog is tied to your mailbox, and my daughter is running down the street crying with no shoes on. Can you watch her while I look for him?" Then I backed off with a wave and started jogging away.

"Oh, ha, ha," she said, laughing. "Thanks for stopping by." She started to close the door.

"NO!" I yelled, less brightly, with a touch of the panic that was pooling in my gut. "Really! Look at her! She's running toward us! Just watch her while I find my son."

The neighbor's daughter came out of the house, too, and they stood with my daughter, their dog, and my dog, a confused and weird little neighborhood subset, and watched while I combed nearby properties for Nico. I willed myself not to think about the nearby lake. Within minutes I found him behind a tree, and he took off again. Then I was running, too, in my Birkenstocks and shelf-bra tank top, trying to catch him before he reached the end of the street. I did, and clamped a strong grip down on his wrist. "LET ME GO!" he screamed. "IF YOU DON'T LET ME GO, I'M GOING TO CALL 911!"

"You don't have a phone," I said between clenched teeth.

We shuffled back to the neighbor's yard. The boy turtled his head into my hip, embarrassed. Neale asked to go inside the neighbor's house. I said no. Then we said goodbye and my children raced back to our house, went inside and watched a cartoon together. I tried to talk to Nico about the running away business, which was prompted in part by his sister not wanting to play with him because he keeps pulling her hair. "Would you want to play with someone who was always mean to you?" I asked.

"Mom," he said. "I'm not listening to your blobbery words."

He fell asleep on the couch that night at 7:15 and I went to bed soon after that. I woke up when Neale came in at 6:25 am and turned on the overhead light. "It's morning time!" she announced. Like that was a good thing.

As we worked on the soothing, Nico's hilarious, creative core occasionally peeked from behind the madness. I walked into the kitchen once to find him making homemade orange juice with a cheese grater. He had cut two oranges in half with a butter knife, and was using the grater to pulverize the pulpy side. "That way it opens up holes so you can get more juice, Mom," he explained. Then he squeezed the orange round into a small plastic cup. "Here," I said, handing him a large bowl. "Why don't you try squeezing it into the bowl?"

"Oh, great, Mom!" he said. He put the bowl on the floor and stood over it, squeezing. His aim was not great. I stood watching. Do you know how much willpower it took for me to just shut up and watch him do this? It was like he was showering the tile floor with fresh brain matter, while simultaneously wasting two of the juiciest, most colorful pieces of fruit that California, Mother Nature, and genetic engineering had ever produced. But I just looked on, chewing on a wasabi-covered roasted almond to prevent me from talking.

He produced maybe a quarter cup of juice, which he divided into four cups so his sisters and I could sample it. It occurred to me as I drank it that great days didn't consist of hours spent making insects out of pipe cleaners (who keeps pipe cleaners in the house?) or hundreds of dollars spent at Target (believe me, I had tried that). Great days consisted of great moments, or even a single great moment: a boy's discovery that he can make juice, a young girl's realization that she can put her hair in a ponytail by herself, a child mesmerized when the tiniest grasshopper on earth has landed on his arm. I realized I needed those small awesome moments to overshadow the many, many bad moments that continued to define our lives. His juicing project simply made him happy, and so gave me hope. *We can do this*, I thought at these moments. *We can find a way to heal his pain.* Betty blamed the Attachment Disorder, with perhaps a little anxiety disorder in the mix. Bob and I talked about the Attachment Disorder constantly, defining and redefining what it meant to us and to our son. It seemed simultaneously complex and simple. The easiest explanation for us seemed to be this: Nico essentially missed a stage of important emotional development—the newborn phase when most babies develop their "secondary brains" which help them feel comforted and secure. As a result, he was a few years behind emotionally. The disorder manifested itself in tantrums and a "fight or flight" reaction to seemingly minor clashes with his sisters or me. When his older sister wouldn't play with him, for example, the rejection debilitated him like a bullet. Younger sister wouldn't share her toys? His heart splintered. He didn't like change; his perfect day involved being housebound with his nuclear family, and perhaps a brief trip to Target. Even going to the beach required strategic planning and rationale.

In short, he sort of sat around waiting for his world to end. But with a catch—he only exhibited the frightening, immature behavior with me, Bob, and his sisters. In school, he continued to shine. There, he didn't just follow rules; he loved rules. We likened it to a low-level nausea he struggled to contain all day long; as soon as he arrived at home—his safe place—he metaphorically vomited all over everything.

He had friends—or rather, one friend—on whom he lavished his attention. Other children were interested in playing with him, but he couldn't handle dividing up his affections. And with his friends, as in school, he was generous, polite, and attentive. It was almost like he was a robot programmed to publicly comply with societal norms, but the computer chip automatically turned off when he was with us.

The tantrums continued. Sometimes they lasted a few minutes, which seemed like progress, and sometimes an hour. When they were over, he would mold himself into me like an infant—*like a newborn molds himself against his mother's chest*—unconsciously craving the measured state in which he didn't distinguish his own skin from that of his primary source of love, nourishment, and comfort.

We made the difficult decision to try medication. He was so young. But nothing could be worse than seeing my beautiful snaggletoothed boy trying to mend his own broken heart over and over again. After a stumbling block or two, we started him on a mood stabilizer that seemed to help. In theory, when he was about to go nutso, the medicine would effectively freeze him in place for a nanosecond, engage his secondary brain, and solicit the right decision—*Okay, I really want to pull her hair right now for calling me a bad brother, but instead I'll just say, "You're a meanie!" and walk away.* Or, *Mom should let me have another cupcake, but instead of tearing out pages of her new Oprah magazine, I'll do what she wants and eat some yogurt first.*

At the same time, Bob and I tried to more fully understand how his little brain worked. At the start of an episode, I began to see the sadness and panic in his eyes, the despair in the downturned corners of his mouth. My newfound comprehension disciplined my own emotions; it was hard to be angry at such utter despondency.

It was still a long damn summer. The daily podcast running in my brain broadcast various incantations of *I don't want to go to the pool! I'm hungry! Can we go to Target? I have a mosquito bite. Will you cook me some noodles? They're being mean to me! I'm never brushig my teeth unless you take me to Target. I want to play on the computer. I have an itchy. I'm not going! I'm moving to San Francisco! I'm never doing what you tell me, ever again. Mom has a fat butt!*

It made for a terrible summer for the girls, who quickly learned that if Nico didn't want to do something, it didn't get done. Neale could be distracted, but Scout understood the injustice. We explained to her that her brother had problems with change and anxiety, but she was only 9 years old. What she saw was her brother getting his way all the time, simultaneously limiting her ability to do fun things.

She also saw how awful I felt after an episode, and it worried her. She often hugged me and asked if I was okay, or yelled at her brother for making me cry. I tried to protect her from such big emotional trauma, but it was hard. She noticed everything.

A few weeks before the start of school, Nico announced that he wouldn't be going. "I want to stay with you," he said, then he put his mouth on my arm and gave me a hickey. He had developed a weird rash all over his trunk, and, convinced it resulted from bugs in his room, he had been sleeping on the couch. "It's my new bed," he said. For weeks he fell asleep there, and any attempts to move him to his bed resulted in violence, so I eventually gave up. We bought him a new Pokémon tee shirt, which peaked his interest in going back to school, and arranged his real bed so it looked like a couch, and he resumed sleeping in his room after a couple of months.

Nico's first grade teacher was one of those extraordinary women he will remember all his life. Ms. B was a big, warm, gregarious woman with a soft, melodious voice and an unabashed love of children. She also had taught Scout, whom she loved, but Nico won her heart. She sensed in him an unquenchable need for acceptance and love, and she doled it out in spades. Nico adored her. As a bonus, she gave no homework, so school-related battles between Nico and us were practically nil.

As fall turned into winter, we had good days—glorious evenings at the beach with the children playing tag in the sand, family dinners telling funny stories, and long, rainy afternoons with the kids playing peaceful games of "school" or "family."

But. There were always the *buts*. Nico's behavior continued to rule the family. His episodes became more predictable, but just as unmanageable. He shoved a camping tent down the toilet. He wrote his name in ink on my bathroom wall. He tore up his father's 50th birthday card. It was difficult, sometimes, to imagine him growing up to be a productive citizen. Demolition expert? Chemist? Pyrotechnician? MMA fighter?

Therapy helped; Betty had a way of peeling away his insecurity like layers of an onion, and just like peeling an onion, the process often resulted in tears. But Nico was still the wild card in everything we wanted to do. Life was a treacherous game of, *What will Nico do next?*

I longed for some type of order in my house, in my brain, in my soul. Each day seemed 40 hours long, and yet they blended together in one long wretched journey with me constantly balanced on an emotional precipice.

I began to yearn for less of everything. Less stuff, less house, fewer clothes … I felt incapable of keeping track of all the crap in our lives, both physical and emotional. Keeping everything straight required my divided attention, and I was running out of pieces of myself.

Nico, though, took the most out of me. "I love him so much," I cried to Betty one day. "I hold him, and console him, I don't know how I could love him more."

"But that's just it," she reminded me gently. "It will never be enough. No matter how much you love him, he'll always want more."

This time, it was a light bulb moment for me, a heart-wrenching, terrible, cathartic realization. This journey had no end. There was no magic pill. I would forever be tethered to my little boy's damaged ego, struggling to protect him from imaginary threats, and filling up his bottomless well of need. On good days, I could use this perspective to understand him; other times, it just compounded my frustration, and my nerves were like a big block of cheese being grated all day long.

We started choosing which battles we fought with him, and found it helpful. "You don't let him get his way all the time, do you?" asked a friend. Well. Not *all* the time. But if he wanted to use the chair with the old, faded cushion because that's what he used every single day, then I hid it from the other kids. If he wanted green eggs and ham for breakfast, no problem. I kept food coloring on hand. He needed to know what came next, how life would pan out for the next five or 45 minutes. Even small changes disrupted his confidence and caused him to lash out. And since change is inevitable, sometimes even getting his way didn't solve the problem.

Nico turned 7. He was growing physically, if not emotionally, into a handsome, polite boy with a shy smile—which continued to make it difficult for people to understand his complicated dynamics. I told someone the story of Nico tearing up his first homework assignment into 14 pieces and feeding it to the dog, and mentioned I was thinking of getting him a tutor to help with the process. She said, "Have you ever thought about just making him do his homework?" *Do people think I'm stupid?* I wondered.

"You shouldn't let him hit you," admonished someone else.

It was demoralizing. *Of course* I had tried to make him do his homework. And I didn't *let* him hit me. But short of straightjackets and torture, there wasn't much I could do. I had a special needs son—but my son's problems were invisible to the eye. When he did act up in public, people assumed it was bad behavior stemming from bad parenting.

He usually greeted people with a shy grin somewhat obstructed by the big wad of gum in his mouth. He might tell them how well he did on his first spelling test, or how much he loved school, Target, and Pokémon. Part of his brain had developed perfectly. He was clever and funny and loving. But hearing the word "No" was like hearing bomber jets overhead. He slipped into a fugue state in which he was a soldier and the world was a well-armed militia.

No one witnessed this happen except us, a handful of close friends, and occasionally strangers. He rarely fell apart in front of teachers or acquaintances—he innately recognized how they would judge him for such behavior, and possibly reject him. But if we, his parents, had done something right, it was to convince at least part of him that we were his forever family, his real parents, anchors to keep him safe no matter what. We would always love him, no matter what. *No matter what.* When he threw Skittles at my head, I loved him. When he broke the sword off my beloved St. Michael the Archangel statue from Guatemala, I loved him. When he told me I was the worst mom ever, I loved him.

But I didn't always like him, and I didn't always parent him appropriately. When his behavior devolved, I couldn't always contain my rage. Once, Bob was off from work and we told the kids we were going to the beach club for the day.

"Yay!" said Scout.

"Sure!" said Neale.

"I don't want to go!" screeched Nico. He slammed himself into me, pulling at my clothes. "I don't want to go, I don't want to go!" he screamed again.

I kneeled down to his level and grabbed his shoulders. "Talk to me calmly," I said. "If you can calm down, we can work this out." Neale wandered into the room to check out the scene, and he turned around and pushed her. Sometimes, seemingly innocuous actions sent me into a rage—that he would push his happy, adorable little sister for no reason other than her mere existence made me lose control. I took him firmly by the arm and forced him into his room and onto his bed, where he flung himself down face first. "I'm not going!" he yelled.

"Why don't you say, 'Hey, Mom, I don't feel like going," I suggested. Inside I was boiling, but still trying to keep calm.

"Fine! Hey, Mom ! I don't feel like going !" he yelled.

"Okay, I'll stay home with you. That's fine."

But he didn't want anyone to go, because that upset his vision of the day. He didn't want anyone having fun without him. At that point, I stopped negotiating and left his room. He followed me into the kitchen and dumped a box of Cheez-its onto the floor.

"Take the girls and just go," I said to Bob through clenched teeth. He seemed unsure what to do. "Just get your stuff and leave right now," I said, sort of fake-calmly. I was so tired of the girls having to witness their brother's meltdowns. It scared them. They left.

For the next hour or so, while my sweet son lay dormant in a secret part of his brain, a wild-eyed rabid animal taunted me. He grabbed a pair of reading glasses and broke them in half. He locked himself in his room and emptied every bookshelf and toy cubby onto the floor.

I cleaned the kitchen, and bit my tongue to keep from screaming, *You stupid little shit* again and again. After destroying his room, he came to find me. "You're the worst mother. I hate you. Make me some pancakes." He picked up a glass of water and watched me as he slowly poured it out onto the floor. And, I snapped.

I picked up a plastic jar of vitamins and cocked my arm back to throw it at him. He screamed and took off, and I followed him. He ran into the living room, and grabbed a lamp as if to smash it.

I stood not far from him; I took aim and threw the vitamin jar at his shoulder, just hard enough to get his attention. He was stunned. I walked over to him, picked up the jar and went back to the kitchen. He followed me, opened the refrigerator and reached for something on a shelf. I picked up the vitamin jar again and threw it at him.

I guess I was in my own sort of fugue state, spewing sarcasm and profanity, filled with loathing for myself and these long, torturous episodes.

Finally, he looked around the kitchen for some kind of havoc to wreak, and noticed an empty water bottle on the counter. Suddenly, I saw his face come back into focus. "Mom?" he asked sweetly. "Can I use duct tape to tape two bottles together and make an hourglass with dirt?" I nodded warily.

For the next hour, he busied himself on the back porch with plastic bottles, sand, rice, and duct tape. Sweat dripped down his cheeks; every few minutes, he came in to get some water and give me a hug. "I love you, Mama," he said, locking his brown eyes onto mine to make sure I understood. "I know you do, honey," I said.

I sat still on the sofa. I've done endurance workouts that didn't so effectively deplete me. My body felt numb and useless, the strength acquired from thousands of push-ups no match for a boy hell bent on testing my resolve.

A few minutes later he came to my side and handed me a piece of paper with three faces drawn on it: one happy, one sad, one angry. There was a square by each face; he wanted me to check one of them to indicate how I felt. I checked the happy face and smiled at him, and he molded his body next to mine. We rested there for a bit, regrouping, like two spiders trying to crawl through an utterly foreign web.

EIGHTEEN

The summer before Nico turned 8, I read a *New York Times Magazine* article entitled "Wonder Dog." It described the relationship between an adopted boy with autism and his service dog, a Golden Retriever named Chance who had been trained as an autism assistance animal. It was the most beautiful, hopeful story I had read in some time. With the dog's help, the surly, incommunicative boy had relaxed into a contented state of awareness, which his parents had described as miraculous.

It planted a seed. Bob read the article, and didn't act surprised when I started Googling. And Googling. And Googling. The Glutton for Punishment part of my brain started sharing space with the Devoted Mom part. They got pretty comfortable with each other.

I also began paying closer attention to the relationship between Nico and our old Chocolate Labrador, Gem. Gem adored him. When he cried, she tried to nuzzle her way into his space. When Nico felt lonely, he'd invite Gem onto the couch so he could lay his head on her belly. But Gem was just a pet. When Nico pushed her away, she moved on to someone else, or plodded over to inspect the pantry. I thought about training her to be my son's best friend, but frankly, I didn't want to invest so much time and money in a project that could be—literally—short-lived.

I convinced myself that getting an autism assistance dog for my son would be the game-changer, the magic pill, the cure for whatever in the world ailed him. It didn't take much convincing. We had become disenchanted with the Attachment Disorder diagnosis—after nearly two years of therapy, we better understood our son, but were no closer to having any semblance of a normal life. Nico's wants and needs still determined the trajectory of our family's routine. Appointments with Betty had become more sporadic—she was sick for a while, her schedule was crammed, we went on vacation. We loved Betty, but we felt stuck and confused. We didn't have any sort of treatment plan laid out, and I foresaw a gloomy future. I feared more than anything that we had reached a permanent plateau: our smart, sensitive son would always be burdened with emotional disability, teetering on the edge of social acceptance. More immediately, his parents would be stuck manhandling his rages, and his sisters forced to sacrifice any childhood normalcy. None of this worked with my parenting plan, in which all of my children became self-sufficient by the age of, say, 9, and went on to be productive, kind, tolerant citizens of the world. So, I kept looking for other answers. I wanted so badly for Nico have some sort of syndrome or disease easily cured by a pill or a shot or a fucking root canal. I easily convinced myself that a dog would solve all our problems. Plus, I love dogs.

I spoke to Betty about the idea; she wasn't opposed—she had two therapy dogs herself—but she also worried, rightly, that I was grasping at straws. At the same time, she became ill and was unable to see us for several weeks, which I interpreted as fate. Nico's new best friend, I decided, would be trained to comfort him when he was upset, lick his face with love, fulfill all of his emotional needs, and generally be the answer to all of our family problems.

For a few weeks it was just an idea. I combed through service dog websites and searched countless word combos looking for what I thought I needed: *emotional service dog; affordable service dog; train your own service dog.* Lots of organizations train autism assistance dogs, I found. But their waiting lists were years long, and their dogs were trained to work with profoundly disabled children. I wanted help yesterday. Plus, Nico wasn't autistic.

I looked at dog rescue groups, but the groups inevitably referred me to an animal that was "very sweet" or "so pretty." They were in the business of saving dogs—I was focused on saving my son. I needed the perfect candidate. And because my son was so young, I really needed to know the history of the dog.

Project Dog became my secret obsession. I didn't tell anyone because I knew it sounded crazy. But Bob checked my browsing history a few times and sat me down for a chat. To our mutual surprise, I talked him into it. He gave me the green light to pursue this crazy, expensive, chaos-inducing plan, an idea so ridiculous it could work. I think he felt as desperate as me for an immediate solution.

We decided to talk to Nico about it, just to make sure he even liked the idea. He did. Who wouldn't? *Hey, son! How about we get you a special dog that will be all yours and no one else's?* But it was a subdued reaction, not gleeful joy or enthusiasm. We explained the concept—*we think this dog will be your best friend, and will help you when you're angry and feeling sad, and wanting to break things*—and that, more than the idea of a dog, seemed attractive to him. At age seven, he had begun to realize he was different than his sisters, though he couldn't pinpoint or verbalize why. But he knew he was punished more often, had to go to therapy, and took special medicine each morning. It was quietly devastating, this inability to understand why unhappiness and rage overtook him. In hindsight, it might have been equally devastating for his parents to essentially say, "Hey, son, you are so fucked up that we think a dog might take care of you better than we do." Hindsight sometimes makes me feel sick.

A few days later, he approached me shyly. "Can I tell you something?" he whispered. "If I get a dog, I want it to be a brown dog, like Gem. And I want to name him Buddy, because he'll be my buddy."

In the meantime, I had found a dog training facility I liked in Wisconsin. The owner, John, travels the country to find Labrador retriever puppies for his program—he handpicks them, and brings them back to his farm, where they undergo advanced obedience training for the next six months. He also specializes in training Search and Rescue dogs. When I first spoke to John, he had no idea what I was talking about. "Let me make a few phone calls," he said. "I want to make sure we have a dog that's right for you." He called me back a few days later. "Okay, I did a little research, and I've narrowed it down to two pups," he said. "I'm leaning towards a chocolate lab named Buddy." Fate had intervened.

And that's how Buddy became our potential Wonder Dog.

Buddy would come to us as a 6-month old pup with basic obedience skills. From that point, I'd work with a local expert to finish the training and transform Buddy into Buddy the Wonder Dog. That was my plan.

It was expensive. Like, trip-to-Hawaii expensive. In addition, I had to travel to Wisconsin to undergo my own training with Buddy, then we'd fly home together. Either it would be life changing, or I'd just have a lot more crap in my life. Or both.

On a pleasant balmy November day in Florida, I flew to the winter chill of Chicago and drove to Wisconsin. I'm not sure why all sitcoms aren't set in Wisconsin. Its level of exotic hilarity must rival that of Alabama. At the Bates-like motel in Wautoma, population 2,200, I seemed to be the only customer not wearing neon to prevent getting shot by a fellow deer hunter. There was a lot of talk about rutting and nubbins and buck urine. Most of the men wore Fire Hose work pants, which, according to billboards, are "tougher than an angry beaver." I ate dinner at the bar of the Moose Inn Supper Club, where the wait staff served pickled herring—cold, wet, gray slugs—as a complimentary appetizer.

Wautoma was the closest slice of civilization to Neshkoro, Wisconsin, which is where Buddy the Wonder Dog lived. Within hours of arriving in the Cheesehead state, I felt as shriveled and chilled as a piece of jerky. But nothing could tame my excitement about meeting the most adorable, well-trained puppy ever to sniff another dog's butt. I swear, this puppy looked at me calmly, and when given permission, walked over and sniffed my hand to say *hello*. His chocolate coat shone in the sun, and his gold eyes melted me.

John had anticipated my wimpy Florida intolerance for cold, and supplied me with hand and foot warmers for my outdoor training day. John and I spent hours in the cold going over Buddy's obedience skills—it was basically a day of school for me. Buddy kept looking at me like, *Don't you know how to heel?* John and his wife taught me how to continue with the work they'd been doing, and how to prepare Buddy to make the transition into being my son's best friend. Two days later, we were home. My level of service-dog-training expertise could have fit on the back of a flea.

We had prepped Nico for Buddy by telling him Buddy would be *his* dog, and would be his best friend. We also had explained how he would be helping in the training and work involved in taking care of a dog. He filtered that part out. But he was only 7—I had anticipated that. What I had not anticipated is how quickly Buddy would bond to *me*. He could sit, stay, and heel. He peed on command. He trotted into his crate when asked. And had zero interest in leaving my side.

For the first few days, Nico acted like he won the lottery. We put the crate in his room, so he and Buddy could sleep near each other. He woke me up at 5:00 a.m. and said, "Mom, I'm ready to take Buddy out." He was so excited.

But soon, Nico lost interest in the work part. This kind of training doesn't just stick; it needed to be reinforced—to the dog, to Nico, and unexpectedly to Bob, who kept shouting out commands at random. *Sit! Heel! Come! Okay! What am I supposed to say again?*

Although Buddy was an extraordinary puppy from the start, he was still a puppy—curious, energetic and, at times, mischievous —and if we failed to follow the trainer's very strict instructions about when Buddy should pee and poop and how to introduce him gradually to the household, mistakes happened. He bit the blooms off my butterfly weed and liked to chew on pine bark. He loved stuffed animals, especially the ones my kids loved most, so I was constantly on alert for signs of dismemberment.

Potty training, I assumed, would be practically done. But Buddy had lived in a barn. He slept in a crate and spent his days frolicking in a fenced corral. John had given me rules about acclimating Buddy to home life, most of which we didn't follow because of the constant state of chaos. Consequently, there were accidents. When I called John, he recommended teaching Buddy to ring a bell near the door when he wanted to go out. Genius! Buddy learned quickly. But it was the holiday season, and every time Buddy heard a Christmas bell, he peed. We nixed that plan and confiscated all the bells in the house.

Poor Gem liked Buddy okay, although I don't think she would have minded had he been just a visitor. She kept looking at me like, *Seriously? Have I not been a good enough dog?* Her anxiety apparently caused her to develop coprophagia. She was eating her own shit, which made me resent her a tiny bit.

I still believed Buddy the Wonder Dog would bring peace and comfort to Nico, and I occasionally glimpsed the potential. One night, after he freaked out because we were out of bologna, Bob brought Buddy over to him and placed our son's hands on Buddy's head. Buddy licked his face and nuzzled his shirt, and we watched as Nico, en route to a mother lode tantrum, visibly relaxed and draped himself on his dog.

It works, I nearly screamed. But I just smiled. It *might* work, I corrected myself. In the meantime, as I had feared, I had a lot more crap in my life.

One Sunday, Nico developed a toothache so painful he started punching himself in the jaw and throwing stuff across the room. Buddy didn't flinch, but he didn't really help, either. I took Nico to the dentist the next day; he had an abscess due to a deep cavity. Good news: it was a baby tooth. Bad news: two teeth had to come out, and he had three additional cavities. "His oral hygiene is terrible," said the dentist, his eyeballs fixed on mine.

Yeah, I knew that. We were choosing our battles in those days. Most nights the choice was: let the boy fall asleep peacefully, drooling on his favorite fuzzy pillow, or pin him down so I could scrub his teeth while he dug his fingernails into my skin until I got so angry I bit off his nails and he eventually passed out mid-scream from physical exhaustion. It was an easy choice.

To fix the abscess, the dentist gave him some laughing gas and a shot of Novocain, and this child, who can't stand to have a mosquito bite, laid quietly in the chair for over an hour while big grownup fingers did construction work in his mouth.

He came home slightly proud and confused, with an enormous tooth to put under his pillow that night. The tooth was so big, with giant pointed roots, which had barely begun to dissolve. I think it freaked Nico out to look at it, and he was glad the Tooth Fairy hauled it away. But listen, the Tooth Fairy kept it. I have it still. I think I might keep it forever. I was spending so much time trying to figure out what was in his head, and this bean-sized piece of enamel was the one thing I knew for sure had been there.

We found a dog trainer to help us with Buddy, and our weekly sessions went really well for two weeks before Nico refused to participate in them. Life started reclaiming my time away from Buddy training, and soon I was more overwhelmed than ever. Three kids, two dogs, a fish, and a husband. My whole life centered on poop, body odor, and food preparation, sometimes all at once. *Gawd*, the poop. And more poop. Buddy the Wonder Dog, for a long stretch, could more aptly have been called Buddy the Pooping, Chewing, Anxious, Thirsty, Enormous Pain in the Ass Dog. He still had a lot of love to give. But he mostly was giving it to me. He stuck to me like a tick. If I stood up, he stood up. If I walked to the bathroom, he trotted alongside me. He loved Nico, but he adored me like I was a slab of bacon. Nico loved Buddy, but still preferred putting together Legos over doing a single thing related to Buddy's basic survival. After a few weeks, our dog trainer noticed how anxious Buddy became whenever I was out of his sight. "This dog has really bonded to you," she said. "He thinks you're his person."

"Gee, you think?" I answered. I walked him. I picked up his enormous pony-sized poops. I gave him treats. I fed him. I corrected him. Of course I was his person. My son adored his new dog, and spent lots of time lounging around with him. But Nico was not prone to chores or prolonged discussions about anything other than Pokémon. It was looking like Buddy would be my service dog, which was not unattractive to me. I felt pretty needy.

But the trainer was concerned. "No, I mean really, really, bonded," she said. "Like he's totally anxious without you." We pondered her words for a moment while Buddy stared at me. "Wait," I finally said. "Are you telling me that this dog, which I bought to help my son with an attachment disorder, now has an attachment disorder?"

"Well," she said. "Sort of." Yes. That is exactly what she meant. So I had two brown-haired, 80-pound mammals sucking the life out of me, and neither of them liked to bathe. At least I was right about one thing: this dog had changed my life.

NINETEEN

Christmas came fast the year Nico turned eight, so quickly I had not taken down my Halloween decorations, and the homeowner's association sent me a notice of code violation. When I finally pulled the holiday decorations down from the attic, I found them covered in rat pee. I couldn't send out Christmas cards because my list of addresses, written on four pieces of scrap paper, had disappeared. Everything, in fact, had disappeared. I was sure my house contained 14 rolls of tape, three reams of paper, enough crayons to pseudo-paint the walls, and a dozen staplers, all of it located in some invisible office supply closet.

The physical stuff in my life was exhausting me. Our house wasn't enormous—2,700 square feet—and it had plenty of storage space, but my perennial lack of organizational skills and the ongoing influx of materials had created a cluttered, half-done décor, which drove me nuts.

As the New Year approached, I wrote this resolution down: I am going to get my life together. I plan to cut back on all of my extracurricular activities (Facebook, drinking, weighing myself obsessively) in order to more effectively fulfill my role as estate manager. If being an estate manager—a mom— is a job, and it totally is, it's without any kind of performance review. Unless they're really, really abominable, moms can't get fired, or reprimanded by anyone other than their over-developed consciences. So I had conducted my own performance review, and it was full of checks in the *needs improvement* boxes. Some mornings I did my job well—the children trotted to the bus stop smiling, with hair and teeth brushed, and bellies filled with eggs and orange juice.

Other days, I dragged my bawling baby girl by the arm threatening to send her to school in her pajamas, and my son ate gummy bear vitamins for breakfast. One morning, Scout walked into the kitchen wearing an old tee shirt of mine that she usually wore for sleeping.

"You need to get dressed for school, honey," I said.

"I am dressed," she replied

At the time I had a knife full of peanut butter in one hand, a cup of coffee in the other, and a dog leash under my foot. Neale was screaming, "Take me potty!" and Nico was screaming, "Come get me dressed right now!" Also, I was trying to figure out why a small plastic rifle was lodged at the bottom of the jelly jar.

So there may have been a little snap to my voice when I said, "No! You can't wear a ratty old tee shirt to school! Go change immediately."

"But ...."

"*No! Just do it!*"

A few minutes later she stomped into the kitchen wearing a different shirt and started making her own lunch while noisily giving me the silent treatment.

"I don't know why you're mad at me, but cut it out right now," I snapped again. "I don't have time for this in the morning."

She looked up at me with tears in her eyes. "*I only wore that shirt to make you feel good because I know you love it and the little kids were making you so mad and I just thought it would make you happy,*" she wailed. The tee shirt featured a quote from one of my stories: *My family, like most Southern gentry before us, thrives on panic and distress.*

Her little bird shoulders heaved and big fat drops welled behind her scratched-up glasses. "I was just trying to help and I didn't do anything wrong and I'm sorry!"

I teared up, and pulled her to my chest, and kissed her hair, and whispered my apologies for several long minutes. Nico muttered *bad mommy* under his breath and kicked a cabinet, while Neale ate chips. Bob sat at the counter reading the news on an iPad, pretending to be oblivious to morning drama.

Later that day, I reviewed the incident in my head. First, this particular nuclear family does not thrive on panic and distress, although it was nonetheless omnipresent. Secondly, the stress of raising Nico was affecting my relationship with the other children—especially Scout.

For years, Scout had been setting an extremely high standard for her siblings. Friends and family often told me that Nico's only problem was being the second child after Scout. "She's perfect," I often said. "She's our reward for the other two." But the tone of family life was changing who she was. My happy, carefree daughter spent far too much time worrying about her overwrought mother, and all too often cried herself to sleep listening to Nico's screams.

One day, Scout was sitting in the living room reading, and when she moved on to her next activity, she left her new eyeglasses on the couch. Brand new. Fashionable two-toned horned-rim beauties, which made her look 16 years old. A little while later, I found the glasses in chewed-up remains on the sofa where she had left them, and my heart sank. Buddy.

Buddy the Wonder Dog, still a puppy despite his advanced training, wanted something in his mouth at all times. Bones and dog toys were merely satisfactory; shoes, stuffed animals and anything inappropriate, far preferable. One morning, his poop looked like a kaleidoscope. "Good grief, it looks like Buddy ate a box of crayons," I muttered.

"He did!" exclaimed Nico. "He ate it yesterday! The whole box! I watched him." I could not convince the kids that leaving their stuff around the house risked their stuff emerging, in pieces,

from the dog's butt. Books, dolls, Legos, stuffed animals, hats—
he wasn't choosy.

So when I found the glasses, I cringed. I knew it would be a
hard lesson. As I told her, I stoically refrained from crying myself
as I watched the tears bubble up.

I tried to comfort her. "I know you're mad at yourself," I
said. "But …."

"I'm not mad at myself!" she shouted at me. "I'm mad at
Guatemala"

That stumped me. "What are you talking about?" I asked.

"If those ladies in Guatemala had been nicer to my brother,
he wouldn't have so many problems. Then he wouldn't need a
dog to help him. And you wouldn't have had to go to Wisconsin
to get Buddy. And BUDDY WOULDN'T HAVE CHEWED UP
MY GLASSES!" She pretty much shrieked that last part, and I
was so shocked by the force of both her words and her anger that
I nearly grabbed the counter for support.

I couldn't argue with her logic, but I was stunned and so, so,
sad that, at age 11, she had put it all together so perfectly, and not
at all casually. She understood Nico had spent hours and hours in
a bassinet, staring at the ceiling or his fingers or maybe the empty
bottle propped up next to him. And she was beginning to intuit
how his resulting emotional development, or lack thereof, would
forever shape not just his life, but hers as well.

TWENTY

I often hated being the family tone-setter. But it was my job. My children represented a collective mood ring, and I was the finger. My kids felt what I felt, they acted how I acted, they reflected the very behaviors I sought to drum out of them, simply because they were imitating me.

One afternoon, I came home from errands to find Neale in a puddle of grief because Nico had chopped off the hair of her Merida doll. Did you see the Disney movie *Brave*? The main character, Merida the princess with tomboy tendencies, has long flowing red hair and shoots a wicked bow and arrow. She's the only Disney princess to end her story happily, without a man.

With her hair chopped off, Merida no longer looked like a princess wild child. She instead looked like a grown-up woman, no time for long hair, ready to tackle a day of wood chopping and bringing large pots to boil. She looked a little like ... Me. I took it as a sign that I needed to do some growing up, and I put it on my list of things to do. And then I got sidetracked by my complicated life.

At age 8, Nico still loved Legos and Pokémon, and was warming up to his furry, chewy, poop factory of a dog. He despised brushing his teeth, going anywhere other than Target, and his adorable little sister. We had reached a plateau in his therapy; Betty had announced her retirement, and we continued to be confused about how to treat this somewhat obscure Attachment Disorder diagnosis. I had this crazy idea that if we moved to a beachfront cottage on a Caribbean island and just turned the kids loose, with a couple of hours of homeschooling each day, everything would be fine. Translation: I was still searching for the magic pill. If a shaman had told me to feed my son the heart of a rare albino sturgeon from the depths of the Caspian Sea, I would have booked the next flight to Kazakhstan.

But I didn't have to go that far. A nationally recognized shaman of sorts practiced medicine right down the road from us, and through a strange turn of events, we connected. For a while we had been hearing about Dr. J., a pediatrician who specializes in autism spectrum disorders. We didn't think Nico was autistic, but he shared many characteristics with children on the autism spectrum—socially awkward, prone to tantrums, rigid in his thought process. My nephew lives with autism, and I had questioned my sister-in-law extensively about it. She was less ambiguous. "No," she said. "I see zero signs of autism in Nico." But she lived far enough away that my brain could harbor lingering doubts without her there to set me straight.

Bob had met Dr. J. shortly before Christmas. His fire engine delivered Santa to the doctor's annual Christmas party, and the firefighters had nothing else to do so they stayed for the party. There were a bunch of autism service dogs at the party, and Bob told Dr. J. we had just acquired an autism service dog. "Is your son autistic?" she asked.

"No," he said. "We don't know."

"Why haven't you been to see me?"

He said he had heard about the eight-month waiting list and explained how his wife had the patience of a rabid toddler.

"Call us! We'll fit you in!" she said, and so we did.

Dr. J.'s assistant sent us a massive questionnaire that took a week to finish, scheduled us for a three-hour appointment, and told us to bring snacks.

It was an emotional afternoon. Dr. J. talked to us, and she talked to our son. She asked him about eating, sleeping, his sisters, poop, dogs, school, Legos—all of life's essentials. Nico's answers sometimes made me cry.

"Suppose you had a choice," she asked, "between being in a classroom with a teacher and doing lots of work, and being in a classroom with no teacher and all your friends. Which would you choose?" Nico chose the room with the teacher, and I could pretty much see his little brain analyzing the options: *no teacher means no rules, chaos, trying to figure out kid games, being worried nobody will like me. I'd rather the teacher be in charge.*

"What do you do at recess?" she asked.

Long pause.

"I swing."

"Who do you swing with?"

Long, fidgety pause.

"Lilly."

"What if Lilly doesn't want to swing?"

Long fidgety pause, fits of eye-blinking. Me holding back tears, biting my quivering lip.

"I swing by myself."

After a while, she sent Nico out to the Lego table to play so she could talk to us. "I don't think Nico is autistic," she said. "But he has horrible, horrible, horrible anxiety. And the fact that I can see that through the medication means it's really severe."

We knew he suffered from anxiety, which we assumed resulted from the attachment disorder. But Dr. J. downplayed the attachment theory. She believes anxiety, ADHD, and a bevy of other childhood psychological diagnoses should be placed on the autism spectrum. She also believes all are treatable through diet and biomedical supplements.

Dr. J. had been a traditional pediatrician until her daughter was diagnosed with autism at age 4, not long after routine injections of childhood vaccines. Despite experts telling her the two incidents were unrelated, she began researching a possible link, and believed she found one. Her daughter, she says, reacted badly to the preservatives found in the vaccinations, and her digestive system began to break down. She soon developed a related theory contending that most autistic children could be healed by treating their guts and their biochemical make-up. Her research convinced her that gluten, a protein found in wheat, and casein, a protein found in dairy, both wreaked havoc with the body's ability to digest and retain healthy bacteria for the belly, and should be eliminated. By the time children reached her office, she told us, years of poorly functioning digestive systems meant the bodies of autistic children were starved for certain vitamins and minerals which needed to be replenished.

If this all sounds familiar, yes, she is one of the fringe autism experts who believe vaccines cause the disorder. At the time, she appeared to us like a savior—she really was the first medical doctor to *see* our son, understand his pain, and map out a treatment plan. The attachment disorder had been an ambiguous diagnosis without end and nearly without hope; this new condition provided a clear solution. She explained, with confidence and authority, the steps we needed to make our son whole:

Step One: Embark on a gluten-free, dairy-free diet

Step Two: Begin a regimen of supplements, including vitamins D and B-12, a probiotic, an L-methylfolate to stimulate the production of neurotransmitters in the brain, and 5-HTP to increase serotonin levels.

She also examined Nico's scalp and back, sites of a mysterious, itchy rash, which had plagued him for years. "I think he's had a fungal infection since the day he was born," she said. She was referring to "yeast overgrowth"—the belief that some foods cause "bad yeast" to develop, which affects brain function. She placed him on an anti-fungal medication, an anti-viral med in case he had some undiagnosed virus, and an antibiotic to kill whatever yeast might be caused by the anti-viral med.

In all, she instructed us to give him five pills each morning, and seven pills each night.

Bob had a more detailed grasp of Dr. J.'s line of thinking. But this is the part I heard: We're going to put him on a bunch of supplements, implement a gluten-free and dairy-free diet, and reevaluate everything in a month, by which time he'll probably be cured. I was cautiously ecstatic.

For the next few days, I researched gluten-free eating options. Scout's diet consisted mainly of pasta, so we were concerned that without it, she might wither away and be dispersed by the next stiff wind. We tried to feed Nico *low* gluten items, which don't exist, and lactose-free dairy products, which still contain casein. Finally, after a week, Bob said, "You know what? We're all in this together. Let's just do it." We explained to the kids we were going to start eating a little differently so we could all be healthier.

Separately, we had spoken to Nico about this new treatment tactic—the diet and the supplements. We explained to him how we were working to make him feel better, and become less angry, and he seemed to understand. But once again, I think what he interpreted was this: there was still something wrong with him, and Mom and Dad were trying something new to fix it.

So on a Sunday afternoon, I stripped the pantry of gluten, disposed of the out-of-date yogurt, and put a hold on buying cheese. Nico asked me if he could have one last granola bar, "so I can remember what they taste like," and I consented.

We started experimenting. The mainstream pasta brands had not yet developed their not bad gluten-free pastas, so we ate a lot of chewy cardboard noodles. Potatoes and rice became staples. I adapted to almond milk in my coffee. And we waited for the miracle.

Two full days into gluten-free life and ten days into the supplement regime, my son came home from school and told me he had four pages of math homework. He asked for a snack, then trudged to his room and didn't come out until he had completed his work. By himself. And he got every question right. Previous homework had been crumpled into balls and thrown for the dog. I nearly wept with hope.

As I reworked our family's meal plans, I became more interested preparing *real* food—unprocessed meats and vegetables, home-baked goods, and healthy snacks. It was more expensive and time-consuming, but I kind of enjoyed it. I let my mind wander backwards to old dreams of more organic living, and began to envision lifestyle changes. I wasted countless hours perusing real estate, thinking we should buy a lot and build a tiny eco-house so we could raise our own chickens. Wherever I went, I talked about being gluten-free, both wanting a referral of decent-tasting bread and dying for someone to tell me it would help. We experimented with mixed results. I made fabulous Rocky Road Rice Krispie treats and *meh* homemade chicken nuggets one night. "They're a little powdery, Mom … but, I'll eat them!" said Scout. I love that girl, because those nuggets tasted like soap.

Our Bible became a book called *Cooking for Isaiah* by Silvana Nardone, whose son was diagnosed with gluten and dairy intolerance.

Nardone's recipes were quick and easy, with simple ingredients and instructions I could interpret. I made coffeecake, pumpkin muffins, pancakes—all some of the best baking I'd ever done. Scout started cooking, too—chocolate chip cookies, brownies, and Rice Krispie treats became her specialties.

The real question was whether the whole process was working to improve my boy's quality of life, and we saw hopeful signs. A couple of weeks after we started the new regime, Nico went to a birthday party and ate gluten-filled pizza dripping with hot dairy cheese, and the next morning, when I asked him to get dressed, he ripped my lampshade in half, broke his doorknob, and told me 30 times I was stupid. "Fucking gluten!" I whisper-shouted to Bob. After the episode ended, I was thrilled—it seemed like further evidence we had discovered the culprit. It was a struggle, but we persevered. We were engaged in a battle, and gluten and dairy were the enemies.

Meanwhile, Buddy. Oh, Buddy. Buddy was not working out the way I planned, possibly because I my planning had been slightly utopian. In hindsight, it might have been unrealistic to think I could buy a puppy and train him to become an autism assistance dog for my son who is not autistic. "Why do you always make your life so complicated?" asked a friend. *But my goal has always been to simplify my life*, I yelled silently in my head. I can see now, though, how I had fallen into an old habit of trying to avoid big problems by creating small problems I can actually solve. Training a kid was complicated, but I could easily train a dog. "I think you just wanted another dog," said Bob. Maybe.

One morning as I packed lunches, I heard three giant *kerfloff* sounds; I investigated. Buddy the Wonder Dog had thrown up three entire socks, each twisted up neatly in heavy braids of bile and slobber. Afterwards, he looked at me with his ears cocked, head tilted, tongue wagging—like, *That's done! Phew! Let's go play!* The incident was the first in a yearlong obsession with socks. At least once a week I cleaned up sock-puke, or helped him expel a sock from his butt. One sock snack led to a $700 midnight visit to the emergency animal care clinic. I hadn't given up hope that

Buddy would become a support animal for Nico. They adored each other; but I continued to be the dog's *raison d'être*.

I assumed, thanks to Dr. J., we had finally found the key to unlocking Nico. With gluten and dairy banned from our lives, Dr. J insinuated, he would eventually develop a permanent penchant for homework, regular bathing habits, and a deep abiding love for his younger sister. And Buddy could just be a dog.

Two weeks into the gluten-free, dairy-free life, Scout and I snuck off for some frozen yogurt, and Nico found a bag of shredded cheese I had missed and ate the whole thing with a spoon. But other than those cheats, we were pretty steadfast, and we definitely noticed a difference in Nico's behavior, though it's unclear now whether to credit the restricted diet, the supplements, or simply healthier eating. It was a strange transformation. He seemed happier, and less anxious, but he also displayed a surprising belligerence, like he finally felt confident enough to brazenly, cheerfully defy us instead of throwing tantrums. I tried to appreciate this change, but it was hard because often he was just being an ass. I generally didn't say that to his face—I just muttered it in the general direction of his stomping-off self. One morning he overheard me. "I heard that!" he yelled. I apologized. "I don't accept your apology!" he shrieked.

God, he was mean. And damn, I was tired. I woke early each day to have 30 minutes to myself before delving into making school lunches, arguing over clothes, and cooking bacon with zero burnt edges, eggs with no brown spots, and toast that didn't look toasted—all while monitoring Buddy and the family's sock population. I picked up so many half-eaten toys I once dreamed Buddy's jaw was surgically removed.

Weekends when Bob was working became my Achilles' heel. I perused Facebook too often and saw other mothers of young children enjoying blissful Saturdays at the zoo or park, or baking cupcakes that looked like dinosaurs, all smiles and happiness and positive energy, and I stamped an invisible FAIL across my forehead. Again and again I tried to redefine successful parenting. One evening, I took the kids to a movie, and afterwards we stopped at a Japanese restaurant so we could sit at a hibachi table and watch our gluten-free meats and vegetables sizzle. When the cooking began, Neale called the chef a Great Lava God. "I wish he was in our family," she said. I spent $60 for the children to see fire and eat white rice, and since the food wasn't particularly good, I feigned nonchalance when the kids turned into uncouth hellions.

We drove home singing that awesome "Thrift Shop" song. *I'M GONNA POP SOME TAGS ... GOT TWENTY DOLLARS IN MY POCKET ... THIS IS FUCKING AWESOME.* Instead of *fucking awesome*, we sang *mmmph-mmmph awesome*, but Scout and I traded secret glances so she knew that I knew that she knew it's really *fucking awesome*. In the middle of it all, Neale let out one of her trademark burps, which honestly sounded like her belly had imploded, and I thought I heard the boy say, "Oh, my feces!" I love when my kids know big words, but that one surprised me.

"Where did you learn that word?" I asked. After some confusion, we determined he had said, "Oh, my geezes!" But they all wanted to know the meaning of "feces."

"Well," I said. "It's like a formal word for poop." The car exploded into hilarious chaos, punctuated by verbal exclamation marks. *Poop ! Feces ! Mom's a feces ! You're a poop feces!* Several surreal minutes flew by, with me driving happily, smiling in the rearview mirror at my brilliant children on a Saturday night entertaining themselves with advanced potty talk. It felt like a success.

We returned to Dr. J. a month after instituting the new diet and the supplement regime. In those four weeks, Nico had gained half an inch in height and lost four pounds. He had started doing his homework voluntarily for the first time ever, and we were seeing a gradual improvement in his ability to verbalize his frustrations. He had explained to me why he hates bathing: he doesn't like being cold when he gets out of the tub or shower. I bought him a space heater.

In addition to suffering through gluten and casein abstinence, Nico was swallowing several enormous pills twice a day with barely a flinch. He knew we were trying to help him; his desperate desire to feel better broke my heart. But it seemed worth the effort: with Nico's inner beast slightly quieted, the whole family dynamic began to change. Family dinners went from short bursts of indigestion to long enjoyable minutes of conversation.

Dr. J. was very excited for us, and she adored Buddy. She recommended a local woman who exclusively trains autism assistance dogs, and we agreed to seek her help in finishing Buddy's training. We were on our way to our Happily Ever After, she assured us. But I perennially see the glass as half-empty; I emphasized the eternal journey in front of us. "I get very frustrated," I said. "I'm impatient, and I lose my temper."

"Well, listen," she said. "You've been through a lot with this child. Sometimes you might be reacting to memories of his previous behavior. It's like you have PTSD (post-traumatic stress disorder)." I practically squealed with joy. An unofficial, spontaneous, random diagnosis of PTSD validated me. Finally, I told Bob, someone understood what we had endured the past few years. Also, I reasoned, if Nico didn't use the service dog, I would. For my PTSD.

We left Dr. J'.s office optimistic, although I remained a bit skeptical. The whole gluten-free thing seemed sort of voguish and genteel, a mere health fad like chia seeds, green juice cleanses, and drinking apple cider vinegar. I had always rolled my eyes at people like me. But anecdotal proof kept building up. I took the children to a birthday party where the picnic tables were decorated with bowls of snacks—pretzels, Goldfish, and crackers. Nico and Neale and some friends immediately found a hiding place at the park and shuttled armfuls of gluten there as though they were stocking up for the apocalypse. And halfway through the party, the Gluten Discs with Melted Casein arrived. Pizza.

"Mom, please, can I have some pizza?" Nico pleaded.

"Honey, I don't think you should," I said. "Please don't." I didn't want my kid to feel weird, so I didn't ban him from anything—I just asked him nicely to abstain, which was pretty unreasonable as I hadn't brought a single piece of gluten-free food for him to eat instead.

"Okay," he said. Then he snuck two or four pieces back to his hideout and scarfed them down like cocaine.

That night, soon after dinner, Nico shifted from 8-year-old boy into child-sized Mephistopheles. The transformation began with his casual obstinance. It progressed into near psychosis. This child was utterly incapacitated—flinging Legos around the room, digging his nails into my arms, screaming, barely able to stand up. He head-butted me whenever he could. He shouted nonsense at us. I didn't rule out taking him to the hospital to be sedated. Bob and I took turns following him around the house, prying breakable items from his fingers and looking at each other in fearful alarm. Our son had shape-shifted from hilarious trickster to malevolent troll in the span of an hour. Near 11:00 p.m., as he slumped facedown on his bed, heaving in exhaustion, I remembered the pizza.

The regression lasted into the next day, and finally began abating mid-afternoon. By that time, I was a convert, and believed gluten was toxic to humans and the cause of nearly every ailment aside from broken bones. Could we really have discovered the key to Nico's happiness and well-being?

No. But for a while, at least, something was helping.

The new dietary plan wasn't particularly hard for the grown-ups, but the kids struggled with it. Scout, in particular, had been forced into a culinary desert. We told her she could order lunches at school, and didn't try to restrict her eating when she was at friends' houses, but her usual after-school snack of noodles and butter was out. Her breakfast of noodles and butter wouldn't work. And her fallback dinner of noodles and butter needed to change.

Neale ate anything, but we couldn't break her addiction to Doritos and Cheetos, which don't include gluten but do include casein because they're made with "real cheese." Yes, for a while we were that strict—we forbade Nacho Cheese Doritos because Dr. J. told us even traces of dairy could cause reactions. We allowed her to eat Doritos when she wasn't with Nico, but wouldn't allow it if Nico was around. And we made our 6-year-old daughter promise to keep the secret from her brother.

Nico's reaction was mixed. He wanted to understand—he knew something was wrong, and he wanted to be better, but he was reaching the age at which he desperately wanted to be like everyone else. The gluten-free diet made him different. I sent in special snacks for holiday parties, and asked for gluten-free options at restaurants, but damn, it was hard. We stopped going to Outback—the kids' favorite restaurant—because Nico couldn't bear to not have the mac and cheese there. We were on the cusp of the gluten-free craze—not everyone was doing it yet—so we were labeled as slightly batty, especially since Nico didn't exhibit his troubling behaviors at school.

A couple of months after implementing the new diet regime, we met my family in Destin, Florida for a beach vacation. On the drive there, I glanced in the rearview mirror and saw Neale fast asleep—and I saw her brother's hand on her arm. I opened my mouth to whisper *Leave her alone* before I realized he was caressing her arm. I looked at him; his head bobbed, and he struggled to keep his dark eyes open. But still his fingers moved up and down on her skin, as if to make sure his connection to her remained fast and tangible. My eyes watered. I could feel his need for her, his need for all of us, his family, his only connection to the promise of a happy life. Later I asked him about the moment, and why he was rubbing her arm. "Because I love her," he said shyly, wrapping his arms around my neck.

He loved her furiously. As Scout grew older, she slowly was leaving her brother behind, forsaking make-believe games of family and school in favor of watching videos and reading books. On this vacation, in particular, Scout and her like-aged cousin spent every minute of every day in the same room. They possibly melded together.

Nico turned instead to his younger sister, and together they built Legos and watched movies and gave their stuffed animals rides on the condo ceiling fans. But our little girly had turned 6 and was marching toward 13. She was a sassy, independent girl who liked to get her way. When she asserted herself, or when she needed some time alone, her brother dove into an inconsolable pit of despair. He pulled her hair, hid her Teddy, and broke her toys. In time, she learned how easily she could manipulate his feelings—a haughty look, or simply a "no, thank you" if he offered her something, was like squeezing the life out of him. So she did it whenever she thought he was being mean.

Nico's tantrums had eased over the previous weeks, but in Destin, he collapsed into an unpredictable, manic, mess of a boy, even though we carefully monitored his vacation diet. He spent long minutes shrieking, laughing hysterically about boobs, saying MOM. MOM. MOM. MOM. Over and over again, or engaging in all three at once. Yeah, it's really possible. At times he seemed downright crazy. After a few days, I called Dr. J. "Something's wrong," I said. "Nico's maniacal. He's acting like he's on drugs. He's screeching and flapping his arms."

"It sounds like an overgrowth of yeast," she said. "I should have thought of this. Let's put him back on the anti-fungal med." That seemed reasonable. There was even a chapter about it in her book.

Nico dutifully swallowed yet another addition to the plethora of vitamins and supplements we gave him twice daily. I had become a traveling pharmacy. And he remained remarkably clear-headed about his behavior. "I'm sorry, Mom," he often said. "Neale just hurt my feelings." Watching his mind process it all was breathtaking. That my 8-year-old son understood his lack of control, and was willing to help us help him … well, it felt monumental, like we'd been climbing a mountain and the clouds finally shifted and we could see the peak.

One thing about clouds, though: clouds always come back. They always, always come back.

TWENTY-ONE

I loved my son so much, especially when he was asleep. But I also thought a lot about military school. The new journey, paved by diet and supplements, had helped a great deal. Physically, he was taller and leaner, with more energy and improved coordination. Mentally, he had progressed as well—he smiled more, did his homework and was willing to try new things. One day he even attempted skateboarding, which previously would have been like jumping from a plane.

Yet insecurities still plagued him like a bad rash, and tainted his behavior. I knew this; I knew he lashed out at his sister because he felt hurt or left out. But it didn't change my frustration level, particularly when I was trying to get something done or be somewhere at a certain time. Sometimes my jaw moved and sounds came out, and I suspected I sounded like The Joker: *Just hit him back. Do you want to go live somewhere else? You're acting like a Butthead. You are mean, mean, mean. Stop ruining everyone's morning! Fine, then, just go outside and beat the crap out of each other.* And finally, the one phrase parenting experts implore you not to say: *JUST. SHUT. UP.*

"He should have been an only child," Bob said regularly. Possibly. But the deeper relationships between Nico and his sisters fit together like a puzzle. They adored each other. Nico depended on them for what little self-confidence he could muster. Making them laugh was Red Bull for his brain, although most of his jokes were wildly inappropriate.

Still, the competition between the younger two children for my attention overwhelmed me. *Mom, help me get dressed. No, wait! First, get ME dressed. Mom, can you find me some socks? Mom, Buddy's got Teddy. I have to go potty. Get me dressed. Mom, I spilled something by accident. Mom I'm so tired.* That's a synopsis of the first 90 seconds of each day. I sometimes screamed words so incoherently Scout ran to me, frightened and alarmed.

One morning, at just such a moment, she took my hand, pulled me away from the younger kids and told me a secret. "When I get really frustrated, I sing this song—'Everybody, everybody wants to love, Everybody everybody wants to be loved ....'" and she launched into the refrain of an Ingrid Michaelson song. "It reminds me that my brother needs extra love," she explained. A minute later, she printed out the lyrics to the song and pressed the piece of paper into my palm. Was this my 11-year-old child, parenting me? It was lovely and magical, this angel girl's willingness to save me from my scary self. She frequently slipped her arms around my neck and kissed my cheek, whispering, "I love you so much," and her words flooded over me like a warm shower.

My son sometimes hugged me the same way with his thicker, stickier arms, often just after pulling his sister's hair, or knocking over a pile of books, or breaking a pencil in half. But he just stared at me, blinking his brown eyes hopefully, silently apologizing for being himself.

I felt his pain in my heart and my brain and even my lungs; he needed my love like he needed air. So I hugged him back, counted the hours until bedtime, and breathed a smidgeon more easily every night after he fell asleep.

As the weeks passed, his verbal acuity shot up, either because of his weekly shots of B-12 or his work with the newly discovered art therapist. Instead of screaming, "No! No! No!" he screamed phrases like, "You're not the boss," and "I love gluten! I miss gluten! I'm going to start eating gluten all the time and you won't even know it!" So, yes, he was aware of being on a diet. He missed granola bars and Subway sandwiches. He missed ice cream. He wanted donuts and those little round cookies from Starbucks, and Kraft macaroni and cheese.

We met Kay, the art therapist, through Dr. J. Nico took to her immediately; she played soothing chakra music and sprayed lavender scent around the room during his sessions, and spoke to him in gentle encouraging tones, which nearly put him in a trance. Somehow she opened him up like a flower. Or maybe more like a shaken can of soda. His feelings had been stuck, gummed up in his brain, I guess, and we'd only had basic knowledge of what was propelling his emotions. He was a 21st century emotional caveman. I knew when he was angry—holes in the wall, hair-pulling. I knew when he was frustrated—the mind-dumbing screeching. Sadness led to tears and snot wiped on my chest. When he was scared, he stuttered. But we often couldn't figure out the impetus for his behavior.

He acted like a sedated bear cub when he was with Kay. "I LOVE him," said Kay after their third or fourth session. The minute we left, he had a meltdown because I wouldn't take him to Target to buy a Monster High doll. He finally eased himself out of tantrum mode by breaking open an ink pen and making blue stains on the leather seats of the car.

As we drove home, we passed the sitter walking with Neale to go feed the ducks. At home, I found Buddy the Wonder Dog eating the mail. I couldn't fuss at the sitter because she continued to come despite an earlier incident during which Nico had threatened her with a pair of scissors.

Buddy had gnawed just the corner off one interesting package, which turned out to be a present from a blog reader.

The reader had sent a gorgeous World Wildlife owl calendar for Nico after reading my blog about how he loves owls. When I gave the calendar to him, he took it as though it was made of glass. He quietly ran his inky fingers over the glossy pictures, and told me in hushed tones that he didn't care at all about the damaged corner. I thought about a story he had written the previous night, the one he had insisted on reading to me before he drifted off to sleep:

Once thar was an iland filled with polar bears in Antartica. It was winter. All of the polar bears loved winter but one polar bear hated winter. He liked summer and spring. Tomorrow was the Polar Bear Plunge. He hated the Polar Bear Plunge. He liked hot water. Cold water was a dislike to him. He wished it was not even inveted. He wondered why the bears liked it. Reasons why he didn't like it: to cold, to deep, to scary because of sharks, to crowded. But then he felt like he should try it the next day. It was time to do it. He got in line. He was the 20th one. He did this because he wanted to act like a big bear. Thar was a bear in line his age. He was new. He said I'm scared to me. I said don't worry it will be fun. It was are turn. Go. We jumped in. When I got in I ghasped and said this is so much fun. My new friend said the same. We did it when it was the Polar Bear Plunge. P.S. The names of the two bears Jeff and JoJo.

Our son was trying. He was trying so hard.

The next day the kids and I engaged in a huge yelling match about a dozen or so different problems. Target was involved. Target always seemed to be involved.

Scout was winning the yelling match, which was unusual because she wasn't usually a yeller. I remained seated in a chair digging my fingernails into my palm, thinking about whether I had enough credit left on my card to flee the premises for a month or so. Then I remembered I would have to bring Buddy the Wonder Dog because otherwise Bob would let him eat all the socks in the house and die, which would complicate my hiatus and trigger my PTSD by reminding me that I spent a fortune buying an autism assistance dog for my child who's not autistic, and then emotionally stunting the animal by loving him too much.

So I just sat there interjecting mild expletives while the kids argued. Finally, Nico spoke up: THIS IS ALL MY FAULT. IT'S ALWAYS MY FAULT. I'M THE ONE TO BLAME. I CAUSE ALL THE PROBLEMS IN THE HOUSE. IT'S ALL MY FAULT.

Everyone was quiet. My first thought was, "Damn straight, man," because it was mostly true. But of course I didn't say that because my very next thought was, "Holy shit, he gets it!"

Oh, my boy. I pulled him into me, and he heaved great big sobs on my chest. It took me several minutes to grasp the significance of the moment—to realize my son comprehended the havoc he wreaked on the family. What a burden to carry! For a long while he remained in my arms, shaking and crying, while I stroked his hair and whispered in his ear: *Shhh. I love you. I love you. Shhh. It's okay.*

A couple of days later he freaked out as we drove to art therapy because he had forgotten something at home, and he came close to coming unglued—but suddenly, like a light switch, he turned off the panic and relaxed.

"Mom, I learned something," he said after a minute. I wasn't sure what he meant, but he was calm, so I went with it. "I learned that if you have a problem, you should go to the ocean, and the desert, and the rainforest, and all around the world until you find a solution," he said. I was speechless. *Oh, honey*, I thought. *You're right. That's exactly what we're trying to do for you.*

TWENTY-TWO

Buddy the Wonder Dog and I continued to bond. He stared at me constantly and I came to think he was the only living, breathing thing that appreciated me. One day, we went to visit my dear friend, Anne, and soon after we arrived, we made giant icy cold gin and tonics and took the kids and Buddy for a beach romp.

Bob dived into the ocean with the kids, and I stood in the sand with Buddy, Anne, and her adorable calm hubby, enjoying the sun and sea breeze. As we chatted, a man walked behind us with a big white German Shepherd. The dog did not seem friendly, and he did a little lunge-snarl at Buddy, which caused Buddy to launch himself into his trademarked vertical airborne jump-spin. I was prepared for the jump! But I was not prepared for the man with the unfriendly dog to malinger, causing Buddy to leap again. The leash was wrapped weirdly around the fingers of my left hand, and—well—the ensuing cracking sound resulted in my inability to wear my wedding ring for the next six weeks. I immediately knew my finger was broken, although it wasn't crazy painful, maybe because of the gin. After the broken bone nausea set in, I quietly instructed Anne's hubby to go tell my hubby I had broken my finger. Bob emerged dripping from the ocean, looked at my crooked, quivering digit, and said, "Just soak it in the gin and tonic. It'll be fine." Reminder: my husband is a *paramedic*, trained for these types of emergencies. He knows better than to prescribe contamination of the only anesthesia on hand, so I overruled him, drank the gin and tonic, and iced the finger when we got home. Honestly, what hurt the most was Bob's willing acceptance of my insistence that I was fine, as though 20 years together had failed to instill in him working knowledge of my martyr-like tendencies.

Over the next 18 hours, I cooked dinner, taught two "Boot Camp" classes, folded laundry, got the kids off to school, and picked up dog poop, even as my finger swelled up and turned the color of prunes. I finally went to the hospital after a chiropractor told me I could lose the use of my finger forever. At the ER, a really hot doctor told me he had good news and bad news. Obviously, the good news was that a really hot doctor was caressing my hand. The bad news: I would not be shooting the bird at anyone with my left hand for a while. Buddy the Wonder Dog was utterly nonplussed by the havoc he wreaked. Everyone was, perhaps because everyone remained fed and relatively clean; our domestic train continued to chug along. The only real disruption was in my head, where those words of a friend kept flashing on the side of my brain: *Tricia. Why do you make things so much harder for yourself?*

The only easy aspect of life in those days was the dependably stable support of my husband, despite him working long shifts. The family dynamics definitely affected our marriage—our date nights usually consisted of me crying about life—but we were in it together. At times, I spoke about the need to get away, to just be alone—for a long time. Bob lovingly catered to me in those worst of moments, silently begging me, *Please don't leave me alone with these three kids.*

Bob was—is—a funny, engaging father. Our frequent dance parties always ended with Bob spasming wildly to Rock Lobster; at the beach, he loved teaching the kids how to bodysurf, or look for the perfect wave. After Neale took an interest in his beloved Red Sox, they spent hours watching games, with Bob explaining the rules and pointing out his favorite players.

His inability to soothe his son broke his heart, and tested his innate desire to comfort those he loved most. I resented being forced to handle Nico alone; Bob resented not being able to help. In the midst of an episode, all three of us often yelled at each other—me begging Bob to take over, him screaming for me to just leave, Nico demanding that I stay.

Bob hated the fighting—we all did, of course—but Bob could hardly bear being so excluded from one-third of his parenting duties. He *wanted* to influence his son; but his son only wanted the influence of me. Eventually, we developed a pattern; when an episode began, if Bob was home, he would take the girls someplace and I would stay home to deal with our son. It felt like the only option, but I still resented him for it. I wanted more sympathy, more credit, and more assurance that I was handling the situation properly. "You have no idea what it's like," I told him furiously, over and over again. He could have said the same words back to me, but he never did.

TWENTY-THREE

City Park in New Orleans was a great big swamp after Hurricane Katrina. Its gorgeous live oak trees seemed drowned and headed for decay. But somehow they survived, and by summer of 2013, many of them continued to be members in good standing of the Louisiana Live Oak Society, an exclusive club of oak trees. (Being a century old is required for membership.) The park includes an art museum, botanical garden, golf course, and lots of bayous for feeding ducks.

My kids love the place, mainly because it also features a little amusement park. The rides tumble under shady branches and meander lazily through the city's ever-present humidity. It's adjacent to Storyland, a gothic-like playground with enormous reproductions of fairy tale characters and structures. Mother Goose floats above the Three Little Pigs' brick house, and Pinocchio sits triumphantly atop an open-mouthed whale.

Post-Katrina, the park opened a satellite location of Café Du Monde, the French Quarter institution that serves beignets and cafe au lait. And there was never a line at the new place. Beignets + strong coffee + no wait + oak trees + breeze = big contented sigh.

The summer of 2013, the kids and I were in New Orleans to visit my family, and one morning, my sister volunteered to take all of the children to Café Du Monde for breakfast. But there was a problem. Beignets are essentially big balls of sugar-infused gluten, deep-fried. I thought about sending the girls along with their cousins, and denying Nico the Café Du Monde experience, but I couldn't bear it. What could I do that was comparable? Make him some gluten-free toast and tell him to eat it outside?

So we all went. Nico promised me he would only have one beignet, kind of like how I routinely promised myself I'd only have one gin and tonic. Later that day, we went to the Southern Yacht Club for lunch, and my dad ordered three plates of popcorn shrimp, delicious, enormous, juicy Gulf shrimp wrapped in GLUTEN and deep-fried, with hot bread on the side. Nico loves fried shrimp. I smiled grimly and watched my happy boy. That morning at the park, he had ridden the Ferris wheel all by himself. Within the next few days, I suspected, gluten consumption would somehow gum up his brain and he would turn into a puddle of inconsolable need.

In the meantime, the vacationing continued. A few days earlier, we had gone tubing on Lake Pontchartrain, and Nico shocked me by loving it more than any other activity ever. Our friend at the helm of the little speedboat took it easy at first, but soon my son was flying over the boat wake and begging to go faster. It had been so long since I had seen such pure, ecstatic joy emanating from him; I choked back a sob or two. For a few minutes, his mere existence had stopped being so hard, and there he was, in the moment, really living and not just surviving.

On the Fourth of July, two days post-gluten feast, Nico spent the morning happily playing with his little sister, whom he thought of as an extension of himself. Neale was six that summer, and developing into an independent, spirited child, not at all interested in following her brother's orders. Nico had trouble understanding the change; it was constantly a mystery to him why the two of them didn't act and think exactly the same. Kay, the art therapist, had been the first to notice it; in his head, she told us, he had joined the two of them as one. Sometimes, when he drew a picture of himself, he unconsciously began drawing his sister instead. It wasn't a gender identity issue—it was a self-identity issue. He had so little confidence in himself he hardly knew who he was, and he found it easier to sort of drift in Neale's wake. So when Neale made a decision to do something besides play with him, it first startled him, and ultimately led to abject despair. Recently we'd been able to help him through these episodes more adroitly, but that wasn't when he was ingesting gluten like it was air, and when we were home, which was his safe place.

On this particular morning, when Neale had endured enough sibling togetherness, Nico had trouble letting go. First he followed her everywhere, then grabbed onto her shirt and wouldn't let go. Finally I dragged him into a bedroom and tried to calm him down. He started chanting: *I wanna go home, I wanna go home, I wanna go home*, interspersed with the occasional *I want Daddy, I want Buddy, I want Daddy, I want Buddy*. Neither Bob nor Buddy had come to New Orleans with us.

I let him rant and flail, even when he marched to the window and tried to open it. We were on the second floor, but the window was painted shut. There was no way he could open it—until he did. There wasn't a screen. And suddenly my hysterical son was a nanosecond away from the roof. I rushed over and pulled him away from the window, and we both fell to the floor, where we alternately struggled and recovered for the next 20 minutes as he tried to escape from both his pain and me.

Finally, exhausted, his tantrum abated. About that time, my cousin came in to see what was happening. She saw Nico and me sprawled on the rug, both of us still in our pajamas. "What are you doing?" she asked Nico. "Get up! Get dressed! It's almost time to go!" We had plans to attend a Fourth of July party.

My son looked at me and said, "Okay." He stood up, pulled out some clothes, and started dressing.

I started crying because I was utterly spent, but also because I could see the disbelief in my cousin's eyes. I saw it in almost everyone's eyes. *This boy? This well-mannered child who loves to hug strangers and dote on his sister? Surely, he's not the problem kid. And if he is, then obviously the real problem is the faulty parent.*

He was like an oak tree, I guess. Most people just saw his strength and height and beauty, and I saw that, too. But I also stared intently at the scars and gnarled roots, and the remnants of a turbulent past. It made me love him more, so I guess I was lucky that way.

TWENTY-FOUR

When a weasel eats a chicken, it bites off the head and sucks out the guts. Then it just leaves the flappy carcass there to scare the bejesus out of the surviving chickens. I know this from personal experience—the first in a series of life-changing moments that took place during our annual summer pilgrimage to Cape Cod. Bob grew up on the Cape and at the time, his mother still lived there; it's also where Bob and I first met. For years, we had been joining Bob's siblings and their families on the Cape for a summer vacation. We drove there, because Bob viewed the trek as a great adventure. He drove most of the time, his headphones in, listening to sports radio. I sat in the passenger seat and developed rotator cuff injuries from constantly reaching back to swat at or throw things at the children.

That year, still the summer of 2013, we had just purchased a Mazda 5, a mini-minivan, which barely accommodated our family on minor excursions around town. But it had been affordable and new, and we mistakenly thought we could make it work. On this trip, we had three kids, two adults, Buddy the Wonder Dog, and zero room for luggage. Really. No room. I made everyone pack their clothes in reusable grocery bags, which came tumbling out of the vehicle every time we stopped for gas. We looked like vagabonds.

In past years, we had rented vacation homes for thousands of dollars, but our dear friends, Isaac and Cynthia, had been asking us to try staying with them, and we finally decided we would.

Bob had met Isaac at his first newspaper job on Cape Cod. When Isaac left to work at *Money Magazine* in New York City, I took his place at the paper. But Isaac had fallen in love with Cynthia, a Cape-based PR manager and business consultant, so he soon returned to the Cape, wrote and published a novel, did some PR work of his own, then settled into being a teacher.

Several years earlier, Cynthia had grown tired of PR and activism work, and decided to try her hand at farming. Over the next few years, she built a chicken coop in her yard, planted colorful plots of flowers and herbs, and leased some property where she could grow an acre of vegetables and more flowers.

Cynthia has two adult children from an earlier marriage, and she and Isaac adopted a child they raise together. The three of them live in a comfortable Cape Cod house surrounded by nature and flowers and chickens. As a farmer, Cynthia has carved out the simplest of lives for her family. They eat real food. They never go to restaurants. Fresh eggs for breakfast, fresh greens with dinner. A small house that stays cool in the summer, warm in the winter. "We have nothing," said Isaac one day, when we were talking about money. But we both knew it was a joke. They have everything.

Even their problems seemed more organically enjoyable than ours. The weasel that had eaten two of Cynthia's chickens also injured a young rooster Cynthia called Rooster Boy. So Rooster Boy moved into the house, and during our visit he slept soundly in a crate right next to the sofa where Scout slept. Among other farmer-like problems: chipmunks were chowing on Cynthia's lettuce and arugula. She put up fencing, which they chewed through. She electrified the fence, and they dug under it. She resorted to peeing around the perimeter hoping to ward them off with her scent. I don't believe she really thought it would work. She just did it out of spite.

The whole point of being on Cape Cod was to spend time with Bob's extended family; but we found ourselves drawn into Cynthia's farming life. When everyone else trekked out to visit the National Seashore, I opted to stay and help Cynthia pull weeds. I was so damn happy. I spent hours pulling weeds, laying down straw, and drinking water from a hose. I ate an apple from a tree. The plot of land is adjacent to a marine estuary, and we could smell the tides as we worked. I got actual dirt beneath my fingernails.

Later, I went to bed thinking of ways to redirect our lives— live more simply, extend our relationship with nature, and maybe even grow a tomato or two. It's not enough, I realized, to enjoy this lifestyle for one week a year. I needed to incorporate it into our suburban existence; how else could we benefit from its spiritual, physical, and psychological gifts?

Early the next morning, as I sat outside drinking coffee, the clucking chickens pecked at their corn and a cardinal sat atop a fence post in front of a wildflower patch. The crickets hummed their morning chorus, and Cynthia tromped about, watering this and cutting back that. After finishing my coffee, I hung some clean laundry up on the clotheslines, which aren't even allowed where I live because of homeowners' association rules, and Rooster Boy started pecking at my foot.

Rooster Boy, since being assaulted by the weasel, had been semi-domesticated. Cynthia rocked him to sleep at night, and he spent his days strutting around the yard. So I was surprised when he dug his sharp beak into my foot. I reached down to pet him and let him know it was just me, Caroline Ingalls, goin' about my chores. And he bit me! I immediately complained to Isaac about it. "You know why he bit you?" he said. "Because he's *turning into a cock*."

Despite the peaceful environment, it was a long 11-day vacation for our son. He tried very hard to adapt to being away for so long, and experienced some moments of happiness—swimming across Dennis Pond, collecting chicken eggs, rocking a baby goat to sleep—along with episodes of inconsolable mania. Cynthia and Isaac witnessed a tantrum one night. "Wow," said Isaac. "That comes from someplace deep inside." Yes. It was visceral. My heart ached for Nico—hurt that his sister wouldn't play with him, frustrated that he couldn't do a cartwheel, angry because I wouldn't give him a donut. But he effectively scratched, screeched, and flailed his way out of my limited supply of empathy, and soon we were equally frustrated.

Buddy the Wonder Dog still wasn't much help back then. We had begun actual service dog training with Dr. J's trainer, and he was doing well, but mostly, Buddy comforted me. Having Buddy at my side reminded me of Nico's calm, loving core, especially when Nico upended his backpack or emptied a bag of chips on the floor. And Buddy reminded me, too, of our family, my life, the good moments. Us, together, me and my man and three children and two dogs, bound by love and commitment.

After living with Cynthia for a week, I returned home more determined than ever to simplify our lives and strip away the inevitable distractions of semi-metropolis living, where the Target sign beckons like a siren, where I need pedicures—a life in which a box of store-bought (gluten-free!) chicken nuggets seems like a reasonable dinner plan.

I spent hours lamenting the suburban blur, wishing we could live more farmer-like and organically. But I felt stuck in the rat race, where our kids panicked when their electronics went low on batteries, I inspected my face for wrinkles every morning, and the neighbors complained about my wildflower patch.

Hopelessly, to torture myself, I again wasted hours online investigating the feasibility of living on a Caribbean island and raising our children to be uninhibited free thinkers who knew how to clean out a chicken coop and grow arugula. I had a yearning for such a life. Maybe, I considered, all Nico needed was the same, to escape from this swirling vortex of modern expectations.

Realistically, though, we were stuck—or at least I felt stuck. We lived in an upscale community in a house we couldn't afford to maintain, but our children attended superb neighborhood schools. Bob had found his dream career in being a firefighter, and his benefits were great, but the pay wasn't. I plugged away doing this and that—writing and teaching—but my main job was raising the kids, and with Nico's special needs, it didn't seem feasible for me to get a day job.

Gradually, I began to formulate a plan. For the first time, I recognized that we could change our lives without selling everything and moving to Costa Rica. "Baby steps," I told myself. I developed a list of initial goals:

1. Real food. I immediately and dramatically reduced the amount of processed food I bought, and started cooking simple dinners from scratch—grilled shrimp and corn, chicken soup, roasted chicken and broccoli.

2. Money. I vowed to keep track of my spending. This was—is—a thorn in my side. I've always assumed I could afford things; it's how I grew up. I *liked* to just assume I could afford things. But I forced myself to understand how stuff adds up—three trips to Starbucks in a week with one kid cost me $30, or $120 a month. That's a lot of humanely raised organic chicken breasts.

3. The outdoors. I still constantly gnash my teeth about this. I wanted my kids to just go outside and do shit. But we needed to teach by example—more gardening, playing tag, horseshoes, whatever.

The very day I wrote my new list, we received a notice from our Homeowners' Association regretting to inform us that we needed to purchase the newly required redesigned wrought-iron community mailbox for $240. I tried not to wallow in regret at choosing to live among people who value uniformity over neighborliness, because it *was* a choice, after all. But I was beginning to find it distasteful, and financially painful. It further motivated me to take the first small steps toward a simpler life.

A few weeks later, with the austerity-simplification plan well underway, we were at the beach watching the sun slip under the horizon when Scout sidled up to me and asked, "Mom? Are we poor?" To emphasize, we were *at the beach*. At our *beach club*, in fact, which we couldn't really afford. "No," I said. "We're not poor."

"Then why are you and Daddy always talking about money?" She rested her soft little hand on my arm. There's a fine line between teaching kids about money and letting financial woes trickle down to them before they're ready to handle it. I realized we had crossed that line. Our new commitment toward fiscal responsibility had subconsciously caused our daughter to worry about our future. She's so good, this girl, always so interested in me and our family—and I was tempted to just spill my neurotic guts and show her our dwindling bank account. I can see how women do that, how they confide in their children and turn them into grownups before their time. But the moment passed, and I recognized her deserved right to believe everything was *just fine*.

"Honey. Listen. Do you have enough food to eat?" I asked. She nodded. "Clothes to wear?" Nod. "A safe place to live?" Nod.

"Nobody who has those things is poor," I told her. "And besides, it's Mommy and Daddy's job to worry about money. That's not your job at all."

"Okay, Mommy," she said.

I sipped my gin and tonic, and we stood still for a while.

I can see myself there, slightly dazed by the scope of the sunset horizon, licking salt from my lips, thinking about nothing and everything. I know now a notion was brewing in me—an intangible momentum to *change everything*. I had somehow gotten turned around on my life journey. I had unknowingly led my family into a metaphorical limbo filled with too much stuff, too much money, and way too much emphasis on what we lacked. And I inherently knew we weren't in a place where Nico could heal. We needed to move.

Literally, we needed to move. That's what I decided, and when I talked to Bob about it, he admitted he'd been thinking the same thing but was afraid to bring it up. We needed to downsize financially. We lived in a 2,700 square foot house—totally reasonable for a three-kid, two-canine family—but the neighborhood was filled with mostly older couples. No kids lived nearby. The house itself needed work we couldn't afford to do.

More importantly, I thought we needed to adjust our way of life.

We had chosen to live and raise our children in a prosperous, fairyland town by the sea—a place where most children want for nothing. Life is a series of soccer games and play dates and surf camps; nobody owns a lawn mower, and everyone goes to college. There's little diversity—we often joked that our children had integrated the neighborhood.

We weren't prepared to yank the kids out of their schools. They were happy and settled, and changing schools for Nico would be like a lobotomy. We decided to stay in the area, but find a smaller home in a more economically diverse neighborhood.

We hired my girlfriend, a superstar realtor, to sell our house. She's not one of those lazy realtors who will show a house when the breakfast dishes are still piled in the sink. She had dragged her eagle-eyed husband into business with her, and he notices every single potential buyer turnoff, including things that may or may not exist. After he walked through our house, we had to hire handymen to fix everything, plus an OCD designer who moved all our furniture around.

We told the kids the plan. Scout was fine with it, because she's pretty much fine with everything. Neale was worried, but told me she'd move if her new room could have either a window seat or double French doors with a balcony.

But Nico couldn't fathom moving, and I made a critical mistake that compounded his trauma. A few months earlier, we had paid an artist to paint a gorgeous octopus mural on his wall. He loved it. Then one night during a tantrum he used the crank from my antique wooden clothes wringer (it might be a butter churn) to bash a hole in the octopus.

Of course the hole had to be fixed before the house went on the market, and after the drywall work was done, the wall had to be painted. Otherwise, the octopus would have had a great white blotch over one eye. I'm sure I explained this to him. But maybe I forgot.

One evening, before the drywall work was done, I was super-exhausted with little patience for his usual weirdo antics. We had a nighttime routine in which I smelled his feet and pretended to pass out. But on this particular night, I didn't want to smell his feet because, first of all, feet are so gross, and also, we had just returned from service dog training at a local mall and he had forgotten his shoes and walked the whole mall in his socks. I was considering putting his feet in bleach. But he insisted on the smelling routine. I let myself get aggravated and I left his room in a huff. To Nico, that meant war. He announced that he would break the wall. And the house. He screamed. He raged. The noise became a soundtrack, and the soundtrack was on an awful, earsplitting loop.

An hour passed; Neale was so tired she could barely hold up her adorable eyelids, but she couldn't fall asleep through the screaming. Scout became furious because her brother wouldn't stop kicking the wall between their rooms. I went to my room on the other side of the house and lay on my bed playing Words with Friends. I tried to re-center myself. I attended a little pity party with just me and Buddy the Wonder Dog as guests. Then I stood up, found my son, calmly grabbed his arm and dragged him outside. He screamed. I calmly told him we were going to walk outside until his tantrum was over. He protested because he wasn't wearing shoes, and I was like, *holy mother of bacteria, you walked an entire mall in your socks*, but I just calmly said, "Too bad," and we kept walking. To be honest, I was walking, and he was being … escorted. And I guess my calm was more like a controlled rage.

But a few minutes of walking did us both good. After a block or so, he relaxed, held out his hand, and we walked back home. He crawled into bed and I held him while he cried the real tears and his lip trembled and he quietly asked why we had to get rid of his octopus. I could see his little heart had cracked. Again. "I feel like you're selling all of our memories," he sobbed. The next day, he tried to scrub the paint off his wall because he thought the octopus might still be there. But it was gone.

By the time we finished all the advanced work, the house looked fantastic. I'd want it! (But we wouldn't have qualified for a loan to buy it.) It looked so great that it sold within six hours despite Nico hanging the For Sale sign upside down each time he passed it.

We arranged to close on the house and rent it back for a month or so. My girlfriend Laura, our realtor, was panicked about where we'd go next, but I was oddly calm about it. My totally unrealistic dream was to build a wide open eco-home using lots of cool recycled materials on a piece of land crowded with moss-draped oak trees. It would take advantage of wind-flow to minimize the need for air conditioning, and even when we were inside, it would feel like we were outside. Scout might sneeze a lot because she's allergic to pollen, but that's Florida life. Otherwise, it would be awesome.

Such property existed, but those lots were well beyond our price range. Also, I wasn't sure if our marriage would survive the building of an eco-house, especially since I wasn't even sure what an eco-house was.

We began looking at a new inland suburb with big new houses and bright green lawns. We still would have been only 15 minutes from the beach. The new homes were Mac-Daddied out, with gorgeous kitchens overlooking huge retention pond lakes, and master baths big enough to be called bedrooms.

This new development had—has—kick-ass amenities: a water park with a lazy river, a zip line, miles of nature trails, and its very own grocery store. It's a great community.

But I realized, as we looked at house after house, I was having to talk myself into wanting to live there, and it took me a while to figure out why: besides being seven whole miles away from the ocean, it was too much. Too much house, too much money, and way too much opportunity for my head to start telling my heart that I needed this stuff to be happy.

The more I thought about it, the more certain I became. "Honey," I said to Bob. "I don't want to move to this place." He was becoming a little disillusioned, too, because their advertised home prices didn't include luxuries like flooring, or actual land. Who advertises a house for sale but doesn't include the price of the lot?

Meanwhile, the packing was underway. Bob's contribution to the process included pulling old boxes out of his closet and piling them onto our bed, then calling, from across the house, "Can you figure out what you want to do with all this stuff?"

It was infuriating, especially since lots of the stuff was his. Evidence: the 1979 electric clock trophy he received for being on his high school track team, and the 30-year-old Peace Corps lab coat that couldn't be washed because it "smells like Zaire." It's a mystery why the Febreze people haven't introduced a scent called Jungle Sweat.

I developed a teeth-gnashing habit. Really, my jaw hurt from it. Bob and I fought a tiny bit, but we both agreed that we had Too. Much. Stuff. And I think we had a lot less stuff than the average family. I purged pretty frequently. Still, we were living too large—our lifestyle had begun to define us even though it wasn't who we were.

I wanted something else for us, a more barefoot existence— an eco-house! Less house to clean, and more reasons to go outside.

"Let's buy a little fixer-upper," I said to Bob. "We'll be able to afford to do whatever we want to it, and we'll put in a huge outdoor living space and an outdoor shower." He did not like the terms "little" or "fixer-upper." But he was blinded by the allure of an "outdoor shower," and I sealed the deal with "built-in summer kitchen" which we totally wouldn't be able to afford.

We started looking for homes in an older established neighborhood just a mile and a half away, still in our upscale community—the kids would be in the same schools—but more economically diverse with solid, small homes. Nothing fancy. Cracks in the driveway and brick veneer siding.

The first home had five college guys living in it. They were chugging Natural Light beer at two in the afternoon, and there was a bong on the porch and dirty underwear on the floor. I couldn't envision it as our dream home. The second property was adorable, but it backed up to a water treatment plant.

One night, right before I went to bed, I checked for new listings, and something popped up. There weren't any pictures yet, but the listing described it as a 1,240-sq.ft. concrete block bungalow built in 1979 with three bedrooms and two baths, located on a tiny cul-de-sac. I knew it would be perfect for us.

We went to see it the next day, before the "for sale" sign had even gone up. As soon as we walked in, a terrible poop odor engulfed us. We traced it to a big gray cat perched in one of the bedrooms. We had scared the shit right out of it.

I peeked in the closet, and saw 12 pairs of sensible black shoes. The pantry held enough bags of Eight O' Clock coffee to fuel the apocalypse. I stood in the middle of the house, breathing through my mouth because of the smell. I looked at the original dark wood doorframes and doors, and the little galley kitchen. "This is my grandmother's house," I said. "I feel like this is my grandmother's house." Except for the smell. My grandmother's house always smelled like pot roast.

"No way," said Bob.

"It has good karma!"

"It's tiny."

"This is it!"

Bob and Laura looked at me, then at each other, to telepathically agree I had lost my mind. The house sat on a huge lot—plenty of outdoor living space—and the price worked for us.

"Let's make an offer!" I practically shouted.

Laura wanted us to think about it. Bob was skeptical. But in the end, we bought it. No one else even looked at it.

The property played host to moss-draped oak trees and a front porch swing, and two-dozen enormous azalea bushes. Confederate jasmine crawled over the mailbox. "We are going off the grid, people!" I told all my friends, but we weren't really. We would continue to utilize public utilities and keep our beach club membership. Still! No more parlor-sized master baths, no formal dining room. No manicured garden. We had work to do, of course—new flooring, updated kitchen, that sort of thing. In the meantime, we rented a two-bedroom furnished condo. In my imagination, this plan worked perfectly.

Contracts signed, we resumed packing, and in the midst of it, Bob brought me a photo slide of a narrow rustic structure with a thatched roof. "Look. My first house." It was the hut he had built for himself in Zaire while in the Peace Corps. "We should do something with this," he said.

Yes, I thought. *We should.*

TWENTY-FIVE

Fact: the simplification of one's life can be very complicated. Subtext: moving sucks. The furniture wasn't the hard part, especially since Bob sold most of it on Craigslist for the low, low price of Whatever Anybody Offered. This decision did not sit well with Nico. When he learned we had sold the couch, he wailed for 20 minutes. "I feel like there's still love on that couch! You're selling our love!" No matter if it was old, musty, love that was tainted with potato chip crumbs and dog slobber. It was still love.

To save money, instead of hiring a moving company, we rented a storage POD. It was deposited in our driveway and we unsystematically threw stuff in there: mattresses, artwork, boxes, and boxes, and boxes of books. Dishes. Baskets of stuff my kids swore they needed to keep, but could live without until we moved into our new home, which was supposed to be only a few months down the road. (No one told us to exactly double a contractor's time and money estimates.)

Bob wanted to throw away everything. One day, I caught him carrying my college yearbooks to the trash. "How am I supposed to know you wanted to keep them?" he asked. When he encountered something he had to keep—i.e., tax receipts— he wrapped it in a plastic bag and shoved it into the back seat of his car. I became mentally paralyzed by the *What Ifs*. *What if* Scout wants her favorite board book when she grows up? *What if* the children hate me for throwing away the Homer Simpson

Santa Claus figurine that sings, "Deck the Halls" with Buddy Holly? *What if* I give away these bags of stuffed animals and Nico one day demands to know the fate of the gray baby seal with lifelike whiskers? And the books! What wordsmith can throw away books? I really, really, really wanted to reread Keri Hulme's *The Bone People* one day. Whenever Bob caught me waffling, he grabbed stuff from my arms and relocated them to the giveaway pile. Otherwise, I shoved them into the POD.

We stuffed the POD as though packing for a lifelong relocation to Mars. When it was full, I transported boxes and bags to the tiny new house, trying not to think about where we'd put it all when renovations began. By the time we officially moved into the condo, we thought we had not much more to bring there than a paltry selection of clothes and some boxes of Important Documents—adoption records, passports, and a few Christmas catalogues I mistakenly thought would prevent any last-minute shopping dilemmas.

Since we didn't anticipate the renovations taking more than three months, we had only rented the condo for that time. Its square footage was slightly larger than that of the new house, so I thought it would be good practice. But by the time we finished moving—the POD was safely stored in a climate-controlled warehouse and we had handed over the keys to the old house—I was stunned and appalled at the stacks of crap we had assembled in our temporary residence. Clothes and paperwork and toys and mementos … and yet we couldn't find a damn thing. Some of the mementos remained at risk. Bob's grandmother had been a personal assistant to the president of United Artists, and when Bob was born, the president (What was his name?) wrote the grandmother to congratulate them on the birth of their grandson. It was very cool to have that letter. The dog thought it was delicious. But it was one less thing to keep track of, and for that I was grateful.

Soon after we moved into the condo, Nico turned nine. Bob and I agreed he had the emotional maturity of a six-year-old, which meant he possibly was starting to grow up. He showed signs of one day being able to accept disappointment and change without triggering the DESTRUCT, DESTRUCT button in his brain. He occasionally seemed to understand how he could control his explosive anger—previously, I think, his meltdowns seemed as natural to him as sneezing, or eating bacon. They made sense to him as a consequence of conflict. Like, *Just do what I say, people, and no one gets hurt.*

He was becoming aware of his temper and how nothing good could come of it. For his birthday, we took another trip to New Orleans, just the two of us. I picked him up from school one Friday and headed to the airport. When he realized he wouldn't be able to pack his own bag—I had already packed it— he panicked, and double-panicked when he saw I hadn't packed his fuzzy pillow. He liked to take Fuzzy Pillow everywhere, which I knew. But Fuzzy Pillow is huge—it's a gigantic non-squishable memory foam pillow, and I didn't feel like lugging it on the plane. So I had packed only the ratty, stained, ripped pillowcase, which is what makes the thing fuzzy anyway. Genius, right?

I should have just poked out his eyeballs. "Then I'm not going," he shouted as we hurtled down the highway. "I'm getting out of this car." He acted like he would climb out the window while I drove. But he wasn't just being belligerent. He was scared—I could see it.

I just kept driving and saying soothing things like, "Everything's okay," and "Do you want some candy?"

Finally, he turned to me and wailed, "Mom, help me. Help me. I can't do it." This simple request was huge. For too long, his traumatic eruptions had been like earthquakes—unpredictable, pernicious, chaotic. His self-awareness made this episode more like a bad storm—all we needed to do was get out of the rain.

I held his hand and took deep breaths with him and turned into a gas station. I wanted to safely calm him, and we needed gas anyway. My son looked around and asked what I was doing. "Well, we need gas," I said.

"I wanna do it! Can I pump?"

"Sure, honey," I said.

He used my credit card to pre-pay, and I helped him load the nozzle and squeeze. "How much does gas cost?" he asked. "Where does gas come from? What do all the numbers mean? Are we going to miss our flight? What kind of plane will it be? I'll do that, Mom!" It was a litany of juvenile questions that could drive a health-conscious person to start inhaling Snickers bars. But for me it was just the re-emergence of my little boy: the real him—inquisitive, helpful, charming, and best of all, excited. Watching him happily pump gas after nearly coming unglued was like witnessing a birth. Love swelled up in my throat and I had to stop myself from enveloping him in my arms. I pushed his hair back from his face and kissed his forehead and told him I loved him.

He smiled up at me. "I think I was just a little confused, Mom," he said. "And hungry."

One morning, I was going through the ritual of getting the younger kids ready for school, and we had ten minutes remaining till departure time. Nico was carrying around an index card reading SHOES TEETH HAIR FACE to remind him of his morning duties. But he and Neale kept getting distracted by the costume accessories leftover from Halloween. Nico had chosen to be an Evil Warlock. "Honey, that's perfect for you," I told him, because he didn't understand irony yet.

The kids were playing with a glow-in-the-dark plastic scythe. They had finished getting ready; I checked to make sure Neale was wearing underwear, and the clock edged closer to the time to leave. The kids played. I watched the clock. My heart raced. The kids played. The scythe swiped near somebody's eye. *"Stop that!"* I screamed. The kids laughed. My breathing quickened. Neale stood on a chair and danced. *"Get down from there!"* I snapped. The kids played. I watched the clock. I breathed deeply to calm myself.

I realized with sudden clarity that I was waiting for something to happen, as though a violent altercation was imminent, or perhaps a fiery explosion, and I was the only one with the fire hose. My kids are playing, I thought. They are doing kid things. And I can't stand it because I'm so afraid it's going to end badly.

Suddenly, I understood Post-Traumatic Stress Disorder, and my little version of it. I'd been so conditioned to expect every moment to end with flailing limbs and broken spirits that I couldn't enjoy life when it was occasionally okay. I walked the kids to the bus stop and watched them as they crossed the street to climb aboard. Nico always ran to his seat so he could lower the window and stick his little arm out to wave for as long as he could see me, and I waved back.

On the way home I thought about Buddy the Wonder Dog. Thanks to more training, he had morphed into an actual service dog. He went with me everywhere—to the gym, the grocery, Target. He and I met a friend out for drinks and he sat under the bar for two hours. He had become my brown, furry shadow.

People always asked me what he was trained to do. I tried out a plethora of answers: I'm training him but he's mine. He's an autism assistance dog for my son who's not autistic. He's a psychiatric service dog. When Nico was with me, I said, *He's trained to be my son's best friend.*

Eventually, we hoped, Buddy would go everywhere with Nico, and help him feel centered when his anxiety heightens. He would indeed be my boy's best friend. But in the meantime, he was mine, and I was really, really grateful.

TWENTY-SIX

House renovation is not a project for the faint-hearted. I became a Pinterest whore. I stalked the site constantly, searching for pins like "small kitchen," and "small master bathroom," and "smallest place you can possibly live with three kids, two dogs, and 10,000 books."

I drew several ideal images in my head for our dream home. But every time I walked into our little gutted bungalow, I thought, *Wow, we've purchased an ant colony!* We couldn't possibly move into the bungalow right away—it was dank, dark, and smelled like cat pee. You can see why we loved it. Our contractor said renovations would take approximately three months and cost around $50,000. I wish someone had explained Building Contractor 101 to us—or, the seemingly universal acceptance that all bid estimates should be doubled upon review.

The two-bedroom condo was spacious, and we were surprisingly comfortable there—the younger kids shared the one spare bedroom, and Scout took over the den. It was our first indication that we were on the right track—we could live larger with less.

But our confidence took a daily hit—we visited the Small House every day because the younger kids took the bus there. Our contractor's workers had done a few days worth of interior destruction—just enough to make to a place hazardous—and were waiting on permitting to start the real work. We'd walk past the dumpster in the driveway, open up the 30-year-old door to piles of drywall dust and construction debris, and feel crestfallen about the possibility of ever living in such a cluttered, fetid space. The kids routinely asked if we could just stay in the condo.

We had moved into the condo in the fall. The holidays came and went without much progress. Around mid-January, we realized we needed a longer-term rental. But the condo was booked. Eviction date: February 1.

While we waited to hear back from more rentals, we began to go through the stuff we had piled in the new house. To start the process, we moved everything onto the driveway, hillbilly style, and incidentally found the enormous box of refrigerated stuff we had lost during the move four months earlier.

Bob again insisted I go through everything and deposit more crap into the dumpster which sat helpfully at my side. The more I saved stuff, the more I panicked about how we could possibly squeeze our big overcrowded life into this tiny demolished house.

That's when I had an epiphany. *We can't just throw stuff away,* I realized. That's just simple de-cluttering. We needed a total lifestyle transformation. Toys must be limited. Christmas decorations: a tree, poinsettias, and candy canes. How many vases did I really need? We could keep just the number of plates and glasses we regularly use. Some lucky soul would get my Cole Haan animal print mule shoes I only wore twice a year. I had to stop buying black tank tops. As for the books—I must share them. I could keep my favorites, and give away the rest.

I tried to reset my brain's auto-response to my frequent anxieties. For example:

Old me: Where will I keep all the beach towels?

New me: Well, we're a family of five. We don't need 24 beach towels.

Old me: I cannot possibly part with the purple paisley shirt Mom bought me in Italy 29 years ago, which I've never ever worn.

New me: Yes. Yes, I can. The shirt doesn't even look good on me.

Old me: If I don't have William Faulkner and Cormac McCarthy books on my shelf, people won't understand my diverse complexity.

New me: Fuck 'em. The people, not Faulkner and McCarthy.

But I hit a snag around photos—boxes and bins and folders full of photos—and the kids' artistic endeavors. I ended up renting a small, affordable storage unit and vowed to deal with mementos later.

I told our contractor we would be moving on March 1, no argument. "Okay!" he said. But it wasn't like, "Okay, that's fine." It was more like, "Okay, I will take that under advisement and laugh at you once I'm safely in my truck."

I was kidding myself, anyway. The house still looked like an NCIS explosion scene.

After hours perusing rental sites, I found a place for us to go—a dilapidated beach house ten miles south of our community with three bedrooms and two baths, right on the ocean. It was a cottage, really, and probably wouldn't pass any home inspections. Its ancient deck boards moaned and bent as we walked around; I warned the kids about splinters.

We moved into it on a sunny Friday in February, and by Saturday the children expressed a desire to live there forever. Within a week, we had all become extremely busy with the life-changing act of being happy. We were miles from anyone or anything, and so spent most of our time ensconced there, lured into calm by the constant presence of the ocean. My children saw the sun rise for the first time ever, and then again and again every morning. One Sunday, they played together for five hours without a single argument. Then we ate a family dinner and laughed until we cried. The kids and Bob went swimming almost every day, laughing and laughing at the chill of the February water. I started waking up early to bake stuff. The dogs were ecstatic.

It was as though we closed ranks, us five, and huddled into the family we've always wanted to be. "Let's just stay here forever, Mom," said Scout. "I love it here. Nobody argues." We had discovered an organic, legal Ecstasy.

Stuff still happened. One morning the two younger children had a big fight about whether a bed sheet is considered furniture and is therefore inappropriate to use outside as a flying cape, and then Nico yelled at me to fix him something to eat and I got so mad I started throwing protein bars at him and he locked himself in the bathroom until we both calmed down and I drove to school holding his hand.

Still. Something was happening. One afternoon, I watched Scout skip down the dune to the sea, her long black hair flying in the air like a silky feathered wing, and I thought: *This is it. Right here, right now, seeing my daughter, all strong arms and legs, leaping off a sand dune with the sun on her back and a foggy cold breeze reddening her face. Leaning into my husband as we watch our young son go swimming in the cold waves. Laughing at the dogs chasing seagulls down the beach. Life.*

But of course, life in all its wonder has glitches. The Dilapidated Beach House did not have a disposal in the kitchen sink; disposals probably weren't invented when it was built. This was a tiny buzz kill, as I love to toss eggshells into the sink from six feet away. I adjusted to not having a disposal, because being able to wake up staring at the ocean gives a person perspective like that. No disposal? No problem! Also, I perched the trashcan up on a stool so I could still throw eggshells from across the room.

But Bob acted like not having a disposal was the same as having a disposal, but without the noise. One night, as he washed a pot, I watched brown water fill up the sink because a bunch of (gluten-free) noodles were clogging the drain. "Remember, we don't have a disposal," I said helpfully.

"I know, I know, I'll clean it out," he said. I looked at him doubtfully. "I will! I promise!" he said.

Well. The next morning, as I made lunches and prepared breakfast, I noticed a bunch of soggy brown noodles sitting in the drain. Is there anything grosser than old, wet noodles? Scout tried to pour something into the sink and asked why it wasn't draining. "Because of those noodles," I said. "Daddy didn't clean them out the way he promised." Daddy was standing right there, and I said it sort of joking but sort of serious. You know that tone, right? Like, *Ha Ha! This is so hilarious, us having a funny family moment, but come fix this fucking problem, dude, right now.*

Bob can take a hint, so he came over to the sink, grabbed a spoon, and started smashing the noodles into oblivion so they'd go down the drain.

"What are you doing?!" I yelled.

"It's fine. We're on the second floor. The pipe just goes straight down. It can't clog."

"Oh my god. Seriously? Stop it right now." Grind, smash. "Stop it! You're going to clog up the drain! Don't do such stupid stuff!"

Bob gave me a withering look. "Can you please not yell like that in front of the kids?"

Some sort of evil force had taken over my brain. *"Then don't do stupid stuff in front of the kids. Anyway, they should know this."* I glanced at Scout. "Honey, don't ever smash noodles so they'll go down a drain without a disposal." She gazed up at me sadly, with hooded eyes, and slunk out of the room, and a miniature shadow of Dr. Phil landed on my shoulder and whispered, "Never, ever, ever fight in front of your children. It changes who they are."

I tried to shut up, but I couldn't. "Don't do stupid stuff!" I bellowed. In case he had developed sudden hearing loss, I said it again, shrilly, with more emphasis. *"Don't do stupid stuff!"* He shook his head at me and walked off, and I yelled after him. "Go apologize to your daughter and tell her it's all your fault because I'm right."

I totally was right about the disposal issue. Just because the noodles don't immediately clog the sink doesn't mean they won't eventually clog the sink, even if the clog starts one story down. Right? Right? I'm right on this. I know it. However. What had gotten into me? Who told me it was okay to berate my spouse and simultaneously teach my kids it's okay to lose my cool over noodles in a drain? I so soured the mood of the morning that Neale started singing the "Happy" song from *Despicable Me* in an effort to repair the atmosphere.

Bob apologized, I apologized, Scout kissed me and went off to school, leaving me alone with the memory of her sad, disappointed face as she retreated from the ugly moment, which had started her day.

I thought about what I had done for a long time. I still think about it. I had—again—abdicated my responsibility to be mood setter and emotional thermometer of the family. I recalled the saying, *If mama ain't happy, ain't nobody happy.* I had always interpreted this as a reason for everyone to keep mama happy. But maybe mama needed to keep herself happy instead.

Bob said I was being too hard on myself, and I guess I was. It was not unreasonable, considering all we were going through, for me to occasionally break down. But at the time, I didn't feel like such painful mistakes were an option, especially when it came to helping Nico.

Imagine two roads in front of you. One road is flat, but curves just beyond your vision and you can't see its end, although you've been told it's where you want to be. The other road leads to a steep, rocky ascent toward the picturesque peak you've been seeking.

We were taking the hard road, and we kept falling. Two steps up, one step back, we moved forward slowly, nursing our bloody knees, and often losing sight of the peak.

TWENTY-SEVEN

Another two months passed, and everybody wanted to know how the remodel was progressing. "Great! Fabulous!" we exclaimed. But we lied. We thought our cabinet guy had absconded to Central America after cashing our deposit, but he showed up one day and spent all night in a frigid house with no electricity installing cabinets in the dark with his wife and daughter. All night. He sent me a text at 5:05 am to tell me they were done. The results: Not Optimal. It looked a little like three people had stayed up all night in a house with no heat and no light to put together some cabinets.

Also: the tile guy began warning us about his prices before he even knew what we wanted. The children were so confused they started missing the old, old house … the one we hadn't lived in for six years. The Dilapidated Beach House developed a fine layer of sand, dog hair, and crumbs on every surface. I held off on changing sheets because what was the point? Everything was infused with sand no matter how much I cleaned.

I still was so excited about the downsizing, the simplifying, the decision to focus on the important parts of life—but I found myself conflicted. We were spending so much money on a complicated project to create a home that allowed us to spend less money and live more simply. Did it even make sense? I wasn't feeling very off the grid, especially since I was short on cookware and kitchen supplies and time so my kids were subsisting on

French fries, Nutella, and bologna. I still made some kick-ass salads for myself because somebody had to stay healthy.

As the beach house lease neared its termination, the small house was nowhere near completion. The house had been drywalled and painted, but the countertops weren't in. We had no closets. Lighting had not been installed. The plumbing wasn't hooked up. The concrete flooring we imagined wasn't working out.

I fell into a dismal trench, or a little figurative wind tunnel. My eyes swelled up from crying. I think I might have looked rabid. *It's too much, it's too much*, I kept wanting to scream. Instead, I just whined the words to the husband, who stroked my hair and let me snuggle with him while he recovered from dropping a 45-lb. weighted bar on his foot.

In reality, nothing was terribly wrong or unfixable. We were moving into our newly remodeled home in mere days, although the house had no appliances, no electricity, no A/C unit, no countertops, and no doorknobs. But we were moving!

When I'm stressed, every little problem, issue and task flies at me in the form of an imaginary arrow and stabs me in the head. When I pull out an arrow, another one takes its place. I imagine myself as a walking zombie with a zillion arrows sticking out of my skull. I make poor choices. I do anything I can to divert my attention from the fact that I should be pulling arrows out of my head.

And I was definitely stressed, with a head full of metaphorical arrows.

• I wasn't being a stellar mother. EVIDENCE: Scout's new favorite breakfast food was a can of corn.

• I wasn't being a great wife. EVIDENCE: Bob winced in pain every time he put weight on his foot, and all I could think about was when he'd be able to carry a box.

242 • The Place of Peace and Crickets

• I was faltering in my role as Chief Domestic Engineer. EVIDENCE: Clean underwear for the kids no longer seemed important.

Most importantly, I was failing in my role as caretaker of my own spirit. I wasn't reading or thinking or meditating or even pondering the jaw-dropping sunrises we saw each morning from the deck of the dilapidated beach house. Instead, I exercised. Every day. Hard. It was the only task I found finite, the one thing I could do consistently right. I lifted and ran and punched and jumped.

At night as I drifted off to sleep, I ran a mental tab of all I didn't accomplish. Didn't order the ceiling fan. Didn't pick out paint color for the bathroom. Didn't get my glasses fixed. Didn't solve the countertop dispute with Home Depot. Didn't arrange Nico's play date. Didn't sign Scout up for camp. Didn't give the dogs their heartworm prevention meds. Didn't call my mother-in-law on her 75th birthday. Didn't return my sister-in-law's email. The list of *didn'ts* made my stomach tighten, and I felt my muscles constrict, trying hard to digest the enormous burden I asked them to carry, and I put my hands on my semi-ripped abs. At least part of me is strong, I thought. Very, very strong.

My strength was tested when, at the end of the beach house lease, the small house still wasn't ready and we had to move into the Marriott with three kids and two dogs. We planned to stay there four days. But after four days, our house still had no countertops, no showers, no stove and no washer or dryer. So I tried to extend our stay at the Marriott. It was full, and the staff politely asked us to make way for actual vacationers. I discovered this conflict one hour before checkout time.

I called a friend who was out of town and asked if we could stay in her house, and delivered half the hotel room crap to her garage. I returned to the Marriott and loaded up the remaining crap to bring to the new house and unloaded it onto the front porch. Then it was time to meet the children and calmly inform them that we had moved into a fourth temporary home. Nico looked as though he might rip out my heart with his grimy hands, so I quickly suggested a trip to Target in order to diffuse the moment. At that moment, Bob arrived home and asked me how the day went, and we had a tiny little enormous fight, then I drank some gin and felt a lot better.

We stayed in my friend's house for several days, although her home was so adorable and perfect I made everyone keep their stuff in the garage, and finally we moved into our remodeled home in the midst of a torrential thunderstorm. Still the construction went on. The drywall guys patched some remaining dents and holes, and although one of them smelled like something died inside him and most certainly was part of a prison day-release program, I was happy the work got done. The carpenters finished off the linen closet and hung some mirrors; the painters arrived to make everything pretty. Then, finally, we began to unpack, and really focus on the simple, clean, living I had originally envisioned. We had completely lost track of how much money it took to renovate. The cabinets did not come out as planned. The concrete floor guy, who coincidentally had recommended the idiot cabinet guy, screwed up the floors and left paint bubbling throughout the house. But everything else was beautiful and perfect and just as I had imagined it.

We were done. But not really, of course.

TWENTY-EIGHT

Throughout the chaos of moving, renovating, moving, moving, moving again, and renovating, we miraculously had maintained Nico's supplement regimen and the gluten-free, dairy-free diet. He also saw his art therapist once a week, and she continued to make great progress helping him express his fears and anxieties.

But his behavior at home was still at times appalling and frightening. Even when he was calm, the tension was palpable. All family plans needed to be vetted through the Nico filter. Even small decisions could have major consequences.

Many of his triggers still stemmed from his little sister's mere existence. He loved her, but he hated her need for my attention, and it frustrated him beyond reason that he couldn't tell her what to do. If she asked me to watch her do a bike trick, I knew Nico would soon be scrambling to do a bike trick, too, and I had to stay outside to watch him, even if a swarm of wasps encircled my head. When Neale waved at me from her bike and I waved back, Nico waved at me, too, and if I didn't wave back, because I couldn't see everything on the planet that happened, he would yell, *Mom, I waved, too*, so then I would wave back at him, and in this way prevent him from flinging himself down on the pavement and wailing until sundown.

But sometimes I was blindsided, and could only mentally flail, try (usually unsuccessfully) to remain calm and keep him from breaking things until the episode ended.

In short, despite the progress of Dr. J.'s regimen and some glimpses of his potential, our son continued to have debilitating issues: terrible anxiety, horrible self-doubt, and a general conviction that life would be perfect if he could be locked in a padded room with me, 40 pounds of bologna, and a limitless supply of Pokémon videos. The improvement curve had long since plateaued. We felt stuck—as a family, as parents, even as people trying to embark on a simpler, happier life. Our "simple" seemed pretty damn complicated, and we had grown weary of no one understanding how difficult our daily routine had become.

Even Dr. J. had doubts about the behavior we reported. She had believed all his problems stemmed from diet and nutrition lapses. She emphasized his need for strict adherence to the plan—and when we reported ongoing problems, she advised more disciplined parenting. Again, we felt misunderstood, and flummoxed.

Every so often, though, someone witnessed a sliver of our reality, and it was almost comical to see Nico's complexity unveiled in public like a controversial art installation.

We had gotten into the habit of occasionally having Smoothie King for dinner. Nico loved smoothies. When Bob was working a long shift, smoothies + a bologna sandwich on gluten-free bread + all new episodes on Cartoon Network = easy-ish night for mama. I just had gin and salad.

One late afternoon, Nico was happily sitting at the kitchen counter sipping his smoothie when the Styrofoam cup slipped from his hands and splattered everywhere.

He fell apart like Humpty Dumpty. His sisters looked at him with pity, kept sipping from their perfectly intact cups, then fled to their rooms in knowing anticipation. I wish I could have done the same thing. But I cluck-clucked my sympathy, and started cleaning up the mess. He fruitlessly used the broken cup to scoop up smoothie puddles, trying to save some, before dissolving into tears. Then this happened:

Him: Mom, go get me another smoothie.

Me: No, honey. I'll make you one—it'll taste even better! But I'm not going to get you another one. Accidents happen.

Him: GO GET ME ANOTHER SMOOTHIE. YOU ARE GOING TO GET ME ANOTHER SMOOTHIE.

Me: No, I'm not.

He found my car keys, went outside, started the van, and sat in the passenger seat expectantly. I followed him, removed the keys, dragged him out of the van, and locked the car. He ran inside after me, frantically trying to get back the keys. As his desperation mounted, he began hurling himself into me. Thank you, gods of fitness, for my outlandish strength. That boy could be a 75-pound rhino when he wanted to be.

I hid the keys, which infuriated him. Suddenly, he got all freaky calm and said, "You want the car locked? I'll lock the car for you." He grabbed something off the table and headed back outside. As I watched from a window, he used a roll of packing tape to wrap up the mini-minivan. He meticulously pressed the tape into the car, and climbed on the van roof to stretch it across the top and back down the other side.

I texted his art therapist: *My son is using packing tape to wrap up the car.*

She texted back: *Do not allow him to do that! That is not okay! Do not let him think that's okay!*

Me: *Okay, I'll make him stop.* I leaned against the windowsill and sipped on a beer.

When he ran out of tape, he came inside with a look of accomplished satisfaction, and surveyed the room. "Now I'm going to break the vacuum," he said. He snarled it, really. I watched as he sat next to the vacuum and ripped off the suction hose. He looked down the hose hole curiously, and then back at the vacuum. He turned the whole thing upside down, then reattached the hose and turned the vacuum on to see if it worked. But his demeanor had changed from fury to curiosity. *Holy shit*, I thought. *He is fixing himself.* As the machine hummed to life, I could almost see its soothing drone driving the toxic noise out of his head. "Mom, can I vacuum the house?" he asked.

"Sure," I said, stunned. He vacuumed. I sat on a kitchen stool and took deep breaths. A few minutes later, my 74-year-old neighbor rang the doorbell. "I know I'm just a nosy old neighbor," he said, stuttering a bit. "But. But. But." He pointed at my car. "I just have to ask …."

I held up my hand to interrupt him. "Wait here," I said. I called to my son, who was vacuuming dog hair out of his bedroom. He looked up at me through floppy bangs and smiled. And his gaze was so open, so trusting and guileless, that I almost left him alone.

"Honey, I'm so happy you're feeling better. But Mr. G. is here and he wants to know what happened to my car." I was shaming him; I expected him to freak out again—he would have been justified—but he acted like I had reminded him to flush the toilet after peeing.

"Oh, right." He turned off the vacuum and followed me to the door. Mr. G. looked at my boy and asked what had happened. "I got a little angry and taped up Mom's car," he mumbled. Mr. G.'s mouth opened and closed comically. He seemed both perplexed and impressed. "Well, I …" he said. "I never … I just never heard …." His voice trailed off and left us in a moment of silence. And then he found a place in my heart forever. Because he said to Nico, "Well, should we clean it up?"

Nico nodded, trudged outside, and began stripping off the tape. I walked closer to watch, and noticed a bunch of chicken nuggets and fries on the roof. "Did you throw your dinner up there, too?" He nodded again. I saw the shame on his face. Verbalizing his behavior to Mr. Gary was, for him, like watching his virtual double in an action movie. He could barely comprehend what he had done. But the facts lay before him, stuck to his brain like the tape on the car. And so my sweet boy kept pulling it off, strip by strip, all the while wondering how in the world it had gotten there.

TWENTY-NINE

As we approached another summer, I felt myself sliding into a chronic state of mental and physical exhaustion. My whole body ached. The arch of my foot hurt. I had unexplained bruises and was swatting imaginary bugs off my chin. The idea of lapsing into a two-month coma was not unattractive to me.

"You're working out too much," said Bob. "No working out today. And maybe not tomorrow, either."

The thought of not working out for two days made me feel more exhausted. At least when I was hoisting weights I experienced a sense of accomplishment.

"I understand," he said. "You're mentally drained. You're panicked about the summer."

Translation: I was panicked about Nico and how he would ruin the summer for everyone. Honestly, that's how I thought about it. But blaming my son for my brooding seemed like bad mothering, so again, I focused on other irritations. *Has my writing slumped? Is Scout growing up too fast? What if we go broke? Why can't the Homeowners' Association leave us alone? I need to spend more time with my husband. Was moving the right decision? My shoulder hurts. My chest feels tight. I'm crying again.*

It wasn't just me falling apart. Scout resented how Nico controlled the family, and she was having a hard time being kind to him. She had become very protective of me—but when I was mean to Nico, she became very protective of him, sometimes even physically guarding him to prevent me from reaching him.

Bob usually was at work when such episodes occurred. But even when he was home, it was difficult for him to help because Nico continued to only want me. If I tried to help him, I quickly lost both patience and my temper. But if I made myself scarce and let Bob handle the problems, Nico escalated maniacally, which caused Bob to lose patience.

"Something's not right," Bob finally decided. We made another appointment with Dr. J. Since moving, we had occasionally let Nico have dairy, and I had run out of some of his supplements without refilling them. Frankly, they were becoming cost-prohibitive. I think I also had grown weary of unfulfilled promises. Our path seemed to have veered off-course. Still, I feared I was in for a verbal spanking.

Dr. J. listened to us rant about our frustrations, and the inanity of living with a kid who couldn't stop kicking our asses. She asked us to describe his diet. Syrup-drenched gluten-free waffles for breakfast, a decent lunch, cookies after school, candy whenever he could get it. Smoothie King every other day. We described the packing tape incident in detail.

Mostly I talked—because I was the one clinging to the proverbial cliff. When I finished speaking, I looked around, half-expecting to see the room flooded with giant 3D versions of the words and phrases I had just spewed forth. Look there! *I can't live like this* is leaning against the desk! Be careful—don't trip on *Enters into a fugue state*. *When will this ever end* is about to crash down on my head.

Dr. J. engaged in some head-shaking and eye-rolling as I spoke, then said, "Your son is addicted to sugar."

I was like, NO. That's impossible. I give all my kids tons of sugar so they'll be immune from the effects of it. Ask their dentist! Nico had two cavities so deep the teeth weren't worth saving. But we started reviewing the episodes I had described: when he dumpster-dived to retrieve a pair of old shoes we had thrown out. The time he wouldn't go to school because his shirt was the wrong shade of blue. When he took back my Mother's Day present and tore up the handmade coupons he had written. How he locked himself in the bathroom because I couldn't find a shoe. All of it could be traced, Dr. J. surmised, to sugar cravings. Part of his behavior was the anxiety, but the escalation, said Dr. J.—his clear inability to control his emotions—were symptoms of addiction.

Whatever, I thought. Because when I say—*When will this ever end?*—what I really mean is, *When can I finally stop making life-altering changes for my son that dramatically inconvenience me?* I gave up wheat bread and pasta. I finally got used to having almond milk in my coffee. I bought him a goddamn dog. And now sugar?

But Bob was all, "Wow, that makes sense." Dr. J. gave us a detailed breakdown about how sugar affects the brain and combined it with a painful lecture on discipline and consequences. I wasn't convinced, but was still desperate for relief. So we gave up sugar. Not all sugars, but most of the added stuff. No more processed cookies. No more gummy bears. So long, Gatorade. I was suspicious of your Red Dye 40 anyway.

Now, keep in mind: I'm highly suggestible. And once again, we all feel better when we're eating right. So it shouldn't have been any surprise that after two days of homemade, nourishing, sugar-free meals, the domestic chaos had dulled to a manageable buzz.

Though I went along with Dr. J.'s latest plan, the seeds of doubt had been planted. She had soundly rejected the possibility that any sort of attachment disorder or truly diagnosable anxiety was affecting Nico. I think she continued to prescribe the low dose of medication to pacify me. She had become like everyone else—she didn't believe us.

For me, it was the beginning of the end of this phase. The healthy eating had helped, because healthy eating helps everyone. The supplements had helped, because proper vitamins also help everyone. Dr. J. had been a key to ushering in this new simpler lifestyle, but she had not been the answer after all.

I was ready to give my son back his pizza.

THIRTY

In the meantime, I was trying to develop my new simplification mindset so we could change how we navigated through the world.

I devoted myself anew to the premise, starting with selling most of my valuables—including jewelry. I gave away fancy clothes I wore once a year. My summer shoe collection included two pairs of flip-flops and one pair of Birkenstocks. With Bob's help, we spent more time as a family during long spring afternoons, and learned to cook together. I began to feel lighter and hopeful, and happy about being on this journey, yet afraid of the niggling little pain in my brain reminding me of the ever-present danger of unexpected curves.

At two years old, Buddy had turned into the best dog in the history of the universe. He gradually had developed into a family service dog. And I was kind of his service human because he adored me so much. Buddy kept each of us centered in his own special canine way. Scout cupped his face in her hands and stared into his gold-brown eyes a dozen times a day. Neale pretended he was a student in her classroom, and he gamely sat in her playhouse and listened to her prattle on about book heroines and Barbie adventures. That's normal dog stuff. But Nico used Buddy to remind himself that he was worthy of being alive. He often pulled Buddy onto the couch, leaned up against the dog's warm bulk, and loudly whispered, "Look, Mom, Buddy loves me," like it was an ever-new revelation. He scratched Buddy's belly until he found *that spot*, which made them both happy, at least for a minute.

The long days of summer—the weeks of limited bathing and extended electronics time and staying up late—were nearing an end, and as the first day of school drew near, Nico's level of cooperation deteriorated. He stopped getting dressed in the morning, and often refused to leave his bedroom at all except to pee. I knew he was nervous; I was nervous, too.

"Just don't get Ms. Bart," said Scout. "She's mean."

"Honey, don't say that. Please."

"Mom, it's true," Nico said. "I heard that, too."

On "Meet the Teacher" day, he rushed to the postings of who was in which class. His best friend had gotten the grade's most popular teacher, a man who spoke with a British accent. Nico had gotten Ms. Bart.

He put on his game face. We scurried to the class with high hopes, and Ms. Bart greeted Nico with a smile and said she looked forward to working with him. He found his assigned spot, and noticed a few familiar names on desks.

As we left, he leaned into me. "She seems nice," he said weakly, and my heart sank.

The first week of school seemed to last 40 days. He held it together during the school day, but by the time he walked into his home, AKA The Safe Zone, his reserves were depleted and all he had left for me was shit. He couldn't verbalize how mentally drained he was—so instead he found something else more tangible to tackle. One day it was not being able to find his Pokémon cards; another day it was the way I measured milk for his oatmeal.

One day it was shoes. I had gone shoe shopping for the girls that day, and although he didn't need any shoes, I had purchased a pair of on-sale casual slip-ons about a half size too big for him. I thought he would like them, and grow into them.

That's not how he saw it. He noticed immediately that his sisters' shoes were the right sizes and had *not* been on sale, and so *clearly I loved them more.* He sobbed. He threw the shoes in the trash, then demanded I return them immediately and buy new ones the right size. He tried to take my car keys. He pushed me away from him, and then followed me wherever I went.

Explaining anything to him was futile—he could barely see me much less hear me. His words were piercing: *Is that how much you love me? You only buy me stuff on sale? What kind of mother are you? I thought you cared. You don't even know what size shoe your own son wears!*

The incident lasted about 45 minutes, and included a lot of pushing, throwing, and grabbing from both of us. Afterwards, I held him in my arms as he took deep breaths and said, "I'm sorry, I'm sorry," over and over, and we talked about how much I loved him and how often I buy him things that aren't on sale and why it shouldn't even matter.

I landed in bed that evening like a felled tree and felt my heart and belly flip-flopping with the stress of the afternoon. I was too tired to cry, too sad to sleep, too worried to talk, so I just rolled on my side and stared at the wall. Bob was at work, which left room for Buddy to jump up next to me and put his paws on my hands. I smelled his paw pads, which seems gross, but they always smell like popcorn to me, and it's comforting. That's how I fell asleep that night, his paws in my hands, one of my beloved brown-haired 75-lb. boys consoling me about the other.

It had not been one of the more alarming episodes, but it was a turning point for me. Over the previous seven years, we had sought help from two psychiatrists, three therapists, and a pediatrician specializing in autism. We had given Nico meds, changed his diet, disciplined him, refrained from disciplining him, punished him, restrained him, hugged him, ignored him, and simply waited for things to get better.

I didn't feel like I could do this any more, this swimming in muck with no solid land in sight. Our exasperation had reached a peak; I didn't even pretend to be sad when he stepped on the bus each day, nor was I happy to see him at the end of the day. "You're too hard on yourself," Bob still said. Everyone said it, in fact. The statement made no sense to me. It was like Nico was trapped under a car, and I couldn't lift the car. *I knew* I shouldn't expect myself to be able to lift it, nor beat myself up because I couldn't. But the fucking car needed to be lifted, right? Who else, but his parents would do it? *Who else?*

I called a friend from book club, a child psychiatrist specializing in special needs children, and we met for coffee. She listened as I rambled in no discernible order about our Nico troubles, then she peppered me with familiar questions until we had this exchange.

"On average, how many positive interactions do you have with Nico each day versus negative interactions?" she asked.

I burst out laughing. "FAR more negative."

"That needs to change right away," she said. He's a little boy, she reminded me, who needs his mother. She advised me to start fabricating positive interactions. If he's sitting on the sofa reading quietly, I should give him a hug. Chat with him on the way to the bus. Support him more profusely when he does something right.

This just seemed like math to me—I needed to create more positive moments so they would outweigh the negative. I could do that.

Next, she pointed out, Nico had become the "identified patient" of the family. Because of all the mental health treatment we sought, he had learned to believe he was the sole problem facing our family. Anything that went wrong, he viewed as his fault.

Finally, she said, I needed more help than I was getting. Eating healthy is great, she agreed. Minimizing sugar—an awesome goal. But, based on our conversation, it was clear to her that Nico's issues were more complicated than a glut of gluten and too many smoothies.

She recommended a behavior therapist she knew. Martin, she explained, didn't work from an office—he made house calls and treated the whole family. She gave me his number, and as we left the coffee shop, we weirdly ran right into him. It seemed like a very good sign, and I emailed him the next day.

THIRTY-ONE

In the free-spirited atmosphere of 1970s-era New Orleans, I started driving at age 15, and soon afterwards became a teenage drinking statistic. I went to my first bar a year later with my first boyfriend. It was 50-cent highball night at The Boot, which is where lots of Tulane University frat boys hung out. I went up to the bar and ordered a highball. "I'd like a highball," I said. The bartender just looked at me. "Uh, what kind of highball?"

The question stumped me. That's how young I was. I thought a highball was a drink. I eventually ordered a screwdriver, and then several more, and ended up with a hickey on my neck that my mother noticed the next day before I did.

I think of that night as the beginning of my formal relationship with alcohol. The high school years were a blur of bars and open parties hosted by kids whose parents were out of town. We all knew the drill regarding area bars: Shanahan's checked IDs but nearly always took fake ones; Fat Harry's never checked; Nick's was nothing more than a long stretch of plywood—you could stand in the parking lot while someone else bought you a drink; ATII's was pretty strict, but if you had a date who knew the bouncer you were golden. We drank astounding amounts for teenagers. And most of us could drive. Drunk driving was more adventure than taboo back then.

I think my mother thought college would calm me down. But Irish Catholic schools with enormous football traditions aren't known for their staid atmospheres. At Notre Dame, our freshman year resident assistant gave us sage advice: *All men are shits, and don't drink the Flanner punch.*

Of course, I drank the Flanner punch, and discovered for myself how all—let's say most—men are shits. And that was just the first semester. By sophomore year, I had been appointed chair of the Tailgating Committee, and was in charge of securing kegs before every home game to raise money for our dorm. My aunt has a great picture of me sitting on a keg handing out cups with dozens of guys handing me dollar bills. It gave me some solid retail experience.

By the time I graduated from college, I had been grossly, awfully drunk more times than I could count. There are dozens of legendary stories—the time I was making out in the dorm's common room with some guy, but kept running upstairs to throw up and brush my teeth before returning to make out some more. The fistfight with a kid in the parking lot. The spontaneous midnight road trip to the Kentucky Derby.

I often thought about how much I drank, particularly on Sunday mornings when I felt near death. I occasionally researched the symptoms of alcoholism and took magazine quizzes: *Do you ever have a drink before noon?* I never drank before noon, so I always told myself I was fine.

I was an expert at nearly all the drinking games. "Quarters" was my specialty because I have a particularly perfect nose; a quarter rolls off of it at just the right angle to bounce into a shot glass. I never wanted college to end, but thank goodness it did. After college, I held several years' worth of jobs conducive to partying. I traveled in Europe and worked in a London pub; I was a tour guide in the Louisiana swamps. And then I worked for two years on the Mississippi Queen steamboat.

On the MQ, we worked 12-hour shifts. The remaining 12 hours were spent drinking, either in the crew rooms or on shore when the boat was docked. My favorite party boy was Timothy the chef; during one shore outing in Greenville, Mississippi, we found a juke joint way outside the city. My clearest memory of the excursion starts with us dancing on the bar and ends with us hitchhiking back to the dock and leaping to the ship deck after the lines had already been untied.

In 1988, I was accepted to the Masters in Journalism program at Boston University, and re-acquainted myself with people who actually read books. A seminal moment came during a discussion about that year's presidential campaign pitting Massachusetts Governor Michael Dukakis against the first George Bush. Kitty Dukakis, the governor's wife, had just said publicly that she was an alcoholic, admitting she had "blacked out" a couple of times after drinking.

I remember working on a group project with classmates, and making fun of Kitty for claiming to be alcoholic. "Really, who hasn't ever had a blackout?" I said.

There was a pregnant pause. "I haven't," said one friend. "Me neither," said the other.

I still can see the light bulb in my brain.

Lots of people have similar stories to tell about youthful indiscretions involving alcohol or drug abuse. The same kind of drinking as an adult seems less harmless. I know a couple of people who don't drink, and never have. I know lots of people who don't drink very much. And I know several people who don't drink anymore because they realized the error of their ways and quit.

But mostly I know people like me, or how I used to be— people who like to drink and drink often and sometimes drink a little too much.

Bob and I don't fight too much. But in those days, we often fought about my drinking. I was drinking too much for a woman with three young children. At my age, three glasses of wine on a school night was too much. In my late 40s, I found wine gave me headaches so I switched to gin. "Gin makes you crazy," said my mother.

"Crazy happy," I said.

If Bob spent the night at the fire station, I made sure I was never too impaired to drive to the hospital in case of an emergency. But looking back, I often would have failed that test.

I drank every night, two or three cocktails. Subsequently, I'd have trouble sleeping, and I'd wake up cranky. On weekends, I drank more—sometimes four or five drinks, and I woke up hungover. But the drinking never kept me from life, or at least I didn't think so. A therapist once asked me if I'd ever thought of not drinking. "No," I said. She looked at me sort of knowingly, and I quit going to her.

The years passed; I kept drinking, and my husband and I kept occasionally fighting about it. "The kids are getting older," he argued. "They're watching you." Was it okay for our children to grow up thinking alcohol is something fun and whimsical and harmless? Why not?

I once had feared developing some kind of a condition preventing me from drinking. As I grew older, I secretly wished for it to happen. I was tired of drinking, but I couldn't seem to stop. I wasn't hiding bottles under the sink or blacking out; but I looked forward to 5:00 p.m. every day, and made sure I never ran out of tonic.

A week after my meeting with my psychiatrist friend and our chance encounter with Martin the therapist, my back started hurting and I had trouble rising out of bed. For days, I could barely manage to get the kids off to school. I Googled "extreme left side lower back pain," "persistent cough," and "armpit pimple," and discovered I was dying and possibly needed to have my spleen removed. Buddy must have sensed this diagnosis, because he sprawled belly-up next to me pretending to be dead. He was so good at playing dead that I frequently checked his breathing.

You know the phrase, "been through the wringer?" It refers to those old-fashioned hand-cranked laundry machines, the kind used to squeeze excess water out of wet washed clothes. I felt like I had been through one of those. I went to the doctor, and I wasn't dying after all. I had a severe case of bronchitis coupled with a weightlifting back injury, and the two simultaneous conditions were competing with each other to see which could take the longest to heal. Coughing too hard hurt my back, and resting my back prevented me from coughing.

I practically begged the doctor to hospitalize me. "Couldn't this all stem from exhaustion?" I asked. "Do you think I need bed rest?"

"Just try to get some rest at home," he replied, like it was even possible, and I refrained from lunging at him because of my back and all.

I was sick for an entire month. I slept on a heating pad, and counted the hours between doses of Advil. My cough sounded positively tubercular, and people walked way around me on the rare occasions I ventured out in public. But something else happened: I stopped yelling. I couldn't yell, because it hurt. Gentle reminder: I have a bad temper. When I'm angry or frustrated, I yell a lot. Sometimes, if I'm in public, I cry instead, and yell later. "Tricia is lots of fun to live with," said no one ever.

Over the years I had mellowed about the small stuff, like the appalling way in which my husband loads the dishwasher or that woman with the weird mole at Target who always gives me the stink-eye. But the kids—the yelling had become a key component of my parenting style. On a purely analytical level, my children deserved some yelling. Nico and Neale have had violent arguments about whose smoothie contained more strawberries and whose imaginary friend had more candy. But here's a mistake us moms make all too often—just because our kids deserve to be yelled at doesn't mean we should actually do it. Because—Dr. Phil is right—too much yelling begins to change them.

A couple of weeks into my accidental sabbatical from loud parenting, I noticed a difference in the household. I found the quieter me much better able to resolve the ridiculous, meaningless conflicts my children invented to torture themselves. Feeling poorly meant I moved more slowly, spoke more deliberately, and considered the consequences of my words.

The result: utter exhaustion by the end of the day. But my kids were calmer. Yes, I spent more time keeping them grounded and content. But in the process, I kept myself in check, too.

I'm not sure the yelling sabbatical would have been as cathartic without the other unintended consequence of the bronchitis and back injury: I accidentally stopped drinking. In the beginning, I was literally too sick to drink. All I wanted to do in the evening was lay in bed with a heating pad and watch NCIS reruns until I fell asleep.

When I finally started feeling better, to my shock, I had lost my taste for booze. The idea of white wine, my previous drink of choice, even nauseated me. Around dinnertime, the traditional start of my happy hour, I wasn't even tempted. *This is so weird*, I thought. It was like my body had unintentionally detoxed.

One morning soon after I felt better, Nico wanted pancakes for breakfast. The first pancake stuck to the pan. The second pancake was burnt, and by burnt I mean cooked. The third pancake smelled like popcorn for reasons I can't explain. The fourth pancake was perfect, but needed a side of cheese omelet. He ate it all while missing the bus.

But the bus makes a loop, so we caught it on the flip side. By then, his regular seat had been taken, so I watched through the cloudy bus window as he sat uncertainly by himself, stretching his neck to make sure his sister was within sight—his sister who attracts friends like she attracts mosquitoes, his sister who dresses like a refugee but works it like she's on Broadway.

I walked back home thinking about how the old me would have handled the morning, how I would have been exasperated after the first ruined pancake. I would have yelled at him for missing the bus, threatened him with losing electronics. I would probably have refused to make him eggs because, let's face it, he just asked for eggs to test me.

But the new me—I'll be honest here, the *sober* me, but also the non-yelling me—remained calm and steady. The new me understood that sometimes, a pancake isn't just a pancake—it's a harbinger of the day. If he can focus on the pancakes, if the pancakes are a mess and he can manage to make the pancakes right, if one stupid fucking pancake can just be cooked and fluffy and yellow-white and soaked in (sugar-free) syrup, then maybe he'll run fast on the playground and his friend will want to play Pokémon at recess and he'll do well enough on his math quiz for his teacher to say, *Good job!* But if none of those things happen— or if say, he accidentally spills a cup of water on a girl and she yells at him, or a classmate teases him because his hair is long—he will come home and pick on his sister and refuse to do his homework, and he won't play outside because he's afraid to make friends and his mother will get mad because he won't listen and then he'll know that YES, he's the bad, unlikeable kid he thought he was, so he might as well punch a hole in the wall and tear up the art project he worked so hard to perfect. So, yes, it's important to at least *start* the day right, and swallow down some hope, because the rest of the day might just suck.

This all came to me in such a sudden burst of comprehension. I had to sit on the sofa to absorb it—the connection between the booze and the yelling and the pancakes and the tone of every hour of every day. It wasn't just the nighttime sobriety. Mornings were different as well. Without drinking, I slept better, awoke more refreshed, and had more energy throughout the day. At 5:00 p.m., instead of pouring my first drink, I found myself chopping onions and working on dinner—and actually enjoying the process. *Not drinking was making me a better mom.* It was a predictable, shocking, life-altering concept, and one I should have known.

THIRTY-TWO

When I had mostly recovered, I finally called Martin, the new therapist. Bob and I met with him to recite Nico's story for the umpteenth time. We gave a synopsis of the previous eight years, then an outline of the present: At age 10, Nico had a habit of attaching himself to one friend only; it seemed difficult for him to focus on more than one non-family member in his life at a time. Although he did well academically, social problems in school had begun to crop up. His current teacher, Ms. Bart, was a yeller herself, and she was hard on children who didn't turn in homework or do well on tests. After a few tearful reports from Nico about Ms. Bart fussing at him for a grade, we had called a meeting with her and the guidance counselor to stop her from doing that. At the meeting, Ms. Bart told us she had noticed how needy Nico was—he wanted to hug her a lot—and she had recently reprimanded him for telling another little boy that he loved him. I stopped myself from telepathically slapping her. "That's normal for him," I said, trying to remain calm. "We say 'I love you' a thousand times a day in our house." She claimed the other little boy was uncomfortable with it.

But Nico did have one best friend who seemed loyal to him, we told Martin, and they frequently played together outside of school. And though Nico for years had refused extracurricular activities, he recently had agreed to do a kids' fitness class twice a week, which was boosting his energy level and confidence.

After the debriefing, Martin came to our house and observed our special brand of lawless living. As is his habit in front of strangers, Nico maintained his composure; he annoyed his sister, but not in any obtrusive way. I pelted Martin with questions afterwards. *What do you think? What's your best guess? Can you diagnose him? Most importantly, TELL US WHAT TO DO.* I was so tired of platitudes, theories, and generalizations. *He has anxiety … he needs discipline … he's very bright.* I needed someone to give me a fucking list of instructions.

Martin asked if Nico had ever been evaluated. We recited the litany of therapists and doctors we'd visited. "But has anyone—meaning a licensed psychiatrist—given him a series of standardized tests, asked him specific questions, and come up with an official, written, diagnosis?" he asked.

Bob and I looked at each other. We felt like idiots. But in our eight years of trying to help this boy, no one had ever suggested doing a full series of testing on him, probably because no one had grasped the enormity of the problem except Betty, and Betty simply had moved forward with treatment.

"That's the first step," said Martin. "We need to know exactly what we're dealing with."

The diagnostician we found seemed like a nerd. Dr. Roberts was a middle-aged man with a mousy beard and a slight paunch who worked out of a nondescript office in a strip mall. Bob and I met with him first by ourselves, and he took furious notes. I felt enormous pressure to make certain he understood our state of despair, so I interrupted Bob frequently with newly recalled anecdotes and crying jags. I left there thinking he would surely diagnose Nico with having a neurotic, hysterical mother.

We scheduled three forthcoming appointments for Nico, and Dr. Roberts handed us a stack of paperwork—some for us to fill out, some to give to Nico's teachers and therapists. A few days later, we brought Nico for his first appointment. He met with Dr. Roberts for nearly two hours, and left with a paper airplane the two had made together.

His second appointment was scheduled for the following week after school one day. From the minute he stepped off the bus, Nico griped about going. We gave him a snack, and he retired to his room for some therapeutic Minecraft—the online game in which users create their own imaginary world. After five minutes or so, we told him it was time to leave. He said no. We gave him five more minutes. He asked for candy. We threatened to take away electronics. He told us to stop being mean.

Finally, gradually, painfully, we lured him into the car. I knew he was nervous, but we had an appointment time to keep, which made me nervous, too. Over the years, Nico had become a human barometer—he sensed my emotional temperature so accurately he actually noticed the way I breathed. So as we drove to the doctor's office, I tried to stay calm. We were halfway there when he remembered he had wanted to bring the paper airplane from the previous week.

I looked at the time. "I'm sorry, honey, we can't go back, we'll be late," I said.

"Please, Mom. Please. Please! I need it, Mom. Please go back!"

"No, sweetie. It will be there when we get back. We don't have time."

I could sense his desperation building, but I was adamant; we didn't have time to go back. He begged one more time. "PLEASE, Mom," he whimpered, crying. I shook my head. And then he opened the passenger door as I sped down the road. I shot my right arm out and grabbed his left, pulling him toward me. The door shut, and I grabbed his right arm so he couldn't reopen the door.

He punched and slapped. By then I was on a highway, and couldn't pull over. With practiced focus I steered with one hand and held my son down with the other. After I parked, Nico climbed in the back seat and refused to get out. I opened the door, and with all my strength, pulled him out of the van. He ran toward the highway. I chased him down and dragged him back to the office building, where he attacked me with a blind rage, dragging me to the ground. I got up and dragged him toward the office.

From inside a nearby Pilates studio, a couple of women watched this scene through the window. I pulled my son toward them, knocked on the window and motioned for one of them to help. When she came out, I directed her toward Dr. Roberts' office and asked her to run for his help. Nico pulled away and ran back to the car. I caught up with him, and tried to secure him from behind but he turned us both around, slamming my back against the car so hard I fell down; I held him tightly, and he fell on top of me. And that's how Dr. Roberts found us when he came running down the stairs a few long seconds later—me crying on my back on the hot pavement, Nico atop me screaming, pounding me with his fists. Dr. Roberts walked quickly up to us, and said, calmly, "Hey, Nico, what's going on?" Nico froze. His face changed from anguished rage to confusion and fright. Dr. Roberts reached out his hand for Nico's, and after a moment, Nico allowed himself to be helped up and walked away while looking back at me fearfully. I sat in my car and wept, defeated and bereft, but thankful that Dr. Roberts had witnessed a sliver of what we had tried to explain.

After three weeks of analysis, Bob and I had an appointment to hear the doctor's findings. He began with a qualification. "I'm a big believer in proper discipline," he said. "Most of the cases I see can be reconciled with more structured parenting." My heart sank. *Same old, same old*, I thought. But I was wrong.

"So I did not come by this diagnosis easily," he continued. "It's actually fairly uncommon. But there's no doubt in my mind that your son suffers from Reactive Attachment Disorder.

"Now, he certainly doesn't have as severe a case as he could. He's obviously attached to you, for example." He nodded toward me. "And in lesser degrees, to the rest of his family.

"He has what's referred to as Anxious-Ambivalent Attachment Disorder."

According to research, children with anxious and ambivalent attachment patterns "exist in a state of being suspicious and distrustful while at the same time acting clingy and desperate. They tend to focus intensely on their parent and are hyper-vigilant regarding the parent's availability or unavailability. They vacillate between over-dependent clinging and angry rejection of their parent or caregiver."[1] I had never read a more perfect description of my son.

Dr. Roberts explained that many of Nico's symptoms were similar to those of children with ADHD. But while an ADHD kid's distractions are external, Nico's were internal, making them hard to observe. He might appear to be listening in class, working on a problem, even concentrating on a book—but inside, his brain was in turmoil: *Do I have any friends? Are they laughing at me? Am I as smart as them? Does Mom love Neale more than me?*

Dr. Roberts gave us anecdotes from his interviews. He had asked Nico, for example, about being adopted. Nico said he had to be adopted because his birth family "didn't have enough food. That's why they had to get rid of me."

Get rid of me. The words hung in the air.

At another point, Nico was asked to create a story. He wrote a tale in which a farmer woman had a pet pig she loved very

[1] Joyce Catlett, PSYCHALIVE.com

much. Then she brought another baby pig in her home, and she loved the new pig more because it was cuter. So he got rid of the first pig. *Got rid of it.*

"I believe the second baby pig is Neale," said Dr. Roberts.

We stared at him, shocked. His diagnosis had brought tears of both relief and grief; selfishly, the report was a vindication of our years seeking help for the nearly indefinable problems we'd had with Nico. And yet such relief was tempered by the enormity of what we'd still face. Our son would always have difficulty with human relationships. His self-esteem was practically nonexistent. He could not emotionally regulate himself without assistance.

"You have a very short window to help Nico," said Dr. Roberts. Soon, he warned, puberty and adolescence would jeopardize our ability to assist him in his recovery.

"So the gluten thing," I asked. "A bunch of crap?"

He sighed. "A healthy diet, physical exercise, all that is important," he said. But, he conceded, gluten, dairy, and sugar were not the culprits. Pizza wasn't making our child crazy. He suffered from an actual condition, a psychiatric illness mentioned in the Diagnostic and Statistical Manual of Mental Disorders. Nico, our handsome, smart, funny, middle child, was not just an average boy.

The process of absorbing this new diagnosis, I suppose, was not unlike discovering your child has a curable form of cancer. Bob and I felt certain we had finally been given the definitive reason for our son's abnormal emotional development, and it was a relief. But it refocused attention on those awful first few months of his life, a brief period of deprivation, which would likely reside within him forever, like a hibernating beast. Yes, we could finally see the road forward. But damn, the road looked like it went on forever.

We asked Dr. Roberts why Neale, who had been through the same traumatic process, even nearly dying from it, didn't seem to be developing an attachment disorder. Children are different, he said, with varying strengths and weaknesses. We know nothing about either child's genetic background, either, he reminded us—perhaps Nico's ancestry makes him more prone to internalizing emotional trauma.

As we prepared for yet another phase of helping Nico overcome his deep-rooted anxieties, shame and regret took up residence in my brain. How could we have given up on this same diagnosis three years earlier? We had subjected our son—the whole family, really—to a severely restricted diet, and forced him to swallow hundreds of dollars worth of vitamins, prescription meds, and minerals. We essentially had convinced him to trust us when the truth is we had no idea what we were doing. I remembered how he bravely swallowed giant pills and inedible chewy gluten-free bread, and listened to me tell his teachers he wasn't allowed to have cupcakes or cookies during school. It made me feel sick.

At the same time, I recognized how the changes had done some good, and the resulting health benefits were exactly what lulled us into thinking we were on the right track. When we cut out gluten and dairy, we all became healthier, which made us feel better; the same happened when we cut back on sugar. Healthier meant happier. In time, I forgave myself for ostracizing Nico so needlessly; it was part of the journey, I reasoned. And, bonus: I had become a better cook.

In the days and weeks immediately following the diagnosis, we met frequently with Martin to come up with a plan of action, which consisted of several parts: proactive, reactive, and safety precautions.

Our biggest issue was handling Nico's episodes. Because he was a strong, healthy, boy, it was no longer easy for me to hold him tightly and keep him from hurting himself or me, or damaging property. Martin taught Bob a restraining method, which worked, although it was super-uncomfortable for Nico, which made him accuse his own father of trying to strangle him. But I couldn't do it for long, and Martin didn't think I should try. If Nico goes off the cliff, he told me, you need a lifeline—someone who can help. Keeping everyone safe, he insisted, is paramount.

Martin said we had spent way too much energy over the past few years trying to prevent Nico's episodes. It's time, instead, to figure out what's sparking them—and to learn how to prevent them. We needed to be *proactive*.

At the core of an attachment disorder, he explained, is the need to feel *safe*—safe from being unloved, safe from anxiety, and even safe from physical harm. In this way, nearly everything we'd done in the past contributed to his fears. When we locked him in the laundry room, his worst fears of being abandoned seemed to have come true. When I screamed at him, he felt threatened. Being physically restrained made him nearly apoplectic with terror. Martin didn't blame us—we had been diligent in our search for answers, he assured us. But now we were essentially starting from scratch.

We began to examine life from Nico's perspective, previewing plans with an eye toward not only what could go wrong, but also how we could prevent Nico from flipping out about it. For example, if Scout had plans and Neale was scheduled to go to a friend's house, Nico was certain to feel left out and lonely. We could preempt his behavior by making plans for him—a trip to buy a new Lego, for example, or renting a movie.

The mac and cheese episode described earlier – the one in which my neighbor Kay came to help—in hindsight had been totally predictable. Nico and Neale had been playing Legos together happily ... but, eventually, I knew, Neale would be tired and want to quit. It was impossible for Nico to understand that his little sister needed to go to bed; he felt abandoned, like she was tired of *him*, instead of just tired. He also had zero confidence that these moments of happiness would ever return. If she quit playing with him now, he reasoned, she might never play with him again. Had I thought about it more proactively, I could have eased the transition by, say, talking about dinner in advance or sitting down with them to play one last game, or even promising to play something special with Nico after Neale went to bed.

Martin also said I had to accept that my proverbial happy place might not be the same as Nico's happy place. My dream has always been for my children to run free like Laura Ingalls, loving nature, climbing trees, building forts, and exploring the outdoors. But when Nico schleps through the door after school, he's exhausted. If he needed an hour on electronics to decompress, we should let him have it. This revelation shocked me—it strangely hadn't occurred to me that my kids might have ideals and interests different from my own.

My new non-drinking, less-yelling lifestyle helped us transition into this new way of parenting. Occasionally, I slipped and lost my cool, which sent Nico to the edge. When that happened, said Martin, it was important for me to regain my composure and *react* appropriately. No more calling Nico an asshole, even if it was true. No more stomping off. I needed to slow down, apologize, give him my full attention, and reassure him of my love.

Nico desperately needed to spend some time—a lot of time—feeling like a regular boy, one who didn't punch holes in the wall because his little sister wouldn't play with him.

It was a big leap for us to go from tough love parenting to laissez-faire parenting. But yet another episode, this one involving a doorknob, convinced us it was the right tact.

The doorknobs in the new house were a beautiful burnished dark brown color. Supposedly the oil in human hands would eventually turn the knobs into a polished, brindle color. I worried we would never find out—because one by one, the doorknobs were being removed. Soon after we moved, Nico and Neale discovered they could lock themselves in their rooms and turn into wizards of chaos—because the beautiful burnished doorknobs were impossible to jimmy open. Twice I'd called a locksmith to help; twice I'd called the builder to ask him to get keys, but he never called back. I'm pretty sure he had been eternally scarred by our complicated process of simplifying.

One night, Nico screamed at me for something or other and locked himself in his room. But after weeks of doorknob-rattling and forcing and jiggling, the knob fell off. In pieces.

"Awesome," I said. "Now you can't lock yourself in your room anymore."

I said it very calmly; still, it was the exact wrong thing to say.

"*Put my doorknob back on right this minute!*" he screamed. "*I want my doorknob!*" My handyman skills are limited to changing light bulbs and nailing, so I couldn't do anything with the doorknob. I walked into my bedroom to hide the fallen doorknob in my closet, and in that minute, Nico locked himself in Neale's room and started banging on her door, dresser, walls, whatever was within striking distance.

Neale started crying; it was her room he was destroying, after all. Scout tried to comfort her; I tried to think. I decided to sit quietly and wait him out. But then he changed the game.

Because Neale's room had been the garage prior to renovation, the circuit breakers were located there, behind her door. Nico opened up the box and started turning circuit breakers on and off at random.

My knowledge of how electricity works is this: never stick a fork inside a toaster. So I assumed Nico was going to set the house on fire or cause the entire region to go off the grid. I swallowed my panic and counted my options. I should call Bob, I thought. That way, if the house does catch on fire, he'll understand the circumstances before he arrives in the engine to put it out. So I did that. "I think I have to call the police," I told Bob, and the girls began to sob. Neale asked me not to send Nico to jail. I wondered whether I was overreacting. But right then, nothing felt more urgent. My 10-year-old son was locked in a room, playing with circuit breakers, threatening to *break the house*, and had reached DEFCON 10 on his rage scale. Anything I said—words of comfort, discipline, love, concern—it didn't matter. All of it filtered through his anger translator, and re-emerged as reason for him to fight.

But I thought maybe the mention of the police would get his attention. I leaned against the door. "Honey," I said, super calmly. "If you don't open the door, I'm going to have to call the police."

"Go ahead."

"Okay. But if I call the police, I want you to know that they're going to ask you a bunch of questions. And if they don't think you're safe here, they're going to take you away."

"Fine."

"They really will, honey. I want to make sure you understand: if I call the police because I'm worried about you being locked in there, they might make you go with them and take you someplace safe."

"Good! Because I'm afraid of you!"

"If you're afraid of me, I can call someone to come get you. You can go sleep at the neighbor's house next door."

"No. I don't trust you. You lie."

I pretended to call the police. I stepped away from the door, held the phone to my ear, and told it my name and address.

"My son has locked himself in a room and is turning circuit breakers on and off, and I'm afraid he's going to hurt himself," I said to no one.

"*Lying*," shouted Nico.

"Yes," I said, answering a nonexistent question. "Uh huh. No, not yet. Yes, I'll hold."

"I know you didn't really call, Mom."

"Yes, I'm here. Well, I just need someone to get him out of the room and make sure he's okay."

"Fine. I'll come out."

"Hold on … I think he might be coming out …."

The next three seconds crawled like days. Nico slowly opened the door and peeked out. I controlled the urge to throw myself at him and pin his arms so he couldn't start the whole thing over again. I didn't because I was still on the phone with the fake police.

"Okay, I think we'll be all right. Yes, I'll call you again if we need help."

Nico came out and sat on the edge of the couch, about three feet away from me. "So," he said casually, "when will the police be here?"

"Well, I canceled them, honey. You came out."

"But I want them to come. I want them to take me away."

I watched him. As in other similar episodes, my son had gone underground; his protector, *the monster*, was controlling the scene. Despite the emotional drama of the previous hour, his face was composed, like a mask.

"Honey, where would you want to go?" He had been waiting for that question.

"I want them to take me to my real family."

I didn't let my face collapse; I remembered to breathe. I summoned strength from the girls, still observing the scene in silence. "We *are* your real family," I said in a strong, clear voice. He sighed as though I was a small child lacking understanding. "Mom, *you know*," he said. He took my hand, and pulled me toward him. "Let's go in my room to talk."

In his room, I sat in a chair; he leaned against the wall across from me. "I think I should go home to Guatemala," he said calmly. "To my family."

We looked at each other for a long moment.

"Honey. I am your mother. We are your family. You were born in Guatemala, and you have a birth mother there, but I am your mother. I will always be your mother. This family isn't complete without you." I opened my arms. He hesitated for only a minute, before he flew to me, sank into my lap, and buried his face in my chest.

"Why would you want to leave?" I asked.

He was crying by then. "I just don't fit in," he sobbed. "I thought maybe if I went back to Guatemala, I'd fit in there, and more people would be like me. I just want to fit in, Mom! I want to be like the other boys! I want to like sports and run fast and have lots of friends ...." I rubbed his back and whispered, "Shhh, shhh," and the pain poured down on us like rain.

I held him for a long time, kissing his forehead and brushing back his sweaty hair.

"Darling," I finally whispered. "We will get through this. You fit into this family just fine. You are perfect. And I know that you feel like you're different, and I know that you want to feel better, and Daddy and I are going to do everything we can to make sure you grow up to be the best possible you. And I'm very proud of you for telling me how you feel. You are a brave and awesome boy, and we love you so much. And I promise you everything will be okay." It was a promise I intended to keep.

As soon as he fell asleep, I wrote down every detail I remembered from the incident and emailed the information to Martin. "We have to tell him he has an attachment disorder," Martin said. "He can't keep thinking this is all his fault. We need to explain it to him."

I dreaded this. We had spent weeks, months, years, convincing this child he was loved and wanted. And now I was supposed to tell him he started life alone and abandoned and unloved. It turned my stomach.

To complicate matters, Nico had begun to loathe Martin's visits. While Kay, his art therapist, was loving, nurturing, and free-spirited, Martin personified rules. He had introduced structure and logic into the household, and as much as he encouraged us to let Nico be himself, he also insisted we hold Nico emotionally accountable when he was unkind. Nico preferred not to be so introspective.

On a scheduled afternoon, Martin arrived to help us explain the diagnosis. As soon as Nico rounded the corner from the bus stop, he saw Martin's car and dashed into the neighbor's house. I followed, and told him we just needed to talk to him for a few minutes. He came out, ran home to our house and locked himself in the bathroom, where he refused to communicate except through notes passed under the door, and then only if I had written the notes.

We passed ridiculous notes to each other for the next 45 minutes.

MOM

Yes?

TELL MR. MARTIN TO GO AWAY

No

Y NOT

He is here to help

IS HE READING THE NOTES

No

I DON'T BELIEVE U

Finally, Martin suggested we adapt our goal to simply introduce the term "attachment disorder," which we could do through the bathroom door. What followed could have been a scene out of a very bad Lifetime movie as parodied on *Saturday Night Live*. Bob, Martin, and I were crowded around the bathroom door. Nico was running water in the sink and shouting, "*I can't hear you!"* And a poorly timed visit from a handyman provided drilling and nailing noises as background music.

"Honey, when you were a baby, you—"

BAM BAM BAM

"—and it's possible you didn't get enough—"

"Hey Steve, did you measure that part?"

"—so sometimes, when you get angry—"

"Stop talking, Mom, just stop talking, I'm not listening!"

"—and so it's not really your fault, you just—"

BZZZZZZZ, BZZZZZZZZ

The barebones explanation took about five minutes. The handyman decided it wasn't a good time, so he left. Martin figured he had done all he could, so he left, too. Nico wrote a note to Bob that said GO AWAY DAD, which he happily did.

When Nico was sure we were in the house alone, he walked out of the bathroom, led me to the sofa, and snuggled into my lap. After a few minutes, I asked him if he had any questions about the attachment disorder. "What's an attachment disorder?" he asked, looking at me furtively. I knew he had heard me while he was in the bathroom; I guess he just needed to hear it again from me.

I repeated my brief, simple explanation. "When you were a baby in Guatemala, living in the house with lots of other babies, there weren't enough nurses there to take care of everyone. And so you didn't always get as much attention as you needed, and so now, even though you're older, you still feel that way, and you get really frustrated and scared when you need something, or when something upsets you, and that's why you have tantrums."

He pointed out, rightly, that I had been lying to him about his earliest months of life, and I said, yes, I had only told him what

I thought he could handle. He asked if any people we knew had "something wrong with them," something with a name, like him. "Oh, yes! I have depression, which makes me sad sometimes!" I said enthusiastically, like it was the best news ever. His best friend had diabetes, I reminded him. His cousin has autism, and his grandfather had pulmonary fibrosis. He nodded, sat a while longer, then told me he was hungry. He didn't bring it up again.

Until he did. A week or so later—I don't even know what started it, and I can't remember why I wasn't in my newly appointed state-of-the-art circle of calm. Perhaps Bob had worked too many double shifts, and I needed a break. Maybe I hadn't slept well. I don't remember what started it, but I remember what I did: When he threw himself at me, I grabbed his shoulders and shook him. When he threw a pair of shorts at me, I used the same shorts to hit him. I roared at him, a deep guttural growl that, even in my maniacal fury, I knew sounded insane. He yelled at me to stop; I did, and he hit me. So I hit him again with the shorts. Back and forth we went for long minutes, until Bob came in and made me stop. He moved to restrain Nico, and I said no, I couldn't bear it. I couldn't bear to see him helpless, screaming he was hurt, shattered because I had lost my cool. At least when I was fighting him, he could end it just by ceasing to fight back. With Bob, he couldn't fight back—Bob held him too securely. We restrained him to keep us all safe, but such reasoning always eluded me in the heat of the moment. "I'm scared! You're scaring me," Nico screamed over and over again. "I don't care!" I snapped, and I didn't, not then. I guess I was having my own episode, forgetting that every single action I was taking was escalating his fear.

Finally, depleted, he gave up, and lay sobbing on the floor at my feet. "I can't trust you!" he cried. "I can't trust either of you!"

"Well, we can't trust you either."

"I thought I could trust you. I can't trust you."

"And I can't trust you."

"I don't feel safe with you. I thought you were safe. Now I can't feel safe anywhere. I only feel safe with Buddy. And my friend Jack. I feel safe with Jack when he makes me laugh. Buddy and Jack, and that's it. And Miss Kay. I'm not safe at school. I'm not safe with you guys. I want to go home."

"You are home," I said.

"I want to go home. I want to see if my birth mother is okay and she has enough to eat and she's alive. My birth mother couldn't feed me and then the people in the orphanage didn't take care of me and now I'm not safe. I've had three really bad stages of my life. I'm sad. I'm angry. I'm scared.

"I want to go to a place where my birth mother had enough for me to eat and those people at the orphanage took care of me, and there's only joy and happiness. I want to go to a place where there's only joy and happiness. Fourth grade was supposed to be such a great year. I was so excited for fourth grade and it turned out to be a big pile of garbage.

"I want to go back to when I was a baby. I want to be a little tiny baby. And you can't just say I'm your baby, because I'm not any more. It seems like that was when I was most—I just—*I just don't want to have a bad life.*"

I swear he said all that. It came out like the rush of a swollen river, in between stutters and sobs and breaths caught in his throat. At some point I crawled down next to him and put my arms around him as he kept talking.

"I'm sorry, I'm sorry," I said. "You're safe with me."

"But you shook me! You shook me! I'm scared, Mom!"

Then a moment later: "I just want a hug, Mom! Please give me a hug!" and I held him as tightly as I could. Later: "I'm not upset," he said. "I'm just sad." He reached for a little photo album where he keeps some pictures of himself as a baby. He opened up to a photo of me holding him, his tiny baby cheek against mine, his swaddled body securely tucked into my arms. "I'm sad because you'll never hold me like that again," he said, sobbing.

It may have been the worst moment of my life, and the best. His heart was wide open; currents of pain stretched between us, and the shock of it was excruciating. I would have joyfully given him my very last breath if I thought it would spare him further, but my presence was a vital organ to him; without me, he would die. And yet his love for me was so intertwined with thoughts of his birth mother, his debilitating fear of abandonment, and an ever-present self-loathing that he couldn't help but question everything in his head. Even as this truth crushed me, I recognized the sliver of hope wedging itself into the moment—Nico was getting it. He was slowly but surely understanding what ailed him. We were moving forward, one step at a time, and for the first time in years, it seemed like real progress.

THIRTY-THREE

One afternoon, Kay, the art therapist, worked with Nico to define his episodes and together they came up with the term "monsters"—the monsters invaded him when he lost control of his emotions. But Kay explained to him how he had power over the monsters—he could refuse them entrance, she said, or make them leave. If he concentrated, he could see them coming, and make them go away.

At home that night, Nico used a roll of duct tape to create a sticky web over his bedroom door. He called it a monster trap. "This will keep the monsters out," he told me. He instructed us to crawl beneath the web to enter or exit his room, and we happily complied.

Dr. Roberts would later discourage us from letting him separate himself from his behavior—but for the moment I understood this as another monumental step. He was controlling the matter the best way he could, and with the most readily available weapon: duct tape.

Meanwhile, mercifully, fourth grade ended and Nico's relief was nearly palpable. It was just a few months after Dr. Roberts' diagnosis, and we were still easing into our new parenting approach. For several days, he slept, played electronics, and watched television. But for week two, I had signed them all up for surf camp.

"I don't want to go," Nico told me.

"That's okay," I said. "You don't have to."

I could nearly read his mind: *Kids will laugh at me. I won't be able to get up on the board. I can't. I can't. I can't.*

"You know," I added, "you could always just go and watch. Or you could go, and if you don't like it, I'll take you home." He said he would think about it.

On the first day of surf camp, I packed an ice chest and helped the girls get ready. "Wanna go?" I asked Nico. He shook his head and snuggled with Buddy.

I brought Scout and Neale to the beach, unloaded their surfboards, lugged the ice chest over the sand, and finally sat down in a chair. The phone rang.

"Hi, Mom."

"Hi, honey!"

"I guess I'll come watch."

"Okay! I'll be right home."

I trudged back through the sand, drove home, picked him up, and started driving back to the beach.

"Do you want to put your bathing suit on?"

"Okay. But at home." We turned around and went home so he could get dressed.

Once at the beach, he tested the waters while I spoke to one of the instructors. "He has severe anxiety," I told her. "He really wants to do it, but he's scared to death, not of the water, but that he won't be able to do it." She was a stunning girl with tattoos and a nose ring, and she walked right up to him and started talking. Before long, they had walked out into the waves together with a board.

Scout surfed like a Florida girl. Neale attacked waves like she was trying to conquer the ocean. But Nico watched each swell approach skeptically, with maybe a smidgeon of hope. Finally, his new instructor friend whispered into his ear before pushing him off toward shore.

Slowly, gripping the surfboard's sides like railings, he pushed one knee into the board while putting his foot flat. The wave bullied its way forward. He pulled his other foot flat; and, in what seemed like slow motion, he released his grip, stood halfway up and rode that damn wave into shore. And then he went back out and did it again.

Safety, said Martin. It's all about feeling *safe*. The need is visceral and chronic for Nico. But is it not the same for me and for all of us? When we cloud our hours and days and weeks with the mind-numbing chatter of news and errands and vapid obligations, we lose sight of what makes us feel safe and secure. We begin to lose confidence in our ability to make a life that's good for the soul instead of good for Facebook.

In this way, our journey of simplifying helped us find a cure for our Nico. Living simply isn't just a decision; it's a mindset. You can't just declutter your house—you've got to declutter the noggin, too, or else the stuff, both material and intangible, creeps back into place, and suddenly you're more laden than ever.

Simple doesn't always mean calm. A day filled with writing, exercise, laundry, grocery shopping, and catering to children certainly continues to have its challenges. But I try hard to enjoy each step. I *like* cooking dinner, and teaching the kids how yummy garlic smells when sautéed with olive oil. I fold clothes deliberately, thinking about when they were last worn.

The hardest part? Forgiving myself for not saving the world yesterday and today and every day. Living simply means being humble, and in a way, tamping down personal ambition. That's not to say I don't make a difference in the world—I think I do—but to regret that my contributions aren't as formidable as, say, Oprah's, is akin to saying the people in my circle aren't important enough to be worthy of my dependable presence, which just isn't true.

Look, not everyone can live simply. Thank goodness there are neurosurgeons and rocket scientists and journalists* and politicians*. (*Some exclusions may apply.) But most of us could do a better job of serving our world if we did a better job of managing what's right in front us—and *simplifying* our ideas about not only what we need, but also what we want. Nearly a quarter-century ago, I was newly married and preparing to move to Florida. I told Bob I wanted a nice house, a dog, a plan to travel abroad, and the option to move if I didn't like it here. I'm so much wiser now. Today all I want is a hot cup of coffee, and maybe a nap later on.

I have continued to remain calm, and I still mostly abstain from drinking, limiting my consumption to one or two drinks on the weekends, if at all. I carefully screen both the people and the distractions I allow into my life—both tend to take time away from my husband and children, and when that happens, physical and mental chaos ensue.

The night Nico lay on the floor and cried to me about wanting to go back in time marked a breakthrough. It was the last episode he had for several months—he had been having them two and three times a week. His next one was predictable—after my father died, at a time when he was struggling with grief and I was unable to comfort him because of my own debilitating sense of loss. He still struggles, of course, but he can dream of a future, and he feels *safe* both within this family and within his own skin. He also has learned to recognize his emotions, and address them appropriately. We recently said goodbye to old Gem, who had developed an age-related neurological disease. Nico insisted on being with me when Gem was put to sleep. Upon arriving home, he paced and paced, looking for something to do. Finally, he found a shoebox. In it he placed: Gem's collar and leash, her favorite toy, a poop bag, her food dish, and a roll of toilet paper. Gem loved to eat toilet paper. He went outside and found a shovel, dug a hole, buried the shoebox, and arranged a circle of stones on the makeshift grave with a capital G in the middle. He had coped with his own emotion, and had he received early admission into Harvard, I wouldn't have been more proud.

Scout and Neale recognized the changes, too, and began to appreciate their brother more for who he is rather than what he does. And as a family, our priorities have changed. We don't emphasize grades; we talk about kindness. We don't pressure our children to play sports; we build bonfires and talk.

One night Neale crawled in bed next to me, and talked about looking at stars and making wishes. "What do you wish for?" I asked, idly wondering about the prices of iPads, battery-operated Barbie jeeps, and new bikes.

"I wish that one day, I could be a really nice girl," she said. It doesn't get much more simple than that.

I began this story to tell you about my son. Really, though, it's a story about me. My husband and I—we believe we saved Nico's life. But it's not an exaggeration to say he saved ours, too. By finding the cure for him, we found the cure for us. And while life isn't perfect, there are gifts in its imperfections. Nico has taught me to slow down, and to say no. He has taught my husband and me to cherish our role as leaders of this special clan, and to celebrate moments as pure as telling a funny story at dinner.

Writers frequently complain about their lists of laments, and I'm no different. Countless times, I have complained about all the writing I *haven't* done in my half-century of living. But I know now—this is the story I needed to tell. No childhood anecdote, no triggered memory—nothing was or is as important as explaining in words this task assigned to me, and how I managed to get it done.

Nearly 11 years ago, we brought home our son. And every single day, we bring him home again. That's how much I love him.

EPILOGUE

Eight years ago, I started writing a blog, and I decided to incorporate an advice column into the mix. I occasionally ran posts entitled Dear Savvy Sister in which I helped real people solve real problems, except that sometimes I made up the problems and sometimes the problems were my own. I was really good at it. If I had pursued a career as a therapist, and been diagnosed with depression earlier in my life, and been interested in going to school for a thousand years, and had a tolerance for annoying people, I would have been an excellent therapist. Ah, well. But my propensity for evaluating problems hasn't gone unused, because I'm now very good at diagnosing myself. I understand my flawed, intricate way of thinking so perfectly that it's like solving a puzzle, except sometimes I solve the puzzle too late and havoc ensues. But still, I solve the puzzle.

A couple of months after Nico's final diagnosis, I began to obsess about getting a third dog. Pure, unfettered, insanity, I know. I had flawed reasoning: Buddy was slowly becoming Nico's constant companion, and Gem barely moved except to eat. We needed a family dog. *Anyone can see that*, I thought. I spent hours looking at puppy pictures on rescue sites. I was done with purchasing purebreds from breeders—I loved my Labs, but I had become more attuned to the travesty of smart, healthy canines without homes. If I believed in the ability of dogs to provide therapy to humans, surely I had to concede that dogs being raised without love were suffering nearly as much as my own boy had suffered without it.

Occasionally, I imagined dealing with the poop of yet another living, breathing being in the house, and came to my senses. But then I'd forget and keep looking. Scout caught me a couple of times. "I want a small dog, Mom!" she said. "Let's get a Pomeranian!" She told her little sister, and soon they were perusing rescue sites, too. Because why not?

"Please stop it," said Bob. "We can't get another animal. We just can't."

"I know, I know," I said repeatedly. "It's just therapy for me. Like watching sports is for you. I'm not actually going to do it."

But after weeks of obsessing, my own primal brain took over and temporarily stole my powers of rational thinking. On a beautiful Saturday morning, when Bob was at the fire station, I took the girls to a pet store where I knew a rescue organization was showing dogs in need of homes. There were two puppies—thin little brindle littermates with long tails tucked firmly between hind legs. The tinier one approached my hand and licked it; Neale threw her hand toward the pup enthusiastically and it cowered back, but then took a timid step forward. Scout knelt down and nearly teared up with emotion. "Mom, we have to get her," she said.

The dog had been brought to a county shelter with her mama and a litter of six. The rescue organization's vet estimated she was by this time nine months old—nearly full-grown. He thought her a mix of boxer and beagle. She was beautiful in a pathetic, fragile way. It seemed contra-indicated for me to bring a pathetic, fragile, soul into our household, but you know where this ends, right? The girls and I went to a nearby frozen yogurt shop, where they promised they would take full responsibility for the pup and walk her and feed her and pick up her poop. In honor of the frozen yogurt shop where we came to this dubious agreement, we renamed the dog Yobe, and she rode home with us that very hour, quivering and afraid, looking like she might throw herself out of the window or purposefully stop breathing just to end her misery.

The minute we walked in the door, I realized my mistake. Yobe shrank into a canine fetal position while Buddy tried to lick off her head; Neale kept picking up her front half while her bottom half drooped down; Scout kept shouting, "Stop, Neale, you're hurting her!" Nico ran around in circles attempting to get a glimpse of her. Gem surveyed the scene like Eeyore, dismayed but not surprised at the appearance of yet more household lunacy. My obsession with getting another dog had disappeared; my new obsession was how to get rid of her.

I fell into a pit of despair. I paced the house. Yobe paced alongside me, like a sheet of paper taped to my calf. I kept tripping on her. I wanted to talk to someone about it, but I still hadn't told Bob, and I was embarrassed to tell any of my friends because they'd rightly ask me if I had lost my mind. The rescue organization said I had a week to decide. I could tell them she didn't get along with my other dogs, I reasoned, or say it was too much work for me. I could let them keep the adoption fee as a donation to lessen my guilt. I could find her a new home, a better home. I could tell them I had suffered from a bout of referred anxiety, and had decided to get another dog in lieu of solving any of the actual problems facing me. But she couldn't stay. It was just too much.

Meanwhile, the girls were ecstatic, although their bubbly enthusiasm was scaring the crap out of the dog. The only place she seemed even partially at ease was curled up in the corner of the couch, which kept leading to a contentious game of musical chairs. Yobe sat on the couch, Nico sat next to her, Neale shrieked "She's my dog!" and pushed Nico away, Nico sat on Yobe's tail,

Yobe jumped to the floor, Neale sat next to Yobe on the floor, Nico shouted, "Neale's being mean to me," and so on for eternity.

When I could stand it no longer, I texted Bob.

I wrote: "I fucked up," and texted a picture of the dog.

He wrote back: "Where did it come from? Where is it going?"

I didn't write back. After a while, he wrote: "Not sure what is up. Let's discuss tomorrow, OK?" He included a little kiss-blowing emoji because he is the best man in the universe.

The next morning, after being up all night running medical calls, my husband came home, met Yobe, then sat across from me and smiled, shaking his head. "You didn't even bother to call me?" he asked. My eyes got leaky, and from my mouth spewed a torrent of excuses and psychoanalysis and unconvincing rationale regarding why the bringing home of Yobe was a terrible mistake that nonetheless could not have been avoided.

"There's so much I don't have control of, and I've been obsessing about things that I can control because it's easier. I'm so worried about Nico, and writing, and money, and I feel like I'm failing at all that, and so I keep finding ways not to think about it, and one way to not think about it is to look at pictures of dogs all the time. I got tired of looking at dogs all the time, because obviously I knew we couldn't get another dog, but I just couldn't stop, and then it seemed like the only way to stop looking at pictures of dogs was to get a dog."

"And you couldn't call me?" he asked.

"I knew you'd say no."

"*Exactly*. That's how we work, remember? You have crazy ideas, and you call me, and I talk you down off the ledge."

We listened to the birds for a few minutes.

"We can give her back," I said. "The rescue organization said we have a week to try it out."

Bob tilted his head and looked at me. "Are you crazy?" I shrugged my shoulders.

"You want to *adopt* a dog and give it to our children—our *adopted* children—and then give it back?"

He is so smart sometimes.

"No," he said. "We are not giving back the dog. We have a third dog, and that's that.

"But let this be a lesson, because you do have control over your life. You do have time to write. We're learning to deal with Nico. Life is good. Every time you look at Yobe, I want you to remember that. Your life is good, and you don't need to keep getting dogs to know that."

On that very day, little Yobe started worming her way into our hearts. She rests her delicate head on my leg as I write, and keeps a thin paw on Neale as they fall asleep together. She flies out the door to greet Scout as she walks home from the bus stop. She adores Buddy the Wonder Dog, and sniffs Gem's ears with affection. She was an abandoned, untethered, unloved youngster who landed here by chance, and by chance we now learn she belongs here. It's a very familiar story.

About the Author

Tricia Booker is a writer, blogger and award-winning journalist. She teaches journalism at the University of North Florida and lives in a small but adorable house with her firefighter husband, three children, and at least two dogs. This is her first book.

ACKNOWLEDGEMENTS

Foremost thanks to Joan Leggitt, my prescient publisher, who read my blog, took me to lunch, and told me I should write a book. Without that prompt, this collection of pages would still be a latent thought in my brain. Thank you for your spot-on editing, your infinite patience, and your faith in me.

Thank you to everyone who has read my blog over the past eight years. Your words of encouragement and support kept my fingers tapping the keyboard again and again, and reminded me always to nourish the writer in me.

Buckets of gratitude to my writer-sister-friends Glenda Bailey-Mershon, Sandra Lambert, Gale Massey, Pat Spears, and Katrina Hodge Willis for frequently bucking me out of the valley of doubts and for helpful early reads. I owe you a bunch.

Forever love and admiration to the exceptional Valle Dwight, who has been my friend for 27 years and counting, and who has never failed to tell me the truth. Giant heart emoji.

Thanks to my earliest writer mentors: Connie May Fowler, Janis Owens, and Dorothy Allison. Your voices will always be in my head. In a good way.

Finally, to my darling, cherished, beloved, perfectly imperfect children and their stalwart treasure of a father, my hot firefighter husband—what can I say? You fill my heart, and you make me better every minute of every day.